Death and Dying in Central Appalachia

Death and Dying in Central Appalachia

CHANGING ATTITUDES
AND PRACTICES

James K. Crissman

University of Illinois Press · Urbana and Chicago

© 1994 by the Board of Trustees of the University of Illinois
Manufactured in the United States of America
1 2 3 4 5 C P 5 4 3 2 1

This book is printed on acid-free paper.

Library of Congress Cataloging-in-Publication Data

Crissman, James K., 1943–
    Death and dying in central Appalachia : changing attitudes and
practices / James K. Crissman.
        p.   cm.
    Includes bibliographical references and index.
    ISBN 0-252-02061-8 (cloth : alk. paper). — ISBN 0-252-06355-4
(pbk. : alk. paper)
    1. Funeral rites and ceremonies—Appalachian Region.
2. Appalachian Region—Social life and customs. I. Title.
GT3206.5.C75 1994
393'.0974—dc20   93-23784
                                                                    CIP

This book is dedicated to
Mary Crissman
and the memory of
Mary Martha Keller Ayres

Contents

Preface

I first encountered death when my maternal grandmother passed away in 1952. Although I was very young, I can still remember my family members gathered around her while she was ill, my mother's reaction when she received the news of the death, the all-night wake with jokes and stories, the trauma of the emotion-filled funeral, and burial in the family cemetery in the mountains of southwestern Virginia. I was too young at the time to truly understand what was going on.

When I was in high school, like many other people my age, I attempted to earn some extra money. Unfortunately, in a small place like Honaker, Virginia, there weren't many places to get a job. In addition to working in the Ben Franklin Store one Christmas and trapping throughout high school, I helped my maternal grandfather work on the family farm. One of my many tasks was filling the sunken graves in the family cemetery with dirt. At that time, I became curious about who these people were, how they had died, why they were buried so far back in the mountains, why I had to keep adding dirt to these burial spots, and why some had headstones and others didn't. In the early 1960s, my maternal grandfather died. While grieving, I was fascinated by the events surrounding his death, wake, funeral, and burial.

In the early 1970s, after my paternal grandparents had passed away, I came across a photograph that belonged to my grandmother. It was a picture of my grandmother's brother, who had died in 1914, lying in his coffin. Once again, I was intrigued. Why was the picture taken? Why was the coffin open? How had he died? What was the wake like? What was the funeral like? Where was he buried? While many of the questions were unanswerable, my interest in death and dying grew.

It wasn't until my college years when I developed my sociological imagination and became well versed in research methodology that I was able to pursue my questions. I decided to focus on my ancestors and what dealing with death was like for them. I wanted to know why the process was much different today from what it had been when settlers first came to the area. Since I wanted to examine these changes, I concentrated on four different sources. First, I used my personal experiences of a life spent almost exclusively in the mountains to formulate avenues of research. Second, I surveyed several hundred books, journal articles, and other written sources. Postdoctoral fellowships from the University of Kentucky and Berea College provided assistance in accomplishing this task.

Unfortunately the literature did not give me enough material. I could not include information on African Americans, Native Americans, Hispanics, or Asian Americans in this book at least partially because there simply hasn't been much written on them in central Appalachia. I hope that despite their small numbers in this region and complications that can arise in making broad cultural comparisions scholars will perform extensive studies of these important groups in the future.

The literature was also woefully inadequate for concrete information on changes in death practices from the early settlement years to the present. I realized I had to interview as many of the older mountain natives as possible, who had lived through many of the changes, before they died and took a wealth of information with them. Beginning in the 1970s I conducted interviews with almost four hundred mountaineers throughout the five-state area of central Appalachia. Most of my firsthand information came from residents over the age of sixty-five, though even informants in their nineties could not testify to everything in the literature. Most of the people I approached were willing to be interviewed, but most also requested anonymity. I have therefore omitted all personal names in this account. Finally, I incorporated the data on music from over one thousand audio recordings made between 1922 and the present in addition to pamphlets, books, journal articles, sheet music, and information gathered by collectors.

Despite this scholarly and professional interest in this topic I am convinced that if I had not grown up in the mountains, if I had not seen a death watch, if I had never found that photograph, and if my grandfather had not employed me to fill in those graves my curiosity about this subject would never have been piqued. I would never have asked all of those questions about death and dying and I certainly would not have started down this road toward resolution. This book is the result of my long search for answers.

Acknowledgments

It is impossible to write a book without the assistance of others. Numerous people made contributions to this book, but I can acknowledge personally only a few.

I am indebted to the multitude of men and women in central Appalachia who provided information through face-to-face interviews and telephone conversations. Some of the discussions were short and others were quite lengthy, but all of the respondents were willing to take time from their busy schedules, and each bit of knowledge gleaned from them was important.

In 1981, I received a postdoctoral fellowship from the University of Kentucky's Appalachian Center to perform an extensive review of the Appalachian literature pertaining to death and dying, and the Appalachian Center at Berea College provided another postdoctoral fellowship in the summer of 1983, which permitted me to conduct interviews throughout central Appalachia. I am obliged to John Stephenson and Loyal Jones for their confidence in my project.

While many funeral directors, museum directors, librarians, and other professionals assisted me in finding material for the book, major contributions were made by R. D. (Bob) Bennett, President, Honaker Funeral Home, Inc., Honaker, Virginia; Martha Smith Cecil, W. J. Smith and Son Funeral Home, Newport News, Virginia; the Kentucky Historical Society, Frankfort, Kentucky; Historic Crab Orchard Museum and Pioneer Park, Inc., Tazewell, Virginia; Richard Stannard, President, J. A. DeDouch Company, Oak Park, Illinois; and Sammy L. Campbell and Sam W. Campbell of Campbell Funeral Home, Inc., Abingdon, Virginia.

My gratitude is extended to Sue Boutwell and Judy Hartman for their help and to my daughter, Jennifer, who tagged along with her dad as he searched for artifacts and had to deal with his inattention on many occasions. I am forever indebted to my mom and dad, Clarence and Mamie Crissman, for all their help with my research endeavors, understanding when I went home to visit and spent my time gathering information, and for just being my parents. A special thanks to my friend and secretary Trish Worth for her help during the project and to the students who assisted with the various phases of data compilation: Edward Schmelzer, Aneela Minhas, Susan McGuire, Katherine Czyzewski, and Kathleen Rogoz.

More than anyone else, I appreciate the love and support of my wife, Mary. She helped formulate the ideas for the research, conducted interviews, walked through hundreds of antique shops, museums, funeral homes, and cemeteries while assisting me in my search for information and objects, attended meetings if I couldn't be present, understood when I had to work on the book and she wanted to do other things, and took a lot of the work at home from my shoulders.

Introduction

Death is an angel sent down from above,
Sent for the buds and the flowers we love,
Truly 'tis so, for in Heaven's own way
Each soul is a flower in the Master's bouquet.
—"Gathering Flowers for the Master's Bouquet"

Many Americans avoid the word "death" if possible. Instead of stating that someone has died they use expressions such as "passed away," "kicked the bucket," "departed," and "expired." A decedent may be "no longer with us," "on the other side," "gone to heaven," or "six feet under," rather than dead. DeSpelder and Strickland in *The Last Dance*, list sixty-seven euphemisms or vague expressions that are often substituted for the words "death," "died," or "dead."[1]

This evasion is a fairly recent development in the attitude toward dying. Until the early part of the twentieth century, death was a part of everyday life in the United States. The average life expectancy in 1900 was only forty-seven years and the mortality rate for all age groups was high.[2] Until medical technology was sufficiently advanced, diseases such as tuberculosis, pneumonia, typhoid fever, and diphtheria took the lives of many people. Epidemics and industrial accidents killed many others. Both women and infants died during childbirth because of insufficient medical care or knowledge.

During the period, rather than living in nuclear families or in even smaller components as they do today, many Americans lived in extended families. Most lived their entire lives near or with other family members. Because of this, a person "couldn't pass through childhood without experiencing the death of several members of the family."[3] Death usually occurred in the home with relatives and friends present. The deceased was prepared for burial in the home and kept there until interment.

To make the reality of death even more apparent, objects were preserved as reminders of the loss of a loved one. People saved locks of hair, clothing, jewelry, and other objects belonging to the departed. When photography was introduced, some Americans kept pictures of the deceased. Black served as a reminder of death for months or even years. Black wreaths were placed on doors. Black clothing was worn to the funeral. Black garments and jewelry were worn, especially by women, as a sign of mourning and to remind others that a death had occurred.

In the early 1900s, the number and quality of medical personnel and health care facilities available in the United States began to increase, and with them so did knowledge and technology, even in rural areas. These advancements have had a tremendous impact on the death rate during the last seventy to eighty years. The mortality rate for women and infants in childbirth has dramatically decreased while the average life expectancy for all age groups has increased. Epidemics have been significantly reduced. Major diseases such as tuberculosis and diphtheria have been conquered or controlled. Machines and procedures make it possible to diagnose and treat illnesses with a much higher degree of accuracy.

The workplace has also become less deadly. Better machinery and an emphasis on safety have curbed accidents in many industries. New child labor laws and requirements of safety devices have been instrumental in saving lives in factories. Particularly significant has been the decrease in coal mining disasters as a result of technological advancements and stress placed on safety inspections and procedures.

This rise of technology has changed the face of dying. With Americans living longer and family size decreasing, most individuals will come in contact with death less frequently. And when people do die, it is usually in a hospital or long-term care facility rather than at home. The improvements in transportation and the increase of business opportunities around the world have helped break up the extended family system. Since many Americans live far away from their families, they are unlikely to be present when a loved one dies. Funeral establishments have replaced neighbors and family as the principle custodians of the dead. Contemporary Americans are less likely than previous generations to dwell on death or carry out death rituals. Such practices as keeping hair belonging to the departed and taking photographs of the decedent are no longer popular. Black as a symbol of mourning has not been eliminated, but it is no longer a dominant cultural trait associated with death, the funeral, and bereavement.

While the twentieth century produced a decline in personal contact with loss of life, beginning in about 1965 impersonal contact with death increased. The mass media, particularly television, has made dying a visible feature of life in the United States.[4] Though wars had been portrayed in movies and documentaries, television brought the Vietnam conflict into the homes of Americans on a regular (almost nightly) basis. Never before had people in the United States come in such close contact with death without encountering it directly. They received firsthand information about draft resistance, viewed corpses on television, and listened to news and debates concerning body counts.

Violence and death on television have increased dramatically since the Vietnam conflict so that it is impossible to watch without coming in contact with them. Increasing numbers of people have spoken out against their portrayal, especially because children have ready access to these images. Cartoons, westerns, detective shows, movies, news reports, and other forms of television programming viewed by children often make references to death. "Although estimates vary, it is said that the average American child has seen between 13,000 and 18,000 deaths on television by the age of 21."[5]

Social issues including capital punishment, abortion, infanticide, euthanasia, and teenage suicide have brought death into public awareness and have personally affected the lives of millions of Americans in recent years. Fear of nuclear holocaust, the war with Iraq, concern about the destruction of the environment, violence in urban areas, international terrorism, the assassination of political leaders and heroes, mass murders, and the rise in AIDS cases have led many individuals in the United States to contemplate their own mortality.

As people contemplate death more frequently, their important health care issues have become more death focused. People are beginning to emphasize the rights of the dying and to react against dehumanizing technology to prolong life. Hospices have been instrumental in delineating and meeting the needs of the dying and their families.[6] A death awareness movement has focused on such topics as the plight of the growing population of elderly citizens, controlling the AIDS epidemic, and improving quality of life for the dying in hospitals.[7]

Death awareness has increased in great part through the establishment of thanatology as a legitimate field of academic study. According to Kastenbaum many scholars assume "that by studying death we will somehow reduce our fears and anxieties."[8] Classic works such as Elisabeth Kubler-Ross's *On Death and Dying*, Jessica Mitford's *The American Way of Death*, and Robert Habenstein and

William Lamers's *The History of American Funeral Directing* have contributed an immense amount of knowledge to the field of thanatology and stimulated other scholars to systematically study people's experiences with death and dying.[9] The number of scholarly works in thanatology has expanded dramatically. DeSpelder and Strickland assert that in 1964 a bibliography of death-related publications consisted of about four hundred references, but by 1975 it had grown to approximately four thousand.[10] Another scholar estimates that more material on death was published in scholarly journals between 1970 and 1975 than in the preceding one hundred years.[11] Over one thousand courses on death and dying are now offered in American colleges and universities. Thanatology has become an interdisciplinary enterprise.[12]

Despite all of this interest, many Americans still avoid talking about death. I doubt it will ever be a popular subject for Sunday conversation (or any other day for that matter). In this book I will illustrate how Americans could have come to such an abrupt change in attitude and behavior using central Appalachia as a focal point. This area offers rich material for study because of its isolation and peculiar settlement pattern. These insular people hung on to the traditions the first settlers brought to the mountains well into the twentieth century. Though many of the old ways are rapidly dying out or have already ceased to exist, some elderly mountaineers still remember and practice the same death rituals that their ancestors did. This juxtaposition of tradition with progress allows for detailed analysis of how and why life changed for these people, what factors influenced them, and how they may treat death in the future.

Appalachia and Central Appalachia

Scholars disagree on the definition and boundaries of Appalachia. In *The Southern Highlander and His Homeland,* John C. Campbell argues that Appalachia "extends from New York to central Alabama."[13] John Gaventa says that it stretches from western New York to northern Georgia.[14] According to Jack Weller, Appalachia is a long range of mountains that runs for 1,300 miles "from Vermont to northern Alabama."[15] Howard B. Lee in *Bloodletting in Appalachia* states that Appalachia "extends in a southwesterly direction from northern New York into northern Alabama."[16] Geographers consider Appalachia to be a vast territory that begins in the Maritime Provinces of Canada and extends southward. I have talked with scholars who place the northern boundary in Maine and maintain that the western boundary extends into southern Illinois.[17]

As defined by the Appalachian Regional Development Act of 1965, the area extends from the Mohawk Valley in New York to the Fall Line Hills in Mississippi.[18] The majority of scholars agree on this definition and include all of West Virginia and parts of New York, Pennsylvania, Ohio, Maryland, Virginia, Kentucky, Tennessee, North Carolina, South Carolina, Alabama, Georgia, and Mississippi in Appalachia.[19] Southern Appalachia, which has received the most attention through the years, excludes New York, Pennsylvania, and Ohio. Central Appalachia, which has been subjected to the most research and scrutiny, makes up part of southern Appalachia and includes Kentucky, Tennessee, Virginia, and West Virginia. In this book I have defined central Appalachia as the Appalachian sections of Virginia, Tennessee, North Carolina, and Kentucky (including the northeastern and southeastern parts extending into the foothills), and the entire state of West Virginia.

Early migration into this region began in the late 1600s. Central Appalachia was settled from east to west by immigrants from the English colonial settlements on the eastern shores of Virginia, Maryland, and North Carolina.[20] It was settled from north to south by Scotch-Irish, English, and German immigrants from Pennsylvania.[21] Most of these people fled Pennsylvania, New Jersey, Virginia, and North Carolina.[22] By 1750 to 1775, settlers were firmly entrenched in the fringes of the central Appalachian Mountains. Caudill notes that these early settlers were "the seed stock of the 'generations' whose descendants have since spread throughout the entire mountain range, along every winding creek bed and up every hidden valley."[23]

The early central Appalachians were not the elite or the aristocrats of the early colonies, but rather almost entirely unskilled or semiskilled workers who moved into the Appalachian mountains to escape.[24] Many were looking for religious freedom and a way to avoid the heavy taxation prevalent in the colonies.[25] In particular, they resisted the exigencies and atmosphere of the Episcopal church: "Many had come from the lowlands of Virginia, where the Episcopal was the established, official church, and all were taxed for its support, whether they adhered strictly to its teachings or not. It was partly to escape the tax and to gain other freedoms of thought and deed that impelled them to make the arduous trek westward. And the lack of emotionalism and strict formality of the Episcopal service did not appeal to their independent way of thought."[26]

Some came looking for adventure and danger absent in the established colonies.[27] Famous trailblazers such as Daniel Boone, Kit Carson, James Harrod, Simon Kenton, John Colter, Jim Bridger, and

Dr. Thomas Walker needed to escape the routine and safety of the East. They all either traveled through central Appalachia or spent a portion of their lives in the area. Some, as fugitives from the law, brought adventure and danger with them.

A large number of the early settlers were indentured servants in the colonies who moved into central Appalachia after they were freed. With the demand for labor in colonial America, orphans, people in debtor's prisons, and criminals were brought from England to satisfy the needs of the wealthy land and business owners. Children were kidnapped off the streets and sold into servitude. In exchange for seven years or more of labor, these people were given food, shelter, and, eventually, freedom. When their terms were up, many of those who felt out of place, or could not afford the price of land in the colonies, moved into the isolated wilderness of the central Appalachian Mountains.

Weller perhaps best captures their spirit when he describes them as the perennial frontiersmen, interested in freedom from the restraints of law, order, and a differing culture, who came to the shores of America in rebellion against the type of society they found already entrenched on the eastern shore.[28]

> The early settlers included, too, many of those on the "first frontier"—those land-hungry, self-sufficing farmers who were in opposition to many of the policies of the British crown and the seaboard regions, particularly on matters of land titles and Indian affairs. They were determined to establish a life as free from contact with law and restraint as possible. In rebellion against a form of government that imposed its rule from the top, these people reverted to a system of private justice based on the personal relationships common to the clan. They thus developed a general ideology of leveling—a system that gave equal status to all and that recognized no authority other than the force of an individual. No hierarchy, authorities, or experts were allowed to form in this society; no pressure from outside was allowed to gain entrance.[29]

Many pioneers sought the solitude of the mountains, which provided a sanctuary that protected immigrants from the foreign culture of the colonies.[30] Some of the settlers only wanted a place to live and land to call their own, but the wilderness and rugged terrain separated them both physically and psychologically from the rest of the United States. While making a subsistence living farming their land, these people became increasingly independent and isolated. The culture and social structure grew out of this isolation and these combined with the virtual inaccessibility of the mountains deterred progress for many years.

There is a lot of diversity among these people despite the seclusion of the area, but most central Appalachians share common cultural characteristics. In a survey of Appalachian literature published from 1898 to 1972, Bruce Ergood identified eleven specific traits of mountain people: independence, religious fundamentalism, strong family ties, life in harmony with nature, fatalism, traditionalism, honor, fearlessness, allegiance, suspicion of government, and born trader.[31] These characteristics grew out of the harsh surroundings, the traditions the settlers brought with them, the immigrants' own strong personalities, and the necessary way of life families built for themselves.

Each family had to struggle to produce enough food to survive. Family members worked together and relied heavily on each other but could not rely on anyone else because the nearest neighbor was likely miles away. The honor, allegiance, and traditionalism of the mountaineers eventually made them resist any attempts at external control of their family or clan and led them to incorporate into their value system what Charles Neville Buck calls a loyalty to "kith and kin above all."[32] The "code of the mountains" rose out of this loyalty, which required reprisal for harm done to any family or clan member by an outsider.

Between fighting against other clans and fighting against the elements, mountain culture virtually revolved around death. Death was commonplace, but that didn't make the death of a loved easy. The peculiarities of this culture and especially family closeness gave rise to a distinctive relationship with death that allowed for honor and dignity for the deceased and grieving and comfort for the survivors. Examining this relationship and the rituals of these people can show us not only how death functioned in this earlier society but also why and how its importance and centrality diminished and what implications this has for the future.

ONE

Familism, Neighborliness, and the Death Watch

In the silent hour of midnight,
In the silence calm and deep,
Lying on her mother's bosom,
Little Bessie fell asleep.

Now up yonder at the portals
That are shining very fair,
Little Bessie now is tendered
By the Saviour's loving care.

—The Blue Sky Boys, "Little Bessie"

U rbanization has had a tremendous impact upon the family in America. The transformation from a rural to an urban environment has produced what Parsons and Ogburn and Nimkoff refer to as a "loss of functions."[1] This means that many of the functions now performed by other social institutions (e.g., the church and the school) were once the exclusive domain of the family. The loss of functions has resulted in the isolation of the family. Kinship units no longer play a major role in the everyday life of family members. The modern urban family now occupies a dwelling separate from the family of orientation of either the husband or wife and is economically independent of the kinship unit. Family members depend primarily on the nuclear family or outsiders, especially for occupational earnings. This loss of functions has wrought changes in the American family including a decrease in family size,[2] a decrease in male family dominance,[3] the establishment of the nuclear family as the dominant family type,[4] and a decrease in familism.[5]

Theodorson and Theodorson in the *Modern Dictionary of Sociology* define familism as "a form of social organization characterized by familial values that emphasize the subordination of the interests and personality of individual family members to the interests and welfare of the family group. It is characterized by a strong sense of family identification and loyalty, mutual assistance among family members, and a concern for the perpetuation of the family unit."[6]

Urbanization has been instrumental in replacing familism in America with a sense of "atomism" or "individualism" in which the individual puts his or her welfare above that of the family.[7] A high value is placed on individual freedom and personal autonomy.[8] Parsons states that the modern nuclear family[9] does not place a great deal of emphasis on family dependence or stress a high degree of familism (i.e., emphasize things like perpetuation of the family unit or family identification). Ties between parents and their families of orientation (families into which they were born) may be weakened or severed. Socialization of children, which is the major function of the family, stresses the child's temporary dependence on the parents (the child remains dependent on the family only as long as is necessary), and the primary agents of socialization (the parents or guardians) do not become enmeshed in family ties.

Concomitant with the decrease in familism has been a growing dependence on nonfamily organizations and individuals. This reliance on "outsiders" adds to the weakening of family ties.[10] The changeover, from an agrarian economy where family dependence was necessary to an industrial economy where the division of labor increased the amount of reliance on persons outside the family, was recognized by researchers such as Emile Durkheim[11] almost one hundred years ago. Durkheim viewed this feature of social change as positive, rather than negative, in that the complex division of labor was an inherent orderly feature of modern urban society.[12]

Familism in Appalachia

When the early settlers moved into the mountains, the family was very important. The nearest neighbor (if there was a neighbor) was many miles away. Family members depended on each other for economic existence and protection. If sickness prevailed, it was the family that took care of the individual until he or she was well (or died). Therefore, familism—the primary loyalty to the family before any other group or principle—became a cultural trait in the mountains. In fact, it was, perhaps, the most distinguishing trait of life in early Appalachia.

While the rest of American society was experiencing major transformation around the turn of the century, Appalachia was undergoing a much slower rate of change. The sociologist George Vincent, after visiting the mountains, called Appalachia "a retarded frontier," while W. G. Frost referred to mountain residents as "our contemporary ancestors."[13] In his *Our Southern Highlanders*, first published in 1913, Horace Kephart reflected that "mountain folk still live in the eighteenth century."[14] While major changes have taken place in the mountains of Appalachia in the last eighty years or so, some contemporary authors report that Appalachia still lags behind the rest of the United States in many respects.[15]

The high degree of familism established in the early years of Appalachian settlement continued into the late 1800s and early 1900s as strong as ever. Vincent, presenting an outsider's view, observed that "family ties seem very strong and arouse, perhaps, the keenest sense of social solidarity to which the mountaineer responds."[16] Kephart noted that "highlanders display an undying devotion to family and kindred."[17] According to Kathy Kahn, Appalachian women transmitted to their children a respect for family unity.[18] Each family took pride in itself. Family members were supposed to be proud of their heritage and if the family name was impugned, each individual was expected in all cases to defend the family's honor. In times of crisis, the extended family network was there for support.[19]

Family loyalty was so extensive at the turn of the century that it resulted in many bloodbaths referred to as "mountain feuds." Vincent observed that this "tribal spirit has been a powerful factor in the feuds and 'wars' that have played so striking a part in mountain life during the last thirty years."[20] "Marriage and other family ties were all the excuse needed to induce a mountaineer to pick up his gun and go to the defense of the neighbor with whom he sided."[21] This means that one did not have to be a relative by blood, marriage, or adoption to be a feud participant. He or she might simply side with one family or the other. Perhaps Kephart puts it most succinctly:

> "My family right or wrong!" is a slogan to which every highlander will rise, with money or arms in hand, and for it he will lay down his last dollar, the last drop of his blood. . . . Your brother or cousin may have committed a crime that shocks you as it does all other decent citizens; but will you give him up to the officers and testify against him? Not if you are a mountaineer. You will hide him out in the laurel, carry him food, keep him posted, help him to break jail, perjure yourself for him in court—anything, everything to get him clear.[22]

The early mountain feuds were numerous. Three of the most notable were the Allen-Edwards war in Hillsville, Virginia, in which feudists "enraged by the outcome of a trial, entered the circuit court-room and shot to death the circuit judge, commonwealth attorney, sheriff and three of the jurors";[23] the White-Baker war in Clay County, Kentucky, where "countless participants died in grim gun battles, some of them on the streets of Manchester, the dusty little county seat";[24] and the feud between the Hatfields of Kentucky and the McCoys of West Virginia.[25] This last dispute brought two states to the brink of war and resulted in at least sixty-five deaths. Accord-ing to Virgil Carrington Jones, "the law promptly stepped in, and the feeling between Kentucky and West Virginia became so bitter that they prepared to send troops against each other."[26]

While familism had decreased in urban America, Appalachian writers in the three decades preceding 1980 were still reporting the clannishness[27] and extreme familism extant within the mountains.[28] According to Brown and Schwarzweller, "In some instances, family loyalty is so strong as to be almost pathological by modern urban middle-class standards."[29] It took precedence over anything or any-body else including the law.[30] The loyalty was extended to cousins, nieces, nephews, uncles, aunts, and in-laws even though the moun-tain feuds were virtually extinct.[31] Though fictional, a good illustra-tion of familism carried to the extreme is Jesse Stuart's *Taps for Pri-vate Tussie*.[32] When Private Tussie is supposedly killed in World War II and his wife inherits a large sum of money, relatives arrive to share in her good fortune. Since they are "kin," they are not turned away. Eventually, with forty-six kinfolk in the house, the destruction to the property became so great that everyone was forced to move.

Jack Weller viewed loyalty as being built into Appalachian cul-ture.[33] Children at a very early age were taught to focus their atten-tion on the maintenance of family solidarity.[34] This cohesiveness continued into adulthood, and children were bound to their fami-lies, particularly the parents, which encouraged insecurity. Both sexes tended to settle not far from their parental home. Family members would gather when there was sickness, death, or some other disas-ter, and outsiders were only consulted when a problem could not be solved within the family.[35] Weller reported that frequently when an individual needed to be hospitalized and a decision made by the family in consultation with the physician, it was the parents of the afflicted rather than the spouse who were called in to make that decision.[36]

Very little research has been done on familism in Appalachia in the last ten years. Studies involving a random sample of respondents living in the Blue Ridge Mountains of Virginia revealed the presence of kin-oriented familism.[37] Data that I gathered in 1987 and 1989 studies indicated that while familism was present among central Appalachians, it was moderate and not significantly different from that of urban dwellers.[38] My first study conducted in Akron, Ohio, compared urban central Appalachian migrants, other migrants, and people who had lived in Akron their entire life. Familism was moderate and central Appalachian migrants were not significantly different from other urban dwellers. The second study of 675 residents of West Virginia delineated a moderate degree of familism that was comparable to that of the central Appalachian migrants, other migrants, and urban natives in the Akron project.

Neighborliness

When the early pioneers moved into the mountains of Appalachia, many sought isolation. They didn't want or need neighbors. "A distant shot, heard faintly across the misty mountains, was enough to cause a frontiersman to pack up his belongings and move on to less crowded quarters."[39] Everything that was needed was available in the wilderness, so each family became a self-sufficient entity dependent upon no other human being. It provided its members with food, protection from the elements of nature, religious spiritualism, and care when they were ill or wounded.

Eventually, neighbors began to appear. Sometimes they were new families moving into the settled area but often they were relatives by marriage that settled close to their family of orientation.[40] The familism of the Appalachian people was logically extended to these relatives. In addition, as areas in Appalachia became more settled, interaction was no longer exclusively with family members. "Families were in frequent contact with their neighbors during an average work day."[41] Chains of communication were informal and there were few secrets in a neighborhood or community. Kai Erikson states that when coal camps began to develop in the mountains, "neighborhoods and villages began to replace families and clans as the basic units of social life."[42] Familism then was extended to others and manifested itself as neighborliness.

Neighborliness was delineated in many ways in the early mountains. When a family moved into a new Appalachian community, the neighbors were there to greet it and provide assistance in moving into the new home. If someone happened to be passing by the home of a neighbor, he or she was asked to "sit a spell," have some nourishment, or, perhaps, even spend the night.

A prominent form of neighborliness was participation (without pay) in social events such as a house raising, a barn raising, land clearing, log rolling, corn shucking, bean hulling, crop planting, or molasses making. One mountaineer describes a land clearing event as follows: "Back when I was growing up, about February you'd go clearing land, clearing it off for a crop. They'd send one of us old boys out and invite everybody in the whole community to come to the working. They'd come, too. I've seen forty and forty-five and they'd just clean off acres a day, pile it ready to burn. They was grubbing, sawing logs, cutting logs, spreading them, piling them in big grips, and getting them ready to burn."[43]

Neighbors also participated in purely social events such as taffy pullings, and there were female activities such as "quiltings" or "quilting bees":

> The womenfolks would come to the house and have a quilting. They'd have two or three quilt tops and you'd pad them with sheep's wool. Man, it was a sight in the world what was going on! There'd be a lot of girls there, seventeen- and eighteen-year-old, helping them quilt. We all would come in of an evening and we'd want to shake the cat. Four girls—one at each corner—would get a hold of that quilt and another one would throw the cat in, and they got to shaking it as hard as they could shake and whichever one that cat jumped toward was going to get married first.[44]

Familism, Neighborliness, and the Death Watch

A limited diet and scarcity of doctors and medical facilities combined with isolation, poor hygiene, and a lack of food preservation facilities made disease and sickness commonplace in the early years of mountain settlement. Babies were born and people died at home, in adverse living conditions, where several individuals crowded together in one- or two-room dwellings. According to Campbell, old and young, sick and well slept together and shared scanty toilet facilities so that "the spread of contagious and infectious diseases [was] naturally rapid."[45] With the prevalence of illness and lack of medical personnel and facilities, it became necessary for the family and neighbors to care for ailing individuals. When someone became ill or was dying, relatives and neighbors offered assistance.

Until recent years, the sick were first treated at home with "home doctoring," "folk medicine," "herbal medicine," or "home remedies." The mountains provided an abundance of materials that could be used for treatment. Since doctors and drugstores were out of reach of most mountaineers, the majority of homes "had supplies of asa-fetida and camphor, as well as bags of dried herbs, leaves, and other materials for making all kinds of tea, salves, and poultices."[46] In a 1979 interview, an elderly woman in Braxton County, West Virginia, explained: "There were no hospitals to take them to, so we used home remedies such as onion poultices for colds and sore throats, sheep nanny tea for fevers, yar for kidney ailments, and kerosene mixed with yellow root for strep throat."

The obvious response when home treatment failed or could not be employed was to go for a doctor. Unfortunately there was often no doctor within a few days' travel. Sometimes relatives or neighbors were prevailed upon to seek help. According to Raine, "in cases of serious sickness any neighbor may be called out of his field, his plowing stopped, and he and his horse requisitioned to go for the doctor."[47] Even then the doctor might not be available. A gentleman in Wood County, West Virginia, pointed out that "he would usually be making his rounds out in the county," and another elderly man in Wood County complained that "sometimes he would be gone to another area and people would just have to handle things themselves."

Seeking help at a hospital was usually not possible. An elderly woman in Lawrence County, Kentucky, said that she didn't know of anybody who went to a hospital. "People were born at home and they died at home." Transporting the individual was a long, arduous, time-consuming task. A doctor in Gilmer County, West Virginia, in 1981 said that "to take a patient to a doctor or hospital could take several days, if they were on horseback (which they usually were)." Mountaineers employed very primitive vehicles to carry the individual to medical assistance. Even in recent years, transportation has been a problem in some of the more remote mountain areas. For example, Fetterman notes that "when illness strikes far up a hollow, a sled is sometimes the only conveyance that can be used to transport the ailing person to a doctor."[48]

In addition to utilizing "home remedies" and attempting to secure professional medical help for an ailing man or woman, relatives and neighbors in central Appalachia also displayed familism and neighborliness by performing the family's chores and supplying food. This permitted the loved ones of the incapacitated person to devote their full attention to his or her care and needs or get some much-needed rest. According to Montell, they would sit up with the sick person at night and tend to the chores and crops of the stricken family during the daylight hours.[49] No monetary compensation was expected. Interviewees throughout central Appalachia confirmed these neighborly tasks: "The family just took the best care of them that they could, and the neighbors would come in and sit up with them and help in any way they could" (woman in Macon Co., N.C., Aug. 1983). "Family and neighbors would help as far as bringing food and offering help" (elderly woman in Parkersburg, W.Va., Apr. 1981). "They took care of the crops. They'd go in and cut tobacco and put up hay" (funeral director in Russell Co., Va., Aug. 1983). "I've even heard of them having bean-stringings and things like that to take care of the crops. Nobody ever got a penny out of it. It was just corn, wheat, and oats, and things like that. Neighbors would come in and cut his corn, or shuck his corn and put it in the crib. Do anything they could" (ninety-three-year-old native of Sevier Co., Tenn., July 1983).

Will D. Campbell asserts that "somehow in rural, Southern culture, food is always the first thought of neighbors when there is trouble."[50] This certainly holds true for early central Appalachia as well. Neighbors would prepare food and take it to the family of the afflicted person or they would go to the home and prepare meals for as long as was necessary. Their provision of nourishment meant that another burden was lifted from the family. A native of Washington County, Tennessee, in 1983 described what he considered to be a typical situation in east Tennessee: "All the neighbors, uncles, brothers, cousins, and all just dropped in and sat out in the yard. And they'd bring food, and they'd make coffee, and they'd talk and visit."

One of the most outstanding examples of familism and neighborliness in the mountains of central Appalachia was the "death watch" (also called a "death vigil" or "sitting up"), provided when someone was believed to be dying. The practice of maintaining a death watch dates back at least to medieval and Renaissance Europe, where a continuous vigil was usually maintained beside the bed of the dying person.[51] Word of a terminal affliction was spread in the days before telephones and funeral notices primarily by word of mouth or the ringing of a bell. An eighty-seven-year-old woman in eastern Kentucky said they had "dinner bells" in her community. When someone was dying, they would ring the bell to notify everyone.

According to Esther Sanderson, it was nothing short of a crime for the neighbors not to "set up" with someone who was ill or dead.[52] In a 1981 interview, a woman in Glenville, West Virginia, referred to the vigil as "an unwritten rule." The practice of sitting up with the sick resulted in relays of neighbors forming to have someone outside the family present with the ill person throughout the night.

In some instances, friends and relatives traveled for many miles to take part in a death watch. It was strictly voluntary and there was never any monetary payment for their kindness. A Russell County, Virginia, native insisted that "they just sat and waited for the person to die. That's what it amounted to."

The number of persons participating in a death watch varied, but generally all the neighbors and relatives who could be present were there to assist the family in its time of need. Sometimes specific people, rather than all of the neighbors and relatives, would sit with the terminally ill and the family. When just one person performed the death vigil it was usually an older person—most likely an older female and frequently a midwife. Midwives were commonly present at childbirth and sometimes ended up participating in a death watch because of the high mortality rate for women in labor. Midwives also took part in vigils that did not involve pregnancy, especially when doctors couldn't be present. Children participated, but not as often as adults. An interviewee in Gilmer County, West Virginia, told me that if a man was ill, men would take part in the death vigil, but if it was a woman, women would be the caretakers. This does not seem to have been the case throughout the mountains.

A death watch wasn't always a short-term affair. Participants didn't show up for one night and then desert the family and the dying individual. They participated for hours, days, weeks, or months if there was a need. Every attempt was made to ensure that the family didn't have to stay alone and take care of the sick, even if there was a danger of catching the disease or carrying it to their own family.

Neighborliness and familism sometimes proved to be more detrimental than helpful, especially when there were too many people there to watch. John F. Day in his *Bloody Ground* noted that he had seen as many as ten people in an airtight room with a person seriously ill. They smoked, chewed, and talked in loud voices while the patient suffered in silence.[53] Similarly, Raine, in an early description of life in the mountains, remarks that in sickness, friends and kinfolk would gather and sometimes seriously impede recovery by crowding in the room and talking continuously.[54] In circumstances such as these, family members were hesitant to ask those sitting up with the ailing individual to leave, because of a fear of "hurting their feelings."

The death watch served a multiplicity of purposes in the early mountain social milieu. First, and perhaps most important, the watchers wanted to be there to help and support the dying individual and his or her family, while assuring the family members that they were not alone. Second, many death watchers desired to show respect for the sick person, especially since it might be the last time they would see him or her alive, and it was not showing the proper interest if they did not participate. [55] For the family, the death watch provided inexpensive and necessary care, which was considered the humane thing to do.

Participants occasionally focused on less humanitarian reasons as well. An interviewee in Gilmer County, West Virginia, told me that the death vigil, particularly in the summer, was to keep animals from bothering the ill. While there are numerous accounts of sitting up during a wake to keep animals away, this is the only instance I know of related to the death watch. Other people got involved because they expected the family of the deceased to reciprocate if the need should arise. Finally, an element of egocentricity was sometimes involved. Some people reveled in the glory of being present when death occurred and took pleasure from describing the death to those not present. Henry Scalf in "The Death and Burial of 'Boney Bill' Scalf" gives the following example: "Cousin Ruth walked back and forth through the house, telling all who came: 'I held his hands for him when he was dying. He wanted it that way.'"[56]

While familism and neighborliness have decreased within the last thirty to forty years in central Appalachia, they continue to be a part of life. Families are still greeted and provided with assistance when they move into a new area. Fewer combined work and social events (e.g., barn raisings, quiltings, corn shuckings) occur, but neighbors and relatives are there for a family when it is in need. In the present-day mountains, the telephone has replaced the horse as an easy means of notifying neighbors, kin, and doctors of an illness or accident. With the widespread access to pharmacies and medical facilities, there is less need to provide "home remedies" (although there are a few who are opposed to outside medical treatment). Doctors, although they seldom make home visits, are available, and helicopters, ambulances, and four-wheel drive vehicles can penetrate most mountain areas. Still, food and labor are provided when someone is ill or hurt so the family can be freed to think only of their terminally ill loved one.

Although not quite as prominent as in the past, the death watch remains a part of central Appalachian culture and continues to be voluntary. With the rise of medical care in the area the site of the vigil, in the vast majority of cases, has changed from the home to the hospital and usually only family members stay with the dying person. Funeral directors I interviewed in the five-state mountain area insisted that only about 10 percent of people die at home.

As they did in the past, when neighbors and kin participate in a death watch they assure family members that they are not alone. Watchers continue to maintain a death vigil out of a sense of respect and a feeling that it is the proper thing to do. Providing free nursing care and being present at the death are still prime reasons, in some instances, for taking part in a death watch.

Premonitions, Visions, and the Death Rattle

As a result of many years of maintaining the death watch, mountaineers learned to observe certain signs or behaviors that indicated death was imminent. Three common indicators were premonitions, visions, and the death rattle. A premonition of death is a precognition, forewarning, or awareness that one is about to die. It can come through a natural sign, an inner conviction, or a supernatural, magical event. Researchers have documented forewarnings of death in both primitive and nonprimitive cultures, past and present. For instance, Ariés, in his discussion of death and dying from the Middle Ages to the present, describes premonitions of death in fictional as well as real-life situations.[57] Among his numerous examples of people sensing the end was near are Launcelot, Don Quixote, and Johann Sebastian Bach.

Superstition has been a part of Appalachian culture since the days of early settlement. Certain happenings were, and still are, interpreted as omens of a death in the near future. For example, a bird flying through the open window of a sick person's room or an individual's dreaming of something white may indicate that a death will soon take place. Premonitions of an impending death continue to be accepted, in many instances, without questioning.

Forewarnings of death may take place seconds, minutes, hours, or days prior to a death. Robert Sparks Walker provides the following account of one mountain man's precognition that he was dying: "I sat beside him, supporting him in my arms. He could not speak, his countenance was like that of an angel. . . . He turned his eyes upward, and with difficulty articulated, 'I am going.'"[58]

Knowing that the end is near, the dying person can prepare for death. In her *Devil's Ditties*, Jean Thomas reports that "if a body had warning of death in the mountains, he chose the hymn to be sung, the text to be preached, and the preacher to 'improve' his funeral 'occasion.'"[59] In addition to planning the funeral, mountaineers have been known to hastily prepare their coffins, select their burial clothes, make out wills (or at least decide who should get their belongings), and pick out their burial plots when they received a forewarning of death.

There is a common belief that each person's life flashes before his or her eyes at the moment of death. Whether this is true or not, it is a certainty that some people experience "visions" of a person, place, or event shortly before death occurs. They are usually images of a dead family member or religious figure and tend to be similar to the visual hallucinations of one who is mentally ill or the delirious response of someone with a high fever. The time span between a vision and death is generally less than twenty-four hours.

Visions have been noted in several cases in the mountains. For example, a minister interviewed in Russell County, Virginia, in July 1983 gave an account of a man who, on his deathbed, saw Abraham, Isaac, and Jacob and conversed with them. In eastern Kentucky, a mountaineer described a woman who saw Jesus and talked to him. A seventy-eight-year-old resident of Macon County, North Carolina, in August 1983 gave a vivid description of a vision that her grandmother had the night before she died:

> The night before Grandma died, she said, "Oh, I want my baby!" Papa was her baby, but she had raised Uncle Rufe's boy, little Leslie, until he died when he was five years old. And she was just hollerin', "I want my baby!" I went to the door, and Papa and a bunch was out in the yard talkin'. And I said, "Come in here, Papa, I can't understand what Grandma's a-meanin'." He came in there and he said, "Ma, do you want me?" She said, "No, Jake, there's little Leslie. Can't you see him, Jake?" Said, "He's right there. Just look at him. Ain't he pretty?" And she was just a-laughin'. And Papa said, "Well, Ma, I can't see him. But you see him." She said, "I see him, Jake." Said, "He's right there." And said, "It just looks like I ought to reach out and touch him." She never spoke many words after that. And so the next morning at 8 o'clock, she died.

She provides a similar account of the death of her sister-in-law: "And she said, 'K., there's little LeRoy! Can't you see him?' Said, 'Don't you remember little LeRoy?' 'No,' I said, 'I didn't get to see him. I remember when he passed on, but I didn't get to see him.' 'Well,' she said, 'there he is, look at him.' I said, 'I know you see him, but I can't see him.' And she said, 'Well, I'm so glad to see him.' And everybody there was just amazed."

It seems that the "death rattle" or "death rattles" (the plural is sometimes used in the mountains), more than any other indicator, served as a dependable sign that death was near. A resident of Berea, Kentucky, in a July 1983 interview noted that "when the family members heard the death rattles, they knew it was time to make preparations for a coffin and burial clothes."

The death rattle is "a sound sometimes emitted by the dying and caused by expulsion of the breath through channels partly filled with mucus."[60] I found that few people in the five-state mountain area of central Appalachia had actually heard it, but most knew about the death rattle. Those who were present when it took place were in basic agreement as to what it sounded like. "It was just a sound down in the chest" (elderly man in Wautauga Co., N.C., Aug. 1983). "Some have the death rattle and some don't. It's an awful rattling in the throat. It's mucus gathered in the throat" (eighty-seven-year-old woman in Berea, Ky., Aug. 1983). "It just sounded like it was somebody gasping for their breath or something. They couldn't get their breath and just rattled" (elderly minister in Russell Co., Va., Aug. 1983).

TWO

Preparation of the Body

She was taken by her weeping friends,
And carried to her parent's room;
And there she was dressed in a shroud, snowy white,
And laid in a lonely tomb.
—Burnett and Rutherford, "Willie Moore"

A rchaeological evidence indicates that human concern for preparation of the dead for burial predates the advent of human history. For example, in Neanderthal burials, over fifty thousand years ago, the body of the deceased was stained with red ochre and placed in a fetal position, which indicates beliefs about the revitalization of the body after death and later rebirth.[1] The ancient Greeks, within one day after death, washed, anointed, dressed, and laid the body in state to await burial. A hero's body was washed, perfumed, and later cremated.[2] Among the Romans, "the body was washed with warm water, anointed, laid out in a white toga, and decorated with whatever insignia of rank the dead had achieved in life."[3]

Early Jews closed the eyes, washed the body, swathed the limbs, and wrapped the entire body in a linen sheet, with myrrh and aloes added to decrease the odor caused by decomposition.[4] Since the corpse was considered to be unclean and not to be touched, designated women, rather than priests or members of the priestly class, prepared the body.[5] The ancient Chinese placed dying people in a sitting position (to facilitate the departure of their souls), pared their nails, and shaved their heads. Followers of Islam, after being faced toward Mecca and given a mixture of water and sugar (or holy water from Mecca), had their mouths closed and tied, their big toes bound together to keep their legs from spreading apart, and their bodies washed and perfumed. During New Testament times in the Middle East, the corpse was wrapped in clean linen and anointed with spices and ointments prior to burial.[6]

Early and developing cultures have exhibited a wide variety of burial preparations. In America, the Ohlones of the California coast placed feathers, flowers, and beads on the corpse and then wrapped it in blankets and skins.[7] The Bara of Madagascar closed the eyelids and tied the mouth shut until rigor mortis set in, then straightened the limbs and placed the body on its back. Some groups in Australia dried the corpse in the smoke of a fire made of acrid green leaves so that it could be hardened and preserved. In some cases, when a prominent member of the community was involved, the body would be carried around for as long as six months while the deceased's clan members moved from place to place. In some circumstances, to prevent the spirit from reanimating, the legs were broken or the body was tied and bound. One group beat the corpse with clubs, cut into it through the shoulders, stomach, and lungs, or filled the body with stones. Another group scraped off the outside layer of skin to expose the white layer of underskin, which symbolized the whiteness and purity of the spirit separated from the body.[8]

The society that placed the greatest amount of emphasis on the preparation of the body was early Egypt. They introduced a mode of preservation that was the forerunner of modern embalming. Mummification consisted of preserving a body with bitumen, spices, gums, or natron.[9] Originally, mummification was reserved for Egyptian royalty. Gradually, however, it became available to anyone who could afford it. Three methods were available, based on one's ability to pay. The first and most expensive involved carrying the corpse to the embalmers, who passed their professional skills down through their family:

> First they draw out the brains through the nostrils with an iron hook, taking part of it out in this manner, the rest by the infusion of drugs. Then with a sharp Ethiopian stone they make an incision in the side, and take out all the bowels; and having cleansed the abdomen and rinsed it with palm-wine, they next sprinkle it with pounded perfumes. Then having filled the belly with pure myrrh pounded, and cassia, and other perfumes, frankincense excepted, they sew it up again; and when they have done this, they steep it in natrum, leaving it under for 70 days; for a longer time than this it is not lawful to steep it. At the expiration of the 70 days they wash the corpse, and wrap the whole body in bandages of flaxen cloth, smearing it with gum, which the Egyptians commonly use instead of glue.[10]

Hundreds of yards of fine gauze and bandages were used. Amulets and stone eyes completed the process.[11]

The second mode of preservation, which was inferior and less expensive, involved preparation in the following manner:

When they have charged their syringes with oil made from cedar, they fill the abdomen of the corpse without making any incision or taking out the bowels, but inject it at the fundament; and having prevented the injection from escaping, they steep the body in natrum for the prescribed number of days, and on the last day they let out from the abdomen the oil of cedar which they had before injected, and it has such power that it brings away the intestines and vitals in a state of dissolution; the natrum dissolves the flesh, and nothing of the body remains but the skin and the bones. When they have done this they return the body without any further operation.[12]

The third, and cheapest, method of embalming consisted of thoroughly rinsing the abdomen with salt of natron, which was a mixture of carbonate, sulphite, and muriate of soda, and then delivering the body to be carried away.[13]

Egyptians mummified not just human corpses. Animals, birds, fish, and reptiles were also preserved. For example, funerals for cats, the most venerated animal in Egypt, were very elaborate. They were mummified, placed in bronze or wooden cases made in their shape, and often buried with mummified mice to nourish them in the afterworld. In Beni, Egypt, in the late 1800s, a cemetery containing over three hundred thousand cat mummies was unearthed.[14]

Central Appalachia before Embalming

Coroner's offices didn't make their way into most parts of the mountains until the 1930s or later. No death certificates or records were kept other than the family Bible. Even when doctors were available, unless they were present when death occurred they would not go to the home to pronounce a person dead. Therefore, the mountain people had to use their own judgment. Since their medical knowledge was limited, they couldn't determine death by taking a pulse. Usually one person would observe the dying person's breathing. When there were several death watchers, each would make an observation and they would jointly decide the state of the individual.

Some watchers held a mirror to the face of the person believed to be deceased. If there was a trace of vapor, he or she was determined to be alive. A funeral director in Russell County, Virginia, related a story of a woman who could not accept the death of her sister. He explained to her that the sister had died in the hospital and was pronounced dead by a physician before the body was transported to the funeral home. She still did not accept the death and asked to see her. Approaching the corpse, she pulled a mirror from her purse and held it to the face. When there was no vapor, the woman agreed that her sister was no longer among the living.

These techniques certainly leave a wide margin for error. A woman in eastern Kentucky in 1977 said that she believed there were times when a person was still alive, perhaps in a coma and barely breathing, but due to a lack of medical knowledge was pronounced dead. It is quite possible that people were occasionally buried alive. I talked with people who had heard stories about "dead" people "coming back to life," sometimes as much as a day after they were determined to be deceased. In the modern-day mountains, however, with the prevalence of embalming, coroner's offices, and medical facilities and practitioners, there is very little chance that someone will be buried alive.

Authors such as William Lynwood Montell in *Ghosts along the Cumberland* and Judy Stewart in "Superstitions" have delineated a variety of superstitious beliefs and practices related to the period immediately following death.[15] Some people believe that if children under one year of age view a dead person, they will die; if people hear of a death on Monday, they will hear about another before the week is completed; if someone sees a dead person's face in the mirror, that person will be the next to die; if a photograph falls in a room with a corpse, the subject of the photograph will die; a clock should be stopped at the moment someone dies; and a mirror should be covered or turned to the wall. My interviewees most frequently were familiar with stopping clocks and covering mirrors.

Most of the people, though, had never heard of stopping a clock when someone died. Of those who had, many did not know the origin of the practice. When they did provide explanations, these varied from one section of central Appalachia to another. I have ascertained at least three logical explanations. First, clocks were stopped to determine the actual time of death. When the turmoil was over, everyone could be sure of the exact time the person died and also provide accurate information for anyone who might inquire later. Second, some of the interviewees believed that if a clock stopped by itself while a corpse was still in the house, a member of the family would die within a year. Finally, stopping the clocks when someone died, and starting them again after burial, was symbolic of the end of one period in the life of the family and the beginning of another. They were starting a new life minus one family member.

Covering mirrors immediately after a death is a practice that predates the settlement of Appalachia.[16] In these mountains mirrors were covered because if they weren't, another death would occur, usually of the next person to look in the mirror. Some residents also believed that the spirit of the deceased would enter the mirror. The mirror superstitions and others concerning the period immediately following death are not nearly as prevalent as they once were. Modern-day mountaineers rarely cover mirrors and stop clocks.

After death was determined, the next step was to notify friends and relatives. In the earliest days of mountain settlement, since there were no neighbors and family members lived close to one another, notification that someone had died was not a problem. When families began to move farther away from one another and neighbors began to appear, there were more people to notify, and there was a greater distance to travel to spread the news. Originally, news that a mountain man, woman, or child had passed away was transmitted by word of mouth. If the distance was not too great, someone (usually a relative or neighbor) would walk to inform those who needed or wanted to know. When the traveling was more extensive and time consuming, the messenger traveled on horseback. Generally, a member of the immediate family of the departed would contact a neighbor and have him or her spread the news. Sometimes children performed the task, and in some cases, a person passing by was accosted and pressed into service. Sometimes family members lived so far away that it was impossible to notify them.

The custom of ringing a bell to denote a death originated in Europe and was first intended to frighten evil spirits waiting to capture the soul.[17] In Tudor England, a "Passing Bell" or "Soul Bell" was tolled to signify the passing of a person in the community.[18] When communities began to develop in the central Appalachian Mountains, "tolling the bell," in addition to announcing an ailing resident, also notified those within hearing distance that a fellow mountaineer had died.[19] Some areas used the church bell to ring out the news while others employed what has been described as a "dinner bell." While not every community used this technique, it was used in some sections of every state within the central Appalachian region. The mode of ringing the bell, and the response of the listeners, varied from one geographical area to another.

An elderly woman in Washington County, Tennessee, told me that the bell would ring one time, there would be a short delay, and then it would be rung again. The process continued for an hour or so. In western North Carolina, an interviewee noted that when the church bell was rung to signify a death, people who heard would go from neighbor to neighbor until they found out which family needed assistance. A funeral director in Washington County, Tennessee, in 1983 reported that whoever rang the bell stayed at the church for a while, and people would stop by to find out who had passed away. They would then spread the news by word of mouth. In Knoxville, Tennessee, in the early 1900s, after the ringing of the bell, people would continue with their work for a few hours until they thought the family was ready for the funeral.[20] Montell, in his study of the eastern Pennyroyal section of Kentucky, related that the dinner bell was rung three times, which meant "help." Everyone within hearing distance immediately stopped whatever they were doing and rushed to the scene.[21]

Normally, the bell tolled the total number of years of age of the deceased. According to Crosby, in Cades Cove, Tennessee, after first ringing the bell to get the the Cove's attention, the age of the deceased was tolled. This was all the mountain people needed to identify the person:

> You can feel the silence pass over the community as all activity is stopped and the number of rings is counted. One, two, three—it must be the Myer's baby that has the fever. No, it's still tolling—four, five, six. There is another pause at twenty—could that be Molly Shields? Her baby is due at any time now—no, it's still tolling. Will it never stop? Thirty-eight, thirty-nine, another pause—who? It couldn't be Ben; he was here just yesterday; said he was feeling fit as a fiddle—no, it's starting again. Seventy, seventy-one, seventy-two. Silence. You listen, but there is no sound—only silence. Isaac Tipton. He has been ailing for two weeks now. It must be Isaac.[22]

Bells continued to be rung until after telephones were introduced. Telephones were scarce in the mountains during the early 1900s since only a few could afford them. As usage expanded, they became the major means of quickly letting people know about a death. Newspapers, when they became available in central Appalachia, often contained an obituary (a published notice of a death that usually included a brief biography of the deceased) or a simple announcement that someone had expired. Until recently newspapers were not available in all areas and even where they were they were sometimes not published daily, mostly because a large portion of the population couldn't read or couldn't afford a subscription.

In some places, such as Berea and Barbourville, Kentucky, in the early 1900s, funeral notices were posted in the windows of local businesses. Similar to the obituary published in a newspaper, they contained the name of the deceased, date of birth and death, and location, time, and date of the funeral. Sometimes the place of in-

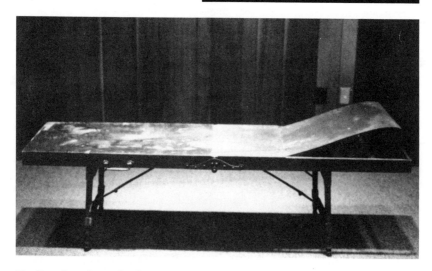

MISS RUTH DAVIS

BORN. MAY 23, 1898
DIED. NOVEMBER 24, 1921

FUNERAL WILL BE HELD AT THE
COLLEGE CHAPEL
AT 2:30 P. M.. SATURDAY. NOVEMBER 26TH
INTERMENT AT BEREA CEMETERY

Funeral announcement that appeared in the window of a local business in Berea, Kentucky, in November 1921.

Cooling board used when embalming was performed in the home. It was carried by a handle, folded to make transportation easier, and resembled a suitcase. (Courtesy of Martha Smith Cecil, W. J. Smith and Son Funeral Home, Newport News, Va.)

terment was included. When they were in town, people would make it a point to go by the shops that usually posted these notices, so they could see who had died.

As far as I have been able to determine, funeral notices are no longer posted in business windows and people no longer ride horseback to convey news of a death in the mountains. Bells are tolled in adherence to tradition rather than as a means of notification. While telephones may not be found in every home, most mountaineers have access to one and can contact people all over the world in a short period of time. Cars, trains, and airplanes make travel to a funeral faster and more convenient. Daily newspapers containing obituaries are published throughout the mountains. In recent years, local radio stations in many areas have begun to provide, on a daily basis, a "deaths and funerals" program that gives complete information on funerals and burial. The mountains, though, still retain their sense of isolation. Even with the advanced modes of communication available, several people I talked with noted that there are times when people find out only after burial has taken place that someone has expired.

CLEANSING THE CORPSE

In the days prior to embalming, the deceased usually died, was prepared, and remained in the home until burial.[23] Preparation of the body was called "laying out" the corpse. While in a few instances it was performed by family members, the laying out was normally done by the neighbors who came to the home for the death watch.[24] Laying out the deceased was sometimes performed on the bed. If the person did not die in the bed, the corpse was often carried there for preparation. However, mattresses made it difficult to keep the body straight and often produced a bowed position when rigor mortis (often called "cold death" or "stiffening" by the mountain people) set in.[25] An elderly woman in eastern Kentucky in 1977 informed me that they would take the feather mattress off the bed and place the body on the ropes or bed slats.

The method most frequently employed in preparing a body was placing it on a "cooling board" (sometimes called a "laying out board"), which has been described as "a board covered with a sheet," "two boards put together," "a scaffold of boards with a sheet," "a big wide board," and "a flat board."[26] The board was usually whatever was available, including a piece of lumber that was handy, a board that was used for ironing, a door that was taken off the hinges, or a table.

The cooling board was either placed on two chairs for support or two sawhorses if they were available. The body was then stretched out so it was straight. Depending on the position of the person at death (some people died while sitting or sleeping in a cramped position), it was sometimes necessary to use warm water or break bones to get the corpse flat on the board so that it would fit in the coffin.[27] Neighbors used a rope, cord, sheet, or something similar to tie the body to the board to keep it straight and prevent it from jerking and scaring people. Even when precautions were taken, "sometimes a corpse that had been straightened would sit up in its coffin in the same position that it had been in when death occurred."[28] The deceased was covered with a sheet until preparation began and remained on the board until placement in the coffin. Bettis and colleagues provide a description of a "cooling board" in one section of the mountains: "The board referred to was a 'cooling board' on which families used to place the body. Each family had its own board that was used by several generations and passed down through the family. The board was usually made of a hard wood like oak. It was about the size of a twin bed. It was often put on saw horses or some other type of support to double as a trestle table at church picnics, barn raisings, etc. Occasionally it was used as an ironing board."[29] A cooling board was also used when embalming was done in the home. To keep the body straight and adequately perform their task so the corpse would fit in the coffin, some embalmers took the board with them as part of their equipment.

In some circumstances, the body remained on the cooling board for an extended period of time, when burial could not be performed right away. For, example, in some remote areas in the winter the ground was frozen so hard that the grave could not be dug with a pick and shovel. A gentleman in eastern Tennessee told a story in which the deceased was prepared for burial in January, but the grave could not be dug because the ground was too hard. The neighbors wrapped the body in a sheet and placed it in the corn crib. It remained there until the spring thaw, when it was taken from the board, placed in a coffin, and buried.

When the corpse was placed on the bed or the cooling board for the laying out, the arms were folded across the chest and the legs were brought together and tied near the feet. If they were not arranged in this manner before rigor mortis set in, it would be difficult to place the body in the coffin. A cord, rope, handkerchief, cloth, or piece of torn sheet was brought under the chin, over the head, and tied to keep the mouth from opening. If it should be open when the body stiffened, it could present what one mountain man referred to as "an ugly sight" at the wake and funeral.

Some people died with their eyes fully or partially open. If they were left open and rigor mortis set in, they couldn't be closed. Therefore, mountaineers placed weights on the eyes to close them and give the impression that the deceased was sleeping peacefully. While stones were sometimes used, coins were the most prevalent means of keeping the eyelids closed. Some people kept coins on hand for this specific purpose. Pennies were most often applied (probably because mountain people didn't have a lot of money and they were more plentiful than any other denomination), however, other kinds of coins were utilized. Pennies were rejected by some mountaineers because they discolored the eyelids. Nickels, quarters, and half-dollars were employed in some instances because they were heavier and did not produce discoloration.[30] A drawback to the heavier coins was that if they were left on too long, they made a noticeable imprint. Terrye Evans and Mark Travis give the following example of weighting the eyes: "'Rather than have the eyes partly open, they'd push the eyelids down and lay a piece of money—usually a penny—on the eyelid to keep it from being partly open at the funeral. They'd make sure that they had the eye pulled down shut, then they put that penny or it could be a nickel on there. When the eye got set properly, they dropped (knocked it off the face) that penny off into the casket and [buried] it with them.'"[31]

The coins remained on the eyes about a day. If they were taken off too soon, one eye or both might be open at burial: "The two old ladies lay on their backs side by side. They were the color of folded white paper. Silver money lay on their eyes. The coin had slipped from the right eyelid of the one nearest John, and the eye stared upward."[32] Since coins were valuable, mountaineers occasionally stole them from the eyes of the deceased. Whether it originated in central Appalachia or elsewhere, the saying that a dishonest person will "steal the money from a dead man's eyes" is still used in the mountains.

Neighbors usually bathed the corpse, which in most cases involved cleansing the face and extremities rather than the entire body, though sometimes they merely aided family members. For the sake of modesty, men usually cleansed male bodies and women washed female corpses. Sometimes, though, women took care of the washing and dressing of the deceased while men made the coffin and dug the grave.[33] In the early years of mountain settlement, when the deceased was laid out, the body was washed with plain water. Later lye soap and water were used. Some central Appalachians also found that applying a cloth dipped in soda water, camphor, vinegar, or alcohol to the hands and face of the departed would prevent them from turning or changing color.[34]

There were also mountaineers who would place a saucer of salt on the chest or stomach of the deceased with the belief that it would dehydrate the body and keep it from swelling.[35] Bettis and colleagues found that in eastern Tennessee, where they interviewed,

> salt was sprinkled on the body to help control the smell of purging (the foaming and dripping that occurred after death). Aromatic cedar chips were used to improve the smell around the corpse. . . . A natural look was preserved by washing the body constantly with wet towels. Sometimes camphor or soda was used on the wet towels to stop deterioration. A saucer of salt was sometimes placed on the stomach or chest. . . . An early method of preservation consisted of putting the body in a mixture that included pine sawdust for about a week to ten days. Turpentine from the pine chips cured the body, but also turned it black.[36]

When the bathing was completed, the hair was combed, but not washed. Mountain people didn't wash their hair as often as they do today (for example, an elderly woman in western North Carolina told me that people in her area only washed their hair once or twice a year), therefore, it wasn't washed after death either. The face of a man would be shaved if necessary or desired. Neighbors ordinarily performed this task, but barbers were occasionally enlisted.

DRESSING THE CORPSE

Coffin, in her discussion of death and dying in early America, says that our earliest American ancestors, when burial occurred, were "wrapped in shrouds made from cerecloth (linen dipped in wax) or wool, soaked possibly in alum or pitch. In some occasions, a fine shroud was sewn from cashmere."[37] It appears that early, as well as some contemporary, central Appalachians were buried in shrouds.[38] These shrouds were similar to robes, less form fitting than dresses, and consisted of a piece of cloth (usually with lace and gathered at the neck) that was draped over the body so that only the face and hands showed. Open down the back, a shroud was easier to get on the body than any other kind of clothing.

Following in the tradition of other societies, central Appalachia had a very specific color scheme for burial shrouds. Richard Huntington and Peter Metcalf report that "although it would be an error to assume that our cultural association of black with death and mourning is universal, there is a very wide distribution among the cultures of the world of the use of black to represent death."[39] Red, white, and black are the three most common colors associated with burial. In many societies, white symbolizes purity and fertility, red represents the good and evil aspects of power and life, and black is symbolic of decomposition and death.[40] In Appalachia most shrouds were homemade and most were black (white was sometimes used for children and women). When funeral homes appeared in the area and shrouds were available in colors other than black and white, the favorite color of the deceased could be used.

Lucy Furman provides a fictional, but fairly accurate, account of what a typical mountain burial shroud was like: "'Oh, hit must be long to her feet, and full, with a ruffle round the bottom, and the aidge notched pretty, and lace full at her neck and wrists, and a cap for her head, too, with two ruffles. Oh, a shroud is what Little Low-izy calls for now—a pretty shroud, a fine shroud, a right shroud, to lay her away in!'"[41]

While shrouds sometimes served as burial garments, most mountain people in the years prior to embalming were interred in their own clothing. Occasionally, the apparel was slit down the back, like the shroud, so that it would fit on the body with a minimum of trouble. The burial attire has been described as the departed's "best clothes," "Sunday best," or "what they wore to church."[42] If possible, the deceased was buried in the outfit they "liked the best," or clothing in which they "looked their best." Many mountaineers only had one or two changes of clothes. In such a case, if it was not possible to make something, interment took place in whatever was available.

Due to the remoteness of the mountains, stores were not readily accessible to most central Appalachians. Even when they were, it was not always possible to afford the price. Because of this, clothing was almost always homemade by the women in the family. If the deceased didn't have anything fit to wear after death, kin and neighbors would get together and make something. In some cases, especially where older persons were concerned, the clothing was made prior to death. According to Sadie Wells Stidham, they made their own burying clothes and "in the summer they would hang them in the sun to make sure the moths didn't cut holes in them."[43]

Men were usually buried in pants and a shirt. As stores became more prevalent, those who could afford them purchased suits to use as Sunday clothes and for burial. While they were the most popular attire for burial, a suit and tie were considered inappropriate for

Bill for funeral goods. (Courtesy of R. D. Bennett, President, Honaker Funeral Home, Inc., Honaker, Va.)

burial if a man was not generally seen in them. Occasionally, people were buried in what might be considered nontraditional garb, such as a military uniform, overalls, or a wedding dress.[44] Babies or small children were sometimes interred wrapped in a quilt or blanket. Women, in most instances, made all of their own clothes, including those for burial. There were few circumstances, even through the 1930s, when a woman was buried in a store-bought dress. It was considered much easier to make women's clothing than to construct a suit or pants for a man. People were normally buried in shoes, but they seldom wore their eyeglasses to the grave.[45]

As with shrouds, black was the preferred color for both burial and mourning clothes.[46] Men were interred in a white shirt and black pants or a black suit. Women usually wore a black dress or shroud. In some instances, women and children were buried in white. Later, when colored cloth and store-bought colored clothes were available, the deceased's favorite color was considered, if possible, for burial attire. Dark clothes, however, were still preferable to those lighter in color.

Central Appalachia after Embalming

While embalming was rejected by the Jews and early Christians and the Greeks preferred cremation, it was used by societies other than the Egyptians, but to a lesser extent. Embalming of sorts was employed by the Romans and was practiced later throughout Europe for sundry prominent and wealthy people, but it was also rejected by some notable figures:

> Alexander the Great is said to have been preserved in wax and honey; Charlemagne was embalmed and, dressed in imperial robes, placed in a sitting position in his tomb. Canute, too, was embalmed, and after him many an English monarch. Lord Nelson, as befits a hero, was returned to England from Trafalgar in a barrel of brandy. Queen Elizabeth, by her own wish, was not embalmed. Developments beyond her control caused her sealed, lead-lined coffin to lie in Whitehall for . . . thirty-four days before interment . . . the body "burst with such a crack that it splitted the wood, lead, and cerecloth; whereupon the next day she was fain to be new trimmed up."[47]

During the eighteenth and nineteenth centuries, several people experimented with preservation techniques. In the United States, embalming gained prominence when it was employed in the preservation of soldiers killed during the Civil War so the corpses could be transported over long distances. Thomas Holmes, "the father of American embalming," who advanced beyond the use of ice for preservation, reputedly embalmed 4,028 soldiers at the rate of one hundred dollars per corpse and returned to his home in Brooklyn, after the war, a wealthy man.[48]

Embalming was popularized when the body of Abraham Lincoln was preserved and taken on a national tour beginning in Washington, D.C., and ending in Springfield, Illinois. Other famous persons were also embalmed. For example, Henry Kyd Douglas in his discussion of the death of Confederate General Stonewall Jackson states that "during the night the body was embalmed and transferred to a neat metallic coffin." Meredith in *Mr. Lincoln's Camera Man: Matthew B. Brady*, presents photographs of embalming performed at Fredericksburg and Gettysburg during the Civil War.[49]

Embalming was first used in the mountains around the turn of the century, though most residents did not practice it until the thirties or forties. Outside the cities and large towns, there "was no undertaker, treading softly with skilled and considerably silent helpers."[50] The first embalmers did not work in funeral homes but came right to the home of the deceased. The embalmer and assistant, with their equipment, traversed the rocky mountainous terrain, where in some cases there wasn't even a road, to accomplish their task. The body was placed on the bed or cooling board, just as it was in earlier years, and then preserved.

Observing an embalming sometimes had a deleterious impact on those who overtly or covertly viewed the procedure. For example, an elderly women in Berea, Kentucky, told of viewing an embalmment through a crack in the door. She had nightmares and wasn't able to tell anybody about her experience for several years. A West Virginian stated that when her father was killed, he was embalmed in the home. While she didn't observe the procedure directly, she later found the evidence in the outhouse, where they threw the cotton, blood, and stuffing. It also bothered her for a long time.

Embalming made slow inroads in the mountains at least partially because it wasn't widely accepted. A funeral director, whose business was started in 1918, estimated that whereas approximately 99 percent of his clientele are embalmed today, only 10 percent were in the early years. The poor could not afford it. Older persons preferred to stick with tradition. Also, people were hesitant about having the body cut so that chemicals could be injected.

The benefits of embalming were slow to make an impression on the residents of Appalachia. A body that was not embalmed could obviously have a disastrous impact on those present for the laying out, wake, funeral, or burial. Roscoe Plowman relates the following story:

> The men had already started digging the grave and I picked a helper to make the coffin. As was the custom, I measured the body: 5'8" by 28". Poplar boards are soft and easy to work with and I soon had the coffin and outside box finished. We covered the coffin and lid with grey cloth, then I looked at the corpse that was outside on the table. The weather had warmed up. The late afternoon sun was shining on the body. To my horror the body was bloating and fluid was oozing all over the . . . table. . . . My helper and I struggled to lift the corpse over in the coffin. It wouldn't go in! "There isn't time to build a bigger coffin!" I said in desperation. With all our weight pressing with both knees; first one side then the other we wedged the body to the bottom of the coffin. The abdomen still protruding an inch above the top of the the coffin, I went for Lena Mae. "I've got to nail the lid

down tight. There can be no viewing of the remains in this condition." She bravely looked at the now puffy face of her husband and turning away said, "Just do what you have to." I pressed the lid down, and we nailed it tight. There was no open casket at the wake that night, nor at the burial the next day.[51]

One bad experience could compel people to change their minds about embalming. The elderly proprietor of a funeral home in eastern Kentucky told me a story about some children who did not want their mother embalmed. On a hot July day in 1935 or 1936, the body was cleansed and dressed and taken to the home. That night, the body began to swell. The next day, they had the funeral and moved the body outside under a tree. Decomposition with discoloration and purging (the sucking that comes from the stomach as a result of the putrefaction of the gastric juices) began. The body was swollen so badly, as a result of the expansion of the gases, that it exploded. The funeral and burial took place as swiftly as possible. A few months later, when the father passed away, all the children came to the funeral home and insisted that they "wanted their father embalmed."

In 1983, an elderly funeral director residing in Washington County, Tennessee, asserted that he had gone to three or four homes where they would not let him perform arterial embalming. So, he did it externally. In his words: "We keep a chemical for external embalming. But that's not good at all. That's temporary. If you're burying them in twenty-four to forty-eight hours, we might be able to control the odor. We do it by just massaging the body with chemicals externally, and it will absorb some, you see. But to really preserve the body, you have to go inside through the arteries."

The earliest embalmers in central Appalachia did not work for, or own, a funeral establishment. In most instances, they either owned or worked in carpentry shops, hardware stores, harness shops, or department stores. Occasionally, a carpenter, in addition to making furniture, decided to use a part of the shop for embalming. Some hardware stores, harness shops, and department stores, while continuing to sell their goods, began to embalm on the premises. Gradually, as the population grew and business increased, "funeral parlors" were established.

Funeral businesses developed at different times in different parts of the mountains. However, by the thirties and forties, embalming and funeral parlors had appeared in most parts of central Appalachia except the most remote and secluded areas. For mountaineers who wanted a loved one prepared for burial, the body was taken to the funeral parlor, where it was preserved, prepared, and taken back

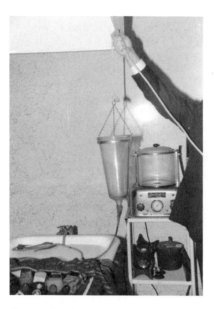

Gravity bottle used in the early years of embalming. It is still used by some funeral establishments in emergency situations such as a power outage. (Courtesy of R. D. Bennett, President, Honaker Funeral Home, Inc., Honaker, Va.)

Modern embalming machine. (Courtesy of R. D. Bennett, President, Honaker Funeral Home, Inc., Honaker, Va.)

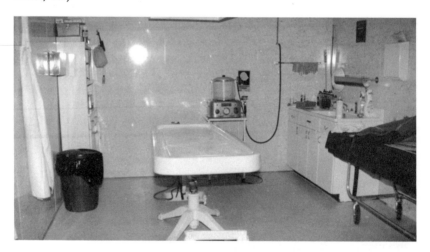

Modern embalming room. (Courtesy of R. D. Bennett, President, Honaker Funeral Home, Inc., Honaker, Va.)

home. In coal mining areas, the company store, in addition to providing coffins and other burial paraphernalia, also handled embalming. A funeral director in Russell County, Virginia, told me that in the twenties the coal company provided coffins in its company store and had a little embalming room nearby. When somebody died, the body was taken there for preparation. There was one embalmer in the area who went to the company store, embalmed and dressed the body, and placed it in the coffin. It was then taken home for burial. He did embalming for the entire county for a fixed fee per person.

As the population increased and houses became too small for wakes and funerals, funeral businesses expanded to handle every phase of the funeral process from death to burial. Even when the corpse was not embalmed, these professionals still cleansed and clothed the body and directed all other aspects of the funeral. People no longer had to "lay out" the body, the funeral home did it for them.

Embalming in Contemporary Central Appalachia

In contemporary central Appalachia, almost no embalming is done in the home, and only about 1 percent of those who die are buried without preservation. The vast majority of the funeral directors I interviewed had not interred an unembalmed body in fifteen to twenty years. Embalming is the preferred means of preservation of the dead in this area, though refrigeration is occasionally used.

While there is a law requiring a funeral home to obtain written permission to embalm a corpse, embalming is not required by law anywhere in the United States, except in certain circumstances (which vary from one state to another). For example, it may be mandatory if interstate transportation is involved, the deceased died as a result of a communicable disease, the corpse will be transported by common carrier (i.e., train, place, bus, or commercial vehicle), or final disposition will not take place within a required number of hours. Kentucky does not require embalming under any circumstances.[52]

Embalming procedures and the materials utilized have changed a great deal since the early years of preservation. The purpose of contemporary embalming is to replace the parts of the body that decay the fastest with a preservative that will retard decomposition. Each embalmer possesses his or her own philosophy and techniques, but most follow procedures common throughout America, including central Appalachia.[53]

When the body of the deceased is received by the funeral home, the embalmer dresses in the proper attire and places the body on a porcelain embalming table. All clothing and valuables are removed and placed in a personal effects bag. The embalmer washes the corpse with a disinfectant and tepid water and then rinses it. During this process, the body is checked for evidence that the deceased died from something other than a natural cause. Body orifices are disinfected, including the mouth, nose, and eyes. Mucous, saliva, and other discharges are removed.

The embalmer shaves both males and females to remove facial hair and poses the facial features. Missing, misfitting, or broken dentures are replaced with dental simulators, and mouth formers are used if necessary. Either a needle injector and wire or sutures may be utilized to close the mouth. The eyes are cleansed and then closed. A nonalcoholic base disinfectant is employed to swab the eyes and remove secretion. Vaseline may be applied to the inside of the eyes to prevent dryness and help hold the eyelids closed. The entire face, including the neck if a carotid incision is not being used, is coated with facial cream to prevent dehydration.

The body is positioned for embalming and supports are placed so as to keep it as flat as possible. The head is properly elevated and turned at least fifteen degrees to the right. The hands are positioned as desired, and the feet are placed approximately twelve to eighteen inches apart. The embalmer clamps a water hose on the table near where the blood drainage will flow. This prevents blood from drying on the table and keeps running water available to the embalmer during the procedure. The temperature of the water is cool or tepid, since hot water will rapidly coagulate the flow of blood and may blister the body.

For arterial embalming the embalmer makes an incision either where preferred or required by the condition of the body. Generally either the carotid artery (at the base of the neck) or axillary artery (under the armpits) is used, with the axillary being the most commonly employed. The blood vessel is raised (i.e., exposed and elevated) from the body part and embalming fluid (consisting basically of formaldehyde, glycerin, borax, phenol alcohol, and water) is injected into it, replacing the rapidly decomposing blood that drains out through a tube inserted by the embalmer.[54] During the injection, the practitioner massages and flexes the body to enhance drainage. When the arterial injection is complete and the drain tube is removed, the incision site is dried. A sealing powder is put on the incision to prevent leakage and it is sutured.

Following arterial embalming, the embalmer performs cavity aspiration (or cavity embalming). A trocar (sharp pointed surgical instrument) with a cannula (tube) is inserted into the abdominal and thoracic areas, fluids are withdrawn, and the embalming chemical is injected. When the cavity treatment is complete, the body is again washed, rinsed, and dried. The hair is shampooed, rinsed, and combed. The embalmer cleans the fingernails and makes final applications of facial cream before enhancing the features of the face with cosmetics. After cleansing the instruments, collecting the trash, and washing the cabinets, floors, furniture, and walls, the embalmer places the body on a cot or dressing table and dresses it.

Unlike dressing procedures in earlier periods, in contemporary central Appalachia the corpse is dressed at the mortuary, rather than in the home by friends and relatives. Burial clothes are no longer homemade. The funeral home furnishes 50 percent to 90 percent of the burial attire (estimates vary from one funeral establishment to another). If it doesn't, the deceased is either interred in clothing owned and worn while alive or store-bought after death. Occasionally burial garments are purchased prior to death or selected during preplanning with the funeral home.

Shrouds have not been used in the mountains for several years. While the deceased was once interred in black or dark clothing or occasionally white, today, burial clothes come in all colors. Every attempt is made to consider the favorite color of the departed when selecting the attire. Generally, men are buried in suits and women are interred in dresses or similar clothing. Several funeral directors told me that their establishments provide a lot of negligees, since they denote sleep. There are still occasions where the deceased is buried in work clothes (their normal and preferred attire).

Belts and shoes are not usually placed on the deceased today. Several embalmers noted that due to the swelling of the body, shoes are occasionally difficult to put on. The dead do wear underclothes. A minister in Dickenson County, Virginia, told of a humorous occasion in which he went with a family to purchase burial clothes. Part of the newly bought clothing was underwear sold in a package of three. As a reward for his assistance, he was presented with the remaining underwear.

THREE

Burial Receptacles and Grave Digging

Sit down the coffin, take off the lid,
Lay back the linen so fine;
And let me kiss his cold, pale cheeks,
For I know he'll never kiss mine.
—Roy Harvey and the North Carolina
    Ramblers, "George Collins"

Oh, Polly, Pretty Polly,
You're guessin' about right.
I dug on your grave
The biggest part of last night.
—Coon Creek Girls, "Pretty Polly"

F or hundreds of years, human beings have been buried in receptacles or containers of some kind. Depending on the culture, people have constructed these receptacles from a plethora of materials including a wide variety of woods, stone (e.g., limestone, granite, basalt, agglomerate, and marble), clay, cement, zinc, glass, iron, bronze, vulcanized rubber, aluminum, papier-mâché, celluloid, india rubber, and cardboard. As technology advanced, crafters became more ingenious in their construction of burial containers, and several very unusual coffins and caskets were designed. For example, a "torpedo coffin" was invented to deter grave robbers; any attempt to steal a body or something valuable resulted in the detonation of an explosive charge. Prior to embalming, ice coffins aided in preserving the corpse.

Wood, stone, and baked clay were employed at various times in early Greek history. In the early eras, most people constructed coffins from baked clay, while chests of cyprus wood were utilized in the later periods. Stone coffins became the most popular, but they were too heavy to be carried in a funeral procession. Therefore, the body was placed on a funeral bier and transferred to a coffin of stone when the funeral procession reached the tomb. Stone coffins (the sarcophagus or flesh eater) made from limestone were ornate, and corpses buried in them completely disintegrated within forty days except for the teeth. Around 1000 B.C., the Greeks began to practice cremation and place the ashes in a clay coffin or urn.[1]

The Romans, like the Greeks, practiced earth burial as well as cremation. Coffins were generally of stone, but many other kinds of materials were used. In Rome during the time of Constantine, the first Christian emperor (314–79 A.D.), a coffin was provided for each deceased person without payment. When the deceased was cremated, the ashes were put into urns that were built into walls around Rome or placed in columbaria.[2]

The earliest containers employed by the Egyptians to protect a body were made of basketwork and wood. The oldest known coffin is the simple wooden container of Mycerinus, an Egyptian king, which dates to approximately 3633 B.C.[3] While the early burial receptacles were rough, simple containers used primarily for the sake of dignity, they became more elaborate in style and decoration as time passed. Later, rectangular sarcophagi made from limestone (wood and other kinds of stone such as basalt, granite, and agglomerate were used in future years), were developed for burial. A wooden coffin could be placed within a sarcophagus for extra protection of the corpse, a practice similar to the modern procedure of placing a casket within a burial vault. During the Middle Kingdom (2134–1785 B.C.), the wealthy were buried in multiple coffins, one fitting into the other, with the outer coffin substituting for a stone sarcophagus.[4]

During the Middle Kingdom in Egypt, the first anthropoid, or "mummy shaped," coffins appeared. Now makers could build the coffin to resemble the mummy itself (corpses of animals were also buried in containers built to match their mummified form). Sarcophagi, both wooden and stone, were also constructed in the shape of the mummy. In the twenty-first dynasty (1085–945 B.C.), rather than construct new ones, sarcophagi were taken from earlier tombs, re-inscribed, and reused.[5]

During the period in which Egypt was under the Ptolemies and Romans (330–305 B.C. and later), the forms of coffins and their decorations changed. A much cheaper process was used to construct them. They were large, rough, badly shaped, and ugly. The poor were sometimes buried in pottery coffins or simply mummified and placed in communal underground chambers where their pitch-soaked bodies were stacked to the ceiling with no coffin or protection of any kind. With the influence of Christianity, the Egyptians gradually abandoned mummification and "were content to lay their bodies in the earth, wrapped in linen cloths only, to await revivification."[6]

While the early Jews and Christians buried their dead, they did not use coffins. The sarcophagus with beautiful iconographic illustrations was first used in the fourth and fifth centuries A.D. During medieval times, the Catholic church began using coffins that were deposited in the church and covered with a black pall prior to burial in consecrated ground. In Islamic societies in the past, as well as today, the use of coffins was forbidden, and the corpse was seldom placed in one.[7]

Burial Receptacles in the United States

The earliest settlers in America were not buried in coffins, since there was little time or technology to construct a burial receptacle of any kind. Actually burial containers date back only about two hundred years in western culture, so they are a relatively new development in disposing of the dead. It wasn't until late in the eighteenth century that anyone, other than the very rich, could afford to be buried in a receptacle of some kind.[8]

As technology advanced Americans could choose from a wide variety of materials for building caskets, including wood, glass, celluloid, potter's clay, zinc, papier-mâché, and india rubber. In 1835, a patent was granted to John White and Associates of Salina, New York, for the construction of burial receptacles from stone, marble, and poured concrete. James A. Gray of Richmond, Virginia, received the patent to manufacture metallic coffins in 1836.[9]

The first coffins in America were made from wood, and their shape reflected the influence of the Egyptians more than any other society. It wasn't until the second half of the nineteenth century, after William Smith of Meriden, Connecticut, constructed the first rectangular burial receptacle, that the word *casket* was used. Today, the term *coffin* is generally used to refer to the six-sided "mummy-shaped" receptacles (it tapers out from the head to the area for the shoulders, where it is widest, and tapers to the feet), while a *casket* is a rectangular container used for interment.[10]

The early coffins were handmade within the community by a relative, neighbor, artisan, or the deceased prior to death. Stores began to carry the hardware necessary for building them, including nails, screws, and hinges. Ready-made coffins appeared around the time of the War of 1812. These early burial devices came with one- or two-piece lids. The two-piece lids meant that only the top half of

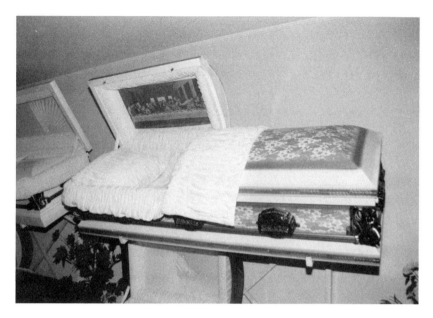

Half-couch decorative casket. (Courtesy of Campbell Funeral Home, Inc., Abingdon, Va.)

the corpse would be displayed, while the one-piece lid meant that if the corpse was to be exhibited, the entire body would be viewed. A coffin with a lid that would slide open a couple of feet for viewing was later developed.[11]

Numerous forms of burial receptacles, in a variety of sizes, shapes, and colors, were introduced in the nineteenth century, including a coffin with a life-preserving device (first made in 1843) that allowed a person buried alive to signal those outside the grave, a cruciform coffin (in the shape of a cross) produced in 1877, and the "preserver" or "corpse cooler" used in the late 1800s. Coffin saw one of these corpse coolers, which "was wooden, paint-grained, with a galvanized liner. Ice was packed around the liner, which extended over the shoulders. A shield at the shoulders retained the ice, and a glass window made the face visible. There were openings to allow replenishing of the ice, and a hose drained water into a bucket beneath the cooler. Before the time of the cooler, bodies were sometimes laid on sod to keep them cool."[12]

Throughout the twentieth century, caskets continued to change and improve. Today, several kinds of caskets are available, including the full couch, in which the entire body can be viewed, and the half couch, which displays the body from the waist up. A hinge-cap casket differs from the half couch only in the placement of the hinges on the molding and paneling, and a lift-lid casket has a removable cover that can be taken off and placed against the wall until time for closure.[13]

Contemporary manufacturers produce caskets in a variety of woods ranging from the cheaper softwoods (pine, chestnut, cypress, and red cedar) to the more expensive hardwoods (oak, birch, poplar, cherry, and mahogany). Most people are buried in metal caskets, such as steel, copper, iron, and bronze, which range in thickness with twenty to sixteen gauge being standard. The lower the gauge, the thicker the metal, the greater the durability and preservation of the body, and the higher the cost to the consumer. Some manufacturers, additionally, provide a sealer casket that is tightly or hermetically sealed for extra protection against nature and decay of the corpse. Cheaper caskets are made of cardboard (for cremation and burial of indigents) and plastic. Finally, people can purchase mail-order caskets, either completely assembled or in kits.[14]

Modern caskets are available in a multiplicity of colors. The lining also comes in a variety of colors and ranges in quality from muslin to velvet. Generally, today's caskets are constructed to denote sleep and comfort. Some include foam rubber, while others have inner-spring mattresses. Terms such as "Perfect Posture," "Colonial Classic Beauty," "Valley Forge," and "Monaco," are used to advertise caskets, and funeral homes now have selection rooms in which they display their wide variety of burial receptacles.

Though vaults are as common as caskets and coffins today it wasn't really until the nineteenth century that the use of a vault became popular, originally among the wealthy. Constructed from a variety of materials including concrete, aluminum, fiberglass, and steel, it serves as an outer receptacle to protect the casket and prevent the sinking of the grave.[15] "The vault, acquired by the bourgeoisie in the nineteenth century, became widespread in the twentieth. This 'super-coffin,' this 'coffin of coffins,' is an index of the 'fever of preservation. . . . It is no longer enough to protect the corpse, we now have to protect what protects the corpse.'"[16]

Burial vaults are now as expensive and elaborate as caskets. For example, the Wilbert Company sells concrete burial vaults with nameplates, decorative handles, the choice of one of four emblems (a wreath, traditional cross, crucifix, or Star of David), and a Strentex lining that provides "hermetically sealed protection." The Wilbert advertisement for the Strentex lining states: "This outstanding seamless lining of pre-formed, high impact polystyrene adds tensile strength to the inner wall of each Wilbert vault for enduring protection. This special reinforcing concept guarantees each vault to be completely airtight and waterproof."[17]

Burial Receptacles in Central Appalachia

Though Christians in other parts of the world had begun using coffins by the time the early pioneers began to move into the mountains, coffined burial did not occur in the United States or central Appalachia for several years. First, there was little time to stop and construct some kind of receptacle for interment. Second, even if they had enough time, few of these early settlers were artisans. Now and then a carpenter, or someone skilled in the use of tools or woodworking, was available, but usually these early pioneers were unskilled people looking for a place to start a new life. Most even lacked the tools necessary to construct a coffin.

Early settlers generally buried the deceased in the clothes she or he was wearing at the time of death. The body might be cleansed and wrapped in a sheet, blanket, or quilt and then placed in the earth with nothing to mark the final resting place.[18] However, like mountaineers today, the early central Appalachian pioneers held such a reverence for the dead, and belief in life after death, that they wanted to be buried in a coffin.[19]

The first containers were probably tree coffins, a receptacle occasionally used in early England where burial mounds have been unearthed revealing skeletons and charred bones in coffins made from hollow logs. While there were no sawmills to cut boards for construction, early settlers could build a burial receptacle from a tree using their primitive tools. Their axes could be employed to cut down a tree and create a log of basically the same diameter from one end to the other. The settlers cut off the top part of the log and hollowed out the inside cavity with a foot adze. The body was then placed inside, covered with the top of the log that became the lid, and placed in the ground. Several of my interviewees noted that this type of burial was practiced in the Marshall, North Carolina, area during the early twentieth century.[20]

After tree coffins, mountaineers constructed boxes of rough or crude boards nailed together with no concern for the way they looked. Through the years, however, mountain people developed an interest in making them more attractive. They dressed up their rough,

Burial without a coffin in West Virginia in the early 1900s.

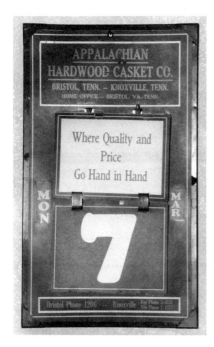

Calendar used as advertisement for the Appalachian Hardwood Casket Co. from the early twentieth century.

Black walnut mummy coffin over one hundred years old that was made for an influenza victim and never used.

rather unattractive lumber with paint or some kind of cloth, usually a cheap cotton fabric such as calico or felt. A few mountaineers chose gray or sometimes white for women and young children, but this fabric was almost always black.[21] According to one author: "For a child, the entire coffin was covered with white material inside and out, including the lid. For an adult, the inside of the coffin was draped with white material and the outside with black."[22] If there was enough time and the appropriate tools were available, the coffin maker planed or "dressed" the wood to present a smooth finish. Later, beautification became easier when mountaineers could choose from varnish, shellac, and stain in addition to paint and cloth.

An attractive wood made a difference in how the coffin turned out, and a wide variety of trees such as pine, oak, poplar, chestnut, cherry, walnut, cedar, maple, and locust are indigenous to central Appalachia.[23] Pine, a soft, plentiful, cheap, but unattractive wood, was the most commonly used, especially by the poor. It was easy to work with, which was important since tools were primitive by modern standards, but decay was rapid when the finished coffin was placed in the ground. Poplar and oak were also often used in the construction of coffins. Poplar, too, was easy to work with and seemed to last longer than pine. It was a rough lumber that when dressed out was smooth and fairly attractive. Oak, a hardwood, also could be made into an attractive casket, especially when stained or polished. It was strong, durable, and popular among high-status mountain people.

Chestnut, walnut, and cherry were nice looking, hard, and durable, but they did not grow in some mountain areas. Mountaineers used them if possible because they not only looked nice but also lasted longer than poplar or pine. For example, a mountain man in eastern Tennessee stated that "pine lasts less than a year, but walnut will last twenty years." Another east Tennessean noted that "poplar was used, but it wouldn't last, not like chestnut or oak." Later, coffins were chemically treated to make them last longer, so the choice of wood was not so crucial.

When the early mountain people began to construct burial receptacles other than tree coffins, they were made by members of the family. The nearest neighbor, if there was one, was many miles away, and there was no one to depend on except other family members. When there was a lingering illness and little doubt that death was imminent, or a person was big or tall and needed a burial receptacle specially built, it was sometimes made while that person was still alive. Elderly mountaineers, in some instances, liked to make final arrangements including the preparation of a coffin. Also, since burial had to take place within about twenty-four hours, it was prudent to have a casket ready when death occurred.

In some cases, family members constructed a coffin when a person was thought to be dying, only to have that person survive. During an epidemic or plague, people hurriedly built coffins and kept them ready for those expected to die. While shopping in an antique store in Sevier County, Tennessee, in 1990, I found a well-constructed walnut mummy coffin over one hundred years old that had been specially made for someone during an epidemic in eastern Kentucky. The person had survived and it was never used. Alberta Hannum provides an example of how ailing people must have felt to know that their coffins were being constructed while people waited for them to die: "Les Alden got 'bad off sick,' and someone of the family sent for the coffin maker. The man came, and went right out to the shed and started hammering. He didn't bother to come in and measure, because everybody knew that Les was the longest Alden of the name. But Les, hearing the racket, asked what it was. When he was told he raised up on his elbow and hollered furiously out toward the shed, 'Quit that! I hain't dead yet!'"[24]

Several scholars have documented accounts of mountain men who constructed their own coffins before they died.[25] This enabled them to select the wood and build it to their own specific criteria. John Parris discusses a situation in which a man planted (in 1885) the tree that provided the lumber for his coffin: "He not only planted the tree, he felled it, supervised the cutting of the boards, and helped shape them into a coffin of his own design."[26]

I encountered several stories while interviewing in central Appalachia of people who bought their burial container (or purchased one for a family member) and kept it in the barn, under the bed, in the attic, or used it for furniture until death occurred. Bettis and colleagues reveal the story of a man who purchased his coffin before death and used it to store tobacco and liquor.[27] An elderly woman in West Virginia told me about a man who bought his coffin early to save money, kept it for years, and used it to store his seed corn. In Washington County, Tennessee, in 1983 I heard from a funeral director the tale of a man who purchased his coffin and kept it in the basement. He liked to lie down in it now and then to see if it still fit. Later, he decided to sell his house and hired a real estate agent. One day she brought some potential buyers to the house, knocked at the door, and received no answer. Finding the door unlocked, she decided to go ahead and show the house to the buyers.

They went through the entire house and just as they reached the basement, the lid opened and the owner sat up in his coffin. It seems that the buyers left in a hurry, and needless to say, did not purchase the house. Lewis Green presents a humorous story of a mountaineer who built a coffin for his wife, determined it was not nice enough, and decided to buy one:

"Ah'd like to buy one o' them white cor'fins like Bushkin 'uz laid away in," Clemmons said. "I'm very sorry, but I don't understand," the man said, shaking his head in a vague and sorrowful manner. "Uh white cor'fin—ah wan' to buy one," Clemmons said. "Well, if someone has passed away, we'd be pleased to show you our units . . ." "H'ain't nobody passed, goddammit," Clemmons growled. "Ah jis' wan' to git one of them white 'uns fer mah wife." "Is your wife dead, sir?" the man croaked, his cold face growing angry. He held his hands before him as if he were praying. "No, she h'ain't dead, dammit," Clemmons said. "Ah jis' wan' to buy her a cor'fin to have when she does die."[28]

While the coffin was sometimes built before death took place, it was usually prepared after the person was deceased. Mountain death was often sudden and there was no time to prepare. Accidents and disease were frequent, and the dying process was usually short. The young didn't worry about death or take the time to make plans because they expected to die when they were much older. In general, like other Americans, the mountain people chose to procrastinate, and when they were no longer among the living, let those left behind take care of the funeral and burial.

Isolated instances in which the husband or son would make the coffin for a loved one continued well into the twentieth century, and on a few occasions, a mountain man even made his own burial container. However, as the mountain population increased and neighborliness became a very important cultural trait, neighbors relieved family members of the burden of constructing the burial receptacle. Whenever they received news of a death, the men would gather the few tools they possessed and meet to begin construction. Some neighbors became skilled in the use of carpentry tools, and they were contacted when a coffin was needed.[29]

With occupational specialization, coffin making became a sideline for mountaineers. Cabinetmakers, carpenters, farmers, blacksmiths, livery stable keepers, upholsterers, and millers sometimes built coffins in addition to their regular work. Louise Murdoch presents the following portrait of a dual-trade coffin maker: "Hen Holiday, who had a natural aptitude for carpentry and a few tools, had also a sympathetic nature and gentle manners, and so was by mutual consent the undertaker for the neighborhood, giving his time and labor, and often the lumber, as he was the miller too, as a matter of course without a thought of pay, and rarely ever receiving any."[30]

These early coffin builders usually had a little shop where they kept at least two or three coffins on hand in case one was suddenly needed. Furniture establishments sold them, and hardware stores, general stores, and dry goods emporiums either sold burial containers or made them. When railroads were built in the mountains, coffins were shipped in large quantities and hauled by wagon from the depot to a store that stocked and sold them along with their regular merchandise.

Coffin making in twentieth-century Appalachia is no longer a sideline. The dual-trade coffin makers have been replaced by funeral establishments that carry a variety of caskets manufactured by companies throughout the United States. Only in rare instances in contemporary central Appalachia is a coffin constructed by someone in the community rather than purchased from a funeral home. Today, hardwood caskets are employed most often for interment, but those constructed from softwood are also used, especially for indigents and those preferring cremation. Oak is most frequently selected, but burial containers made from cherry, mahogany, walnut, cedar, and maple are available. Poplar and pine caskets can still be purchased, and, when finished, they are more expensive than some that are made from metal.

Metal caskets were not used in most parts of the mountains until the thirties and forties. While they were expensive in the beginning and could only be purchased by the wealthier mountain people, the price eventually became affordable, and as the cost of wooden caskets increased, interment in a metal casket became the preferred mode of burial. Mountaineers prefer them for more than their looks, which suggest eternal comfort. They last longer than wooden containers and provide better protection from air, water, animals, and insects. Several people I interviewed even maintained that metal caskets are less expensive than the factory-produced wooden containers. Like those in mainstream America, metal caskets in central Appalachia are available in a variety of metals, shapes, and colors and range in price from a few hundred to several thousand dollars.

CONSTRUCTING THE COFFIN

When coffins were still custom-made, the first step in building one was to take the measurements of the body. Although each custom-

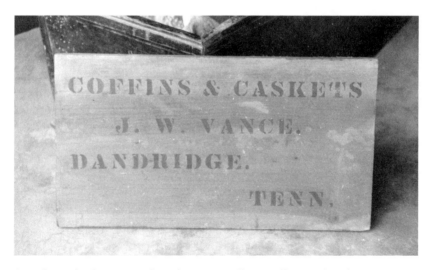

Bill for a casket and the opening of the grave dated December 28, 1943. (Courtesy of R. D. Bennett, President, Honaker Funeral Home, Inc., Honaker, Va.)

Sign from the late 1800s for a business selling coffins and caskets.

Grooves were cut into the side boards of a coffin so that it could be bent into the mummy shape.

made coffin was approximately eighteen to twenty inches at the head and foot,[31] before starting the coffin maker measured the length of the body and the width of the shoulders to determine the length and width of the coffin. A stick (sometimes two sticks) was typically used for this task.[32] Measurements were important because these early coffins were oblong and six-sided, fashioned after Egyptian mummy containers. Developed with plenty of elbow room in mind, it was small at the head and foot and wide at the shoulders. Descriptive terms, depending on the section of the mountains, included "mummy coffin," "toothpick toed," "toe pincher," "squeezing casket," "bent corner casket," and "heel squeezer."

After taking measurements, the coffin maker had to acquire lumber. Sawmills, when they were easily accessible, generally had seasoned wood that could be used. Neighbors would sometimes contribute boards they had in their possession, however, most mountain families had their own lumber on hand. In many instances, they took their best wood and stored it so that it would season and a coffin could be built when a family member expired.[33]

Construction of the mummy coffin, or heel squeezer, commenced as follows: "To begin a coffin a carpenter would cut a board the shape of the bottom. Then he would saw through one half the width on the sideboards. About five of these slits would make the wood bend. . . . Soaking the boards in water or steaming the wood would make it bend easier. . . . The lid would be nailed down."[34] "Some were constructed narrow at each end and wider at the shoulder area. The coffin maker would saw part way through the board in the area where he wanted it to bend. Several such cuts would be made at half-inch intervals. Then boiling water would be poured on the wood to soften it until it would bend without splitting."[35]

Coffins were made so that all of the body was revealed by removing the entire lid. Hinges were not frequently used, since people preferred to remove the lid and set it aside for viewing. Later, the half-lid, partial-view coffin was introduced and hinges were occasionally employed, though the half-lid took more time to install than making a plain lid did. In the southern and central Appalachian sections of the United States today, the half-lid casket is the most popular receptacle for burial, while the full-lid is found more frequently in the northeastern states. The lids were flat, and the early coffins had no handles. They were either carried by holding them underneath at the ends and the sides or were attached to poles on the shoulders of pallbearers. Eventually, when handles became fashionable, they were made from a small straight tree, handles from a wash tub, or anything that was available. Hardware stores and funeral establishments eventually stocked them. They later carried hinges too and plates for the lid, which could include a name, short epitaph, or insignia.

When the coffin was completed, the deceased was placed inside and a cloth or veil was put over the face. Anyone who wanted to look at the corpse had to remove the face covering and then replace it when finished. The lid was then nailed or screwed to the rest of the coffin prior to burial.

Since the deceased was not embalmed, the coffin had to be completed as soon as possible. The time it took to make one varied, depending on how easy it was to get someone to construct it, the time and season of the death, and the availability of construction materials. If someone was available to make the coffin, or a business establishment had some on hand, the corpse could be placed in the burial container within a few hours of death. There were times, such as the one portrayed by Virgil St. Cloud in *Pioneer Blood*, when no one at the death scene knew how to build a coffin:

When this man died, his close friends, as was the custom, set about to get a coffin made for him. Death did not come often to this sparsely settled territory and when it did some kindly neighbor, who was handy with saw and hammer, would make the coffin. But on this day the friends of the deceased came to an impasse. They could find no one to make the coffin. One craftsman was sick abed, another had no suitable material, another was off on a deer hunt and so it was with all who had the skill to perform this important adjunct to the sad rites that, because of the warm weather, must be performed that day. The committee had agreed at the onset that it would be a waste of time to ask Uncle Tobe to do the job. His enmity toward the dead man was so bitter and of such long standing, and he was so "hard headed," and so "sot in his ways," that they knew beyond the shadow of a doubt that Uncle Tobe would, in no uncertain terms, turn them down. . . . As the spokesman broached the subject to Uncle Tobe his voice was apologetic and carried a note of despair and one of timid, hesitant supplication. Before he had said a dozen words Uncle Tobe abruptly cut him off. "Hell yes," he said, "I'll make a coffin for him. I've been a'longin' for that job, lo these many years."[36]

When the deceased expired in the morning or in the winter, there was more time to construct a burial container than if death took place late in the day or during the summer when decomposition was rapid. If lumber was available at the home of the deceased, construction could commence sooner than when it had to be obtained elsewhere. Sometimes a source for lumber was hard to locate or distant. In these cases and many others, coffin makers worked well into the night to complete the caskets prior to burial the next day.

Sometimes the deceased did not fit into a coffin when the coffin maker either didn't measure the corpse or took incorrect measurements. Sometimes the body swelled to such an extent that it would not fit. Harriet Arnow gives an example of what could happen if the burial container was too small: "And then she must have swelled a little or something, or maybe Keg Head had measured in too big a hurry or not measured at all, but, anyhow, the coffin wasn't quite wide enough and they had to turn her a little sideways; and by then she was too stiff to do much with and her head kept turning with her thin wide shoulders and stuck up in the air, and they had to squeeze to get the coffin lid down."[37]

During the days of custom-built coffins, the age, weight, and height of the deceased didn't really matter, since each burial container was made to fit the corpse, even though the coffin maker didn't always succeed in this. However, when coffin making became a profession and caskets were ready-made, there were only two sizes, one for children and one for adults. Some coffin makers only made one size, in which both children and adults were interred. A funeral di-

Modern infant's casket. (Courtesy of Campbell Funeral Home, Inc., Abingdon, Va.)

Marker indicating that a mother and infant son are buried in the same grave.

rector in eastern Kentucky in 1983 told me that in the early 1900s coffins were available in three sizes: one for an infant, another for a middle-sized child in the teens, and a large one for an adult.

Occasionally more than one person was interred in the same coffin. For example, when a mountain woman had twins or triplets that died in childbirth, family members were killed in a mountain feud, or both mother and infant died during childbirth, they were sometimes placed in a common burial receptacle. I talked with sundry mountaineers who had either built a coffin for twins or had seen one constructed. A few gravestones in central Appalachian cemeteries mark mothers and children buried together. When three sons of Randall McCoy were killed during the Hatfield-McCoy feud, he decided they should be buried in one coffin: "Thus, looking at the three bodies Randall McCoy would get a mental picture that time would never erase. . . . The coffin of the three boys, although similar to other coffins in two of its dimensions, was three times as wide, the biggest coffin in the State of Kentucky before or since."[38]

THE LINING FOR COFFINS AND CASKETS

The first true coffins in central Appalachia were not lined. In some instances, the body was wrapped in a sheet, blanket, or quilt before burial in an unlined container. An elderly man in eastern Tennessee told me that he had seen several burials in the early 1900s, long after lining coffins was an established cultural trait, in which the deceased (usually poor) was wrapped and interred in an unlined coffin. Makers of these crude coffins often focused on the appearance of the outside rather than the comfort of the dead. When lining was first employed, it was usually anything that was handy. Instead of wrapping the deceased before interment, the body was dressed and a sheet, blanket, or quilt was used to line the coffin. Some mountain people would save a favorite quilt for their burial.

Men constructed the coffins, but women were responsible for the lining.[39] The first step was to pad the coffin for the "comfort" of the deceased. While several kinds of padding were used, such as straw, potato sacks, and blankets, the most common were quilts and cotton batting or "batten."[40] If there was a choice, mountaineers preferred something soft that denoted sleep and comfort. Almost every mountain family had quilts, which were usually prepared for comfort while alive. Sometimes an individual, especially an elderly person, made a quilt and kept it for burial. In other instances, it was made by a neighbor, friend, or relative and used when death occurred. The quilt inserted in the coffin was almost always the best the family possessed. Later, cotton batting replaced the quilt as the choice of most mountain families for padding. If possible, people purchased rolls of cotton batting to make quilts and pad the burial container before the lining was installed. The lining was generally constructed so that additional cotton could be added later if necessary.

If lining was used rather than a quilt or blanket, it ordinarily consisted of black or white cotton or a grade of cotton such as muslin (bleached or unbleached) and calico. The traditional black lining predated Appalachian settlement when the clothes of the mourners matched the lining of the casket in a symbolic joining of loved ones. Gradually white, suggesting purity, replaced black, especially for young or female decedents.[41] These black or white materials were cheap and families usually had some on hand at the death of a relative. Linen, cambric, taffeta, silk, satin, and velvet were also used to line burial receptacles. Silk, satin, and velvet (or cheaper materials that resembled them) were desired, because they looked nice and delineated luxury, smoothness, comfort, and peaceful sleep.[42] It took approximately ten to twelve yards of material and two to three hours of work to complete the lining. Either nails or tacks (glue was also used in later years) attached the lining. When it was available and the family could afford to purchase it, lace or ribbon was used around the edge of the coffin as a final decoration.

If there was no material available, mountain people used whatever they had to cover and line the burial receptacle. Skidmore provides a fictional, but accurate, portrait of the extent to which a family would go to make the coffin look nice when it was placed in the ground: "Maw had brought two long black, gored skirts from the cabin and torn them apart for him to stretch and tack over the box. In his hurry to get home he had neglected to get black cotton for the purpose. When this was done she brought out a heavy quilt, helped him fold and place it so it would best serve as padding for the crude pine board. . . . She passed into the house and returned with a clean pillow and placed it at the end of the home-made casket."[43]

These pillows, extra cotton, or a quilt were popular additions because they added the look of comfort and peaceful sleep when the deceased's head was raised a few inches up on them. An elderly native of eastern Kentucky said that the lining was "draped from the sides and lapped over in the middle so if the head wasn't high enough, they could insert more cotton or bunch up the quilt more. Many people had a cushion of feathers which was used if necessary."

Today pillows to cradle the heads of loved ones can be purchased with caskets and are available in a wide range of colors and fabrics.

The lining in the modern central Appalachian casket is factory installed. It is available in many colors other than black and white and in many fabrics too, including some of those used in early coffins. The most commonly used linings range in price from twill as the cheapest followed by satin, crepe, and velvet as the most expensive.

Digging the Grave

Death in the mountains was truly a community affair. In addition to preparing the body for burial and constructing a coffin, friends and neighbors gathered to dig the grave.[44] Relatives, but generally not members of the immediate family, sometimes participated. Immediate family members took part only when it was necessary, but even then they merely observed or gave advice. Male neighbors and friends went to dig a grave because they considered it part of their community duty. They also wanted to relieve the grieving family of a major burden and show their respect for the deceased. It was an honor to help the family and serve the community. For some, it was a chance to socialize and gossip. A few did it for recognition. Regardless of the reason for their participation, the men performed the work without any expectation of being paid.

The number of participants varied, but an elderly minister in Russell County, Virginia, told me that he had seen as many as twenty-five to thirty people show up to dig a grave. An interviewee in West Virginia in 1980 stated that "when someone died, they didn't have to ask people, they came in droves to help dig the grave." Usually, the grave digging team consisted of four to six persons.

The time for digging a grave depended on when death occurred and varied from one section of the mountains to another. In some instances, the men worked well into the night to finish their work. While not necessarily true for all areas in central Appalachia, Bettis and colleagues provide the following description of grave digging: "If the person died at night or morning before daylight, the grave was dug in the afternoon. If death was after midnight, the deceased was never buried before the day following his death. If he died before midnight, he was buried the following afternoon. If digging a grave began a day before the funeral, the excavation was never completed until the day of the funeral. To leave a completed grave open during the night was inviting trouble."[45]

Only males would partake in this task.[46] Men did the digging, while young boys supplied drinking water, transported tools, or carried out other assignments. Women often prepared a meal for the workers and, on occasion, took it to the cemetery where the work was in progress. This food was only necessary, however, if the digging took a long time or the men had to work through the noon or evening meals.

With interment in a family or church cemetery, the first task was to cut the weeds, brush, trees, and shrubs in the cemetery, as well as those on the route to be taken by the burial procession. Then, under the direction of an older or knowledgeable person, the site for the grave was selected and marked off with respect to length and width. This procedure was called "laying off the grave."

Graves in family and church cemeteries were dug by hand. Appalachians used the pick (also called a coal pick), mattock, and shovel most often. A pick was especially useful for marking the dimensions of the grave and digging into semifrozen ground. An adze, axe, or broadaxe was sometimes employed when tree roots were encountered or the men wanted to smooth the edges of the grave. The younger men did the digging, but there was always one or more old-timers who went along to provide company and offer advice such as how long, wide, and deep, in what direction, and how the grave should be dug.

Grave digging involved working in shifts. When the men reached the cemetery and laid off the grave, two men would begin to work while the others waited for their turn (or supervised and gave directions). One person would break the earth with a pick and then the other would shovel the loose dirt onto a pile nearby. When the diggers had worked for several minutes, two others would relieve them. The process continued until the work was completed.

Digging the grave was generally a social affair. While two people worked, the others reminisced about past experiences with the deceased that they had enjoyed, told tall tales and true stories, discussed the latest news of the community, and talked about other graves that they had dug. A West Virginian in 1980 remarked that "grave diggers talked about everything under the sun." Alcoholic beverages were sometimes consumed. A gentleman in southwestern Virginia said that participating in the digging of a grave was fun, and it was the only time, when he was a boy, that he heard people tell dirty jokes and saw them drink liquor.

Central Appalachians, from early settlement to the present, adhere to a tradition of digging the grave in an east-west direction, with the feet toward the east and the head toward the west so the deceased faces the rising sun. This cultural practice has been so important to some mountain people that I once heard men get into an argument, while digging a grave, because they couldn't come to an agreement about which way the sun would rise. Placing the body with the face toward the rising sun continues to be important to many mountain people who believe that the Second Coming of Christ on Judgment Day will be from the east and the dead will view and take part in the event. In Christianity the rising sun is symbolic of the Resurrection.

Prior to the use of metal and concrete vaults in the mountains, graves were dug six feet deep. Suppressing the odor from the decomposing body and deterring grave robbers were partial reasons for this procedure, but the major purpose was to prevent animals from digging up the corpse. If the body was buried six feet deep, it was less likely to be disturbed by animals. This didn't always work. Wooden coffins without protective vaults decayed, and the animals had access to the corpse. For example, in December 1990 I stood on a mountain top in Virginia near the final resting place of a man buried in 1932. The grave was sunken and there were several groundhog holes. When vaults (metal and concrete) and metal caskets came in vogue, rigid adherence to the six-feet principle was no longer necessary.

VAULTS IN CENTRAL APPALACHIA

The first step in the evolution of the vault in central Appalachia was to dig the grave in two sections rather than one. About twelve inches was added to the width of the coffin when laying off the grave. In the first section, the workers dug about four feet into the ground and then decreased the width about four to six inches on each side to create a bench or shelf. Then they dug about two feet further, creating a second section the width of the burial container. Later, when burial took place, three or four layers of boards were placed on the shelf over the coffin. When the dirt was shoveled into the grave, the boards helped to form a vault that prevented the coffin from being crushed, delayed its decay, and made it difficult for animals to reach the corpse.

Similar to the Egyptian practice of placing a coffin in a sarcophagus, the next step entailed constructing a second coffin from wood (usually pine or poplar), making it slightly larger than the coffin, and then placing the coffined body inside. The grave digger would measure the width of the wooden vault (also called a "rough" or "ruff" box because it wasn't planed or finished) rather than the coffin, dig approximately three feet into the ground (the extra height of the vault meant decreasing the depth of the first section of the grave approximately one foot), decrease the width of the grave about six inches on each side, and dig another three feet. When burial took place, the vault was deposited in the grave and the coffined body was put inside. A wooden lid was placed on top or layers of boards were positioned on the shelf. The grave was then filled with dirt.

In the early part of the twentieth century, metal and concrete vaults replaced those made from wood as the major means of providing extra protection for the corpse. In contemporary central Appalachia, they are required in many public and some church cemeteries because they not only protect the body from the elements of nature and don't deteriorate as rapidly as wooden vaults, they are stronger and can withstand the weight of the heavy equipment used when graves are dug nearby.

Metal vaults are available in copper (most expensive), stainless steel, and steel (seven, ten, and twelve gauge), with twelve-gauge steel being the least expensive. Concrete vaults are not used as often as metal ones. With the movement toward interment in public or perpetual-care cemeteries, however, many funeral homes are getting out of the vault business, and some no longer sell them at all. Except in family and church burial grounds, cemetery or funeral home personnel generally dig and fill the graves and supply the vaults.

PROBLEMS ENCOUNTERED WHEN DIGGING A GRAVE

Digging a grave was not always easy. Because of the rugged mountain terrain, a large number of graveyards in central Appalachia, especially family cemeteries, were established on a hill or mountain. During certain seasons, and in inclement weather, sometimes it was difficult to get to the burial ground to dig a grave and even more problematic to transport the deceased to the grave for interment. Even when the grave diggers could get in the cemetery it was sometimes hard for them to determine where the grave should be dug. Many of the graveyards were old, and when there were no headstones, they had to find someone who knew where bodies were buried. Some mountaineers possessed an expertise or ability to check the ground and ascertain whether a grave could be dug without disturbing one already present:

> The . . . grave digger says that he can hit the area of ground where he is about to dig with a hammer or stamp on it with heavy shoes and tell by the sound of the earth if there is a body there already. Because the ground never settles back as solidly as it was, it sounds hollow when hit with the hammer. Sometimes he uses an iron rod and, by

punching the rod into the earth, can tell if he is digging into an old grave. If there is a grave there, the rod will go through the earth easily. If he is disinterring a body, the earth he digs into is like fine sand. The marks of the pick and shovel can still be seen in the walls of old graves.[47]

Nature provided a variety of obstacles to grave digging in this area. In the winter, before heavy machinery was available to do the work, mountain people had to deal with frozen ground that picks and shovels could not penetrate. They were sometimes able to build a fire on the ground at each step that the grave was dug,[48] but that took a long time. On many occasions, the deceased was placed in a cold back room or wrapped in a sheet and placed in an outbuilding until the grave could eventually be dug. Graves could fill with water as the men were digging so that it was impossible to place the deceased in the ground. This created major problems, especially in the summer when there was accelerated decomposition.

The major barrier to digging a grave in most mountain areas was rock. It was, at times, impossible to dig beyond a certain point. Until the advent of coal mining in the area, sledge hammers and hand drills were the primary tools for breaking rock. Miners used dynamite to remove the rock, though care was needed to prevent the disturbance of other graves when the explosion occurred. A funeral director in eastern Kentucky told me that even with explosives, there were circumstances in which "3 ½ feet was all you could go." Encountering rock generally meant a delay of a day or so before burial.

Olive Tilford Dargan in *From My Highest Hill* gives an example of what could happen when it was necessary to dig a grave:

> "We meant," explained Uncle Dan'l, "to lay Nathe by his fust wife, Ponnie, but when we dug down there we struck a rock that would 'a' had to be blasted out, an' we's afeard it would shake up the graves. We couldn't lay him t'other side o' her, 'cause her two children wuz there, an' then come Lindy, his last wife, so we decided to dig jest beyant Lindy. But about four feet down we come to water that turned ever'thing inter mud—it wuz that spring, I reckon, that sinks inter the ground above the graveyard—an' we had to go to the upper row where Callie an' little Rufe an' Lu wuz layin'. We couldn't put him by Lu, 'cause she wuz in the aidge o' the Ponder lot, right next to Randy Hayes in Bill Hayes' lot, an' it had to be Callie or nothin'."[49]

DIGGING THE GRAVE IN CONTEMPORARY CENTRAL APPALACHIA

The decrease in the number of burials in family and church graveyards in central Appalachia and the increase in burials in public or perpetual-care cemeteries has resulted in a substantial decrease in the amount of graves dug by neighbors and friends. Interment in a public cemetery is important to many people because of the continuous care that is provided. While many church and family burial grounds have fallen into a state of disrepair because there is no one responsible for their upkeep, public cemeteries are obligated to take care of the graves of their patrons.

Since almost every death is handled by the funeral establishment, it is the responsibility of the funeral director to see that the grave is dug. The proper officials in public or perpetual-care cemeteries where the deceased is to be interred, when contacted by a funeral home, have their caretakers open a grave. Friends still do much of the digging in church or family cemeteries, but this varies from one area of the mountains to another. For example, a funeral director in Russell County, Virginia, said that while most of his burials are in perpetual-care cemeteries, about 40 percent take place in family graveyards where 90 percent of the time friends do the digging. A funeral director in North Carolina stated that graves in his area are almost always excavated by paid diggers. However, he told me about two communities where they are always opened and closed by friends. An elderly minister in Dickenson County, Virginia, told me that he knew of only one grave in the community cemetery in his town that was dug by a funeral home. Friends continue to dig the grave out of a sense of duty and respect or because the family can't afford to pay to have it done.

Time has changed grave digging too. Heavy machinery, especially the backhoe, has replaced the pick and shovel in opening a grave, except in cases where it is impossible to get it to the burial site or friends do the digging. The social atmosphere has changed. It is now more of a job rather than an honor. Graves are not as deep today and it is no longer necessary to dig them in sections. Vaults, metal and concrete, have lids and offer protection for the body. Burials in central Appalachia have been transformed from a social, family-oriented task into just another profession.

FOUR

The Wake

And when friends have gathered 'round,
And look down at me;
Will they turn and walk away,
Or will they sing one song for me?
—John McCutcheon, "Who Will Sing for Me?"

T he vast majority of anthropologists agree that all known civilizations have had some formal process of disposing of their dead[1] that generally has included the preparation of the deceased, viewing the dead body, a funeral service, and disposal of the corpse, usually by earth burial or cremation.[2] A major facet of the funeral process in most societies has always been the wake, also known as the "visitation," "calling hours," and "waking the dead." The term *wake*, which was originally *lyke-wake* or *liche-wake*, is derived from the Anglo-Saxon *lic*, for "corpse," and *wake*, which means "to watch" or "to keep vigil."[3] According to Habenstein and Lamers, ancient peoples, including some preliterate groups, observed the custom of keeping the corpse laid out after death and keeping a "watch" or "wake" over it.[4] Since then the wake has taken on many forms.

Among the early Greeks, friends and relatives viewed the corpse to guarantee that death had occurred. Female mourners ritualistically wailed, and after a day of lying in state the corpse was accompanied to the tomb by a funeral procession. If the deceased had been a prominent member of the society, the time for disposal could be extended up to seven days.[5]

In early Roman society, people usually died in the presence of their immediate family members: "The body was then put upon a funeral couch, feet to the door, to lie in state for a period of three days to a week depending upon the prestige of the person in life. Flowers were strewn about the funeral couch, incense was burned, and outside the door, cypress or pine boughs were set as a warning of the possible pollution of death."[6] Where the wealthy were concerned, professional undertakers took care of the entire funeral process, including the wake. In contrast to the Egyptians, the corpse was not preserved for eternity but to retard putrefaction so that it could be viewed prior to disposal.

While the ancient Egyptians devoted considerable attention to death and life after death, they appear to have placed more attention on preservation of the body and the funeral process than on the wake. According to Panos Bardis, a part of the funeral consisted of mourning and praying in the dead person's house.[7] The Egyptians believed that life continued unaltered after death, and since the body was preserved for future reanimation (within three thousand years) through mummification,[8] the wake marked respect, honor, and the future "life" of the deceased, rather than a need to sit up with the corpse to protect it from predators.

The early Jews used the wake as a precaution against premature burial. The body was laid on a couch in an upper room. Relatives and close friends were permitted to view the face of the deceased, and an interval of eight or more hours was required before burial.[9] The wake was (and still is) simple, and the use of flowers, plumes, velvet palls, and the like, as well as show and display of wealth, were prohibited. In contemporary Israel, "uncoffined burial is the rule, and the deceased is returned to the earth in a simple shroud."[10] The early practice of corpse watching for payment is still practiced by the Jews.

The early Christian wake, which was adapted from several cultures, continued the Jewish practices of giving comfort to the bereaved family and scrutinizing the dead for signs of life but broke with the Jewish belief that the corpse was unclean by introducing the "kiss of peace" bestowed on the body of the deceased.[11] Further, instead of the wailings of the mourners (who may have been hired for the purpose) and having the wake at the grave in Jewish society, the Christians kept their emotions in check and transferred the wake to the home or church. Huntington and Metcalf describe the early Christian wake as a continuation of the deathbed gathering, taking place in the same building or same room, and being held on the evening after death.[12] Early Christian law required that "the body should be decently laid out, with lights beside it; that it should be asperged with holy water and incensed at times; that a cross should be placed upon the breast, or, in lieu of a cross, the hands should be folded; and that it should be buried in consecrated ground."[13]

One of the most interesting and controversial forms of the wake is the Irish wake. In the days before embalming, it was a three-day affair and mourners sat up all night with the corpse, which lay on cakes of ice for preservation.[14] It was always a lively time with singing, dancing, drinking, and laughter, and Coffin points out that there were occasions when "the corpse was stood up in the corner" to enjoy the festivities.[15] Around the fourteenth century, the Irish wake focused on "rousing the ghost." Participants tried, through black magic or witchcraft, to enliven the hours and frighten superstitious relatives by playing practical jokes by raising or calling back the departed. Things sometimes got out of hand and people were injured. This form of raucous behavior was so important as a cultural practice that, according to Habenstein and Lamers, at one time in Ireland "a woman was given a penance of fifty days on bread and water for wailing after the death of a layman or laywoman."[16]

The American Wake

Since early American society was not homogenous but rather a collection of widely ranging cultural practices, numerous manifestations of the wake were extant. As a more distinctive American culture developed, the wake in the United States became an integration of various customs. The wake took place on the night following the death. It was a social event in which friends and relatives gathered in the house where the body was laid out (either in an open coffin or on a tabletop) and took turns watching over it, generally to share in the ritual of mourning and to make sure that there were no signs of life. Children often took part, and participants sometimes slept in the same room as the corpse.[17]

Embalming, introduced in the nineteenth century, brought about significant changes. Health risk was no longer a problem and the body could be preserved and displayed for a longer period of time so that relatives and friends could make the long journey to the funeral. As the crowds grew larger, the site of the wake moved from the home to the church or funeral home chapel.

The viewing of the body preceding the funeral service is still employed in over 75 percent of deaths in the United States,[18] primarily because viewing the corpse is considered healthy. Actually seeing the loved one dead helps many people recognize the reality of the situation and enables them to resolve their grief. Now commonly referred to as the visitation, it takes place in either the funeral home, church, or the private home (in rare instances), and continues to provide a chance for social interaction.[19]

Early Central Appalachian Wakes

Like the United States in general, the central Appalachian area was settled by people from a wide variety of cultural backgrounds. As a result, the wake in contemporary Appalachia contains elements of the Greek, Roman, Jewish, and early Christian wakes. However, due to the large number of early Scotch-Irish immigrants, the Irish wake had a powerful influence on the cultural pattern that developed in the mountains.

Mountaineers, before preservation, were concerned, as were the early Jews and Christians, with making sure that the person was actually dead. Interviews conducted in central Appalachia revealed several tales of individuals, believed to be deceased, who suddenly displayed signs of life. One interviewee told the story of a person, supposedly dead, who while being conveyed by wagon to his freshly dug grave suddenly sat up, rubbed his eyes, and asked what was going on.

In the years before window screens and insect repellents, bugs were a problem at the wake. Janice Holt Giles argues that "the most ghastly thing about the watch was the bugs."[20] Kathleen Morehouse depicts a scene in which one participant at a wake was "fanning off the greedy flies, the long tailed moths who dropped around the candle."[21] Especially in the summer with the body decaying rapidly, friends and relatives had to maintain a twenty-four-hour vigil to keep the insects from the corpse. In addition to the bugs, the farmsteads were infested with rats, and an all-night wake was necessary to protect the corpse from these rodents.

Since neighborliness and familism were so important in the mountains, it was natural for friends, neighbors, and the family to attend the wake and pay their respects to the departed. According to Montell, the "principal reason for this practice was respect and affection for the deceased."[22] Interviewees in Mars Hill, North Carolina, and Honaker, Virginia, however, indicated that people in their areas showed up to honor the members of their community as well as the deceased.

A major factor in the etiology of the wake in the mountains, according to numerous sources, was protection of the corpse from cats. Cats would mutilate and even eat the eyes of the corpse.[23] Folkloric evidence indicates that one should never permit a cat near a corpse, because it will attack the face of the decedent, tear it with sharp claws (the face is usually attacked first), and feed on the flesh.[24] Some people even believe that the cat will take the soul of the deceased. Bettis and colleagues report that when the wake was held in the home, cats were attracted by the smell of the corpse and "would come from as far as half a mile away to eat the dead."[25] In Franklin, North Carolina, a mountaineer described an instance in which a cat got to the deceased and ate the fingers before it was discovered and removed.

Another explanation for the mountain tradition of sitting up with the dead is an ancient fear that the dead body might be "carried off by some of the agents of the invisible world or exposed to the ominous liberties of brute animals." Some central Appalachians believed with many other Americans that the "delay between death and burial served a psychological need in gradually conditioning friends and relatives to the changed condition brought about by death." This resolution of grief, so widespread today, dates back to preliterate societies. Some mountaineers were even afraid that body snatchers might steal an unguarded corpse and sell it to a medical school.[26]

The time between death and burial was generally twenty-four hours, with an all-night wake and burial at about two o'clock in the afternoon. This was especially true for most babies and young children. The gap between death and burial, as well as the determination of whether or not a wake was held, depended on a number of variables. If the death was the result of an incurable or contagious disease, burial was quick, but if disease was not a factor, the body was held until the family arrived. Odor from the decaying body expedited disposal. Summer weather especially increased the need to rapidly dispose of the body. According to Allebaugh, "this hot weather made it rough. Couldn't keep them up over one night in hot weather. I had a brother-in-law that had a stroke and died. Had to make his casket and everything. We set him out in the yard the last night and the dew fell on him. Next morning we had to nail him up hard and tight and put him in the box. Never could open him up. I hauled him to the cemetery. Fellow had to ride on top with a branch to keep the flies off."[27]

Infrequently, the body was kept up for more than twenty-four hours to accommodate the arrival of a relative. For example, Slone notes that "usually a body was only kept up one night after death, but Mother wasn't buried until the third day, because it took that long to get Flora word and bring her home."[28]

Time of year, inclement weather, and location were determinants in the extension of the wake. Flooding, mud, and bad weather, as well as rocky soil, could delay burial for an indeterminate period. One mountaineer, in an interview, described an instance in which her grandmother passed away and was to be buried the next day. It was in the winter and the ground was frozen. Attempts at digging the grave failed, and Grandma had not been embalmed. The only thing they could do was place Grandma on the front porch in a rocking chair, where she was preserved by the cold weather until burial could take place. The wake continued with the "wakers" in the warm house and Grandma outside in the cold.

Finally, the period of the wake may have been extended, or it might not have taken place at all, since preachers were not always available when someone died. The deceased was sometimes buried without a wake or funeral, usually after a brief graveside service, and the funeral was conducted later, occasionally many years after the death.[29]

THE SOCIAL CONTEXT OF THE WAKE

Before the wake started, the family placed the prepared body on display in the home, usually in a coffin, where it remained until the funeral and burial. The site was usually the living room or parlor. It was exhibited on either a table or two chairs. When the home was ready for the viewing, friends, neighbors, and relatives arrived to visit, provide assistance, or just sit with the corpse to ensure that it was not left alone prior to burial. Usually people would remain through the night. In some instances, one group stayed up with the body until midnight and another sat up from midnight until daybreak. On many occasions, a young person sat up with the dead, and occasionally this became the context of a date:

> One of us would side up to her and invite her to "set up" with the corpse, as this was the custom in the mountains. Usually she'd agree. We stayed there at the house, and about midnight all the old people would go back home and leave us younger ones. After they had gone, we would close off the room where the corpse was and all go to the kitchen. Our dates would set-in and cook us a big dinner in which we all set down and ate. After the dinner was off the table and dishes washed, we would make candy, this would usually take us to the early hours of the morning. While we were eating and making candy we were also getting more acquainted with our "dates." We were not necessarily interested in the eating and candy making though this helped our intentions. While everyone was trying to get organized and confusion reigned, we would attempt to slip out the door and head for the hay loft.[30]

In the days before embalming, a major chore of the wakers, which was begun during the laying out of the body, was to spend the night applying a cloth wet with soda water, camphor, or alcohol to the

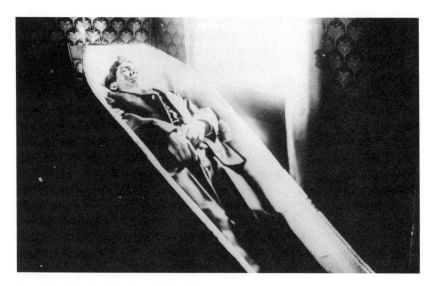

Deceased displayed in a mummy coffin during his wake, June 30, 1914.

face of the corpse to keep it from changing color.[31] One informant noted that "they'd fix a solution of soda water and they'd keep that rag wet all night. And put it on their face." Some mourners placed a saucer of salt on the stomach or chest during the preparation of the body and constantly changed it throughout the wake. The salt was supposed to soak up moisture and keep the corpse from swelling and bursting. An elderly woman in eastern Kentucky reported that she knew a number of people who swelled so badly they burst the casket.

By the time the body was prepared, "sympathetic neighbors were dropping in with supplies of food."[32] Adams holds that food was "plentiful for a midnight snack with plenty of coffee or hot tea to drink."[33] On winter nights, "a pot of hot coffee was kept hot on coals at the edge of the fireplace. The watchers ate teacakes and gingerbread and sweet potatoes roasted in the ashes."[34] An elderly couple in Fall Branch, Tennessee, told me that at one wake a whole pig was roasted and consumed with food brought in by the neighbors. According to Cooper, "women began baking and cooking additional foods. Green coffee beans were parched in a skillet, ground in a handmill between the knees, then brewed in a large iron pot above the fireplace coals."[35]

Meals were consumed in the room where the deceased was displayed. Even when death resulted from a plague or contagious disease, friends and neighbors responded to the needs of the family, but in a somewhat modified form. A woman in Mars Hill, North Carolina, recounted that during a flu epidemic in 1922, friends would bring in food and leave it on the porch. Ellyson gives the following example: "Other sympathetic neighbors came to the gate with cakes and pies, cookies and apples, baked chickens and boiled ham, as was the custom in time of death. This time they left them on the gate post in baskets and stood at the other side of the road calling out their sympathy to whomever came to the door.[36]

Religion was often the focus of conversation. Wakers speculated on the afterlife and the future of the deceased in the hereafter. For example, would the departed go to heaven, and would family members be with him or her when they expired? Grieving was open and unashamed. There was prayer and hymn singing, and in some instances, a service similar to the actual funeral. Wakers also reminisced about the deceased and recalled fond memories. Participants recounted good times and shared activities, like hunting, fishing, or cooking. The virtues of the dead person were extolled, but shortcomings were never mentioned.[37]

The character of the wake depended more on the family and its religious background rather than on the geographic locale. Some families preferred to keep the wake quiet, following in the tradition of gathering sympathetic relatives and friends in the home of the deceased, paying respects to the dead, and attempting to dispel the grief of the members of the family. Some families made the wake into a gala affair, and in fact this type of wake became the norm across central Appalachia. In Berea, Kentucky, a woman remarked that it seemed to her that there was a time when wakes were very quiet and respectful, but they became almost like a party with joke telling, laughter, stories, and staying up all night. Russell notes that they were more like celebrations than wakes.[38] Watchers were supplied with firewood, food, and whiskey, and they drank, ate, and gambled during the night. Cooper, who argues that as time passed and the wake, after a preliminary period of solemnity, became an occasion for songs, laughter, games, gossip, and courtship, provides the following description of sitting up with the corpse:

> As the evening wore on, the wake became more festive. Jokes were told and riddles propounded, then came a round of tongue twisters. A young lady sang "Black Jack Davis" and "Barbara Allen," a young man played the banjo which he had brought along, while an elderly man cut the pigeon wing. Two men started the game of Morris and

two other men tried their hands at Fox and Goose. The young lady who had done the singing and her boyfriend went outside and courted in the moonlight on the farther end of the porch. Inside the kitchen young ladies had their fortunes told from the formation of coffee grounds in twirled cups. As the night progressed, the hungry ate and drank coffee at intervals, a jug of whiskey was repeatedly passed to those who craved a drink of moonshine.[39]

Several interesting stories about behavior at the wake were related to me during interviews in the mountains. People told me that sometimes the corpse was placed in the corner or carried into another room to provide space for dancing, singing, or game playing. In the morning, it was returned to the table or chairs to take part in the funeral. An elderly woman in West Virginia remembered a death in which the family wanted the deceased left where he died until burial. He died sitting in a chair in the living room, so they left him there, sat with him during the night, sung hymns, and then buried the body the next day. Another West Virginian recollected that wakers pitched pennies on the hearth, and later, when the drinking started, they removed the corpse and took turns lying in the coffin.

PHOTOGRAPHY AND THE WAKE

When cameras were introduced in the mountains, taking photographs of the deceased certainly did not become universal (some mountaineers were superstitious about having their pictures taken), but there were occasions when a picture of a departed loved one was important. Before photography, water color paintings, which were distributed to family members and friends as well as displayed openly, were common.[40]

There were few cameras in the mountains until the very early 1900s. According to an elderly native of Glenville, West Virginia, most people in the mountains couldn't afford a camera, but after World War I there were "traveling camera men," and if they came through at the time of a wake or funeral, the family sometimes seized the opportunity to have a picture taken of the decedent. Most often these pictures were taken during the wake so that the formality of the funeral or the emotions of the mourners would not be interrupted. Occasionally photos were taken of the body both inside and outside the coffin and also sometimes at the grave site prior to burial.

Since photographs were rarely taken while anyone was alive and since families were so close, pictures furnished evidence that the person was dead, as well as recalled them as living. The grieving process was made easier with an image to help remember the loved one. These photos were normally kept and cherished by family members, but sometimes they adorned tombstones or monuments. To make things easier, sometimes people had photographs of themselves taken in their burial clothes or in their coffins prior to death. In James Still's *River of Earth*, the mother climbs to the graveyard at the top of the hill and proclaims, "I wisht to God I'd had a picture tuck of the baby so it could be sot in the arbor during the meeting. I wisht to God I'd had it tuck."[41] In a similar vein, Day writes: "When it looked as though the last bit of emotion had been wrung from them somebody would pass around a photograph of Blinky Shade in his coffin. Blinky Shade lying there so white and still and natural like."[42]

The Wake in Contemporary Central Appalachia

In the vast majority of deaths in contemporary central Appalachia, the deceased is kept overnight in a church or funeral parlor instead of the home. At least 99 percent of the bodies are now embalmed.[43] Therefore, while one night is still the standard, the visitation can be longer without causing problems. For example, a minister in Clintwood, Virginia, stated that the wake in his church consisted of two nights, with a song service the first night and a preaching service the second.

Since there is no longer a need to sit with the deceased to keep the cats, insects, rats, body snatchers, and other predators away, the contemporary wake is not an all-night affair, except when it is requested. A funeral director in Barbourville, Kentucky, reported that only about one of one hundred visitations involved a request to sit with the deceased all night. The "viewing," as the wake is termed today, generally lasts from about 6 P.M. to 9–10 P.M.

The viewing today is still a social event. There is a chance to see friends one hasn't seen in years, show respect for the deceased and the family, comfort the bereaved, reminisce, or just interact socially. While interviewing in a funeral home in North Carolina, a citizen dropped by to see if there was to be a wake that afternoon. She apparently needed a chance to socialize.

Neighborliness is just as extensive as it was in previous years. Food is still provided for the bereaved. However, it is not brought to the site of the viewing and participants do not eat in the presence of the deceased. Unless there has been an accident or debilitating illness the body is still, as it was in the past, displayed in an open casket. Occasionally families decide to have the casket closed.

Photographs are still popular in some circles in central Appalachia. Even though there is a plethora of cameras, and plenty of photographs are taken while living, the need for a final image of the deceased leads many mountain residents to seek photographs of their loved ones after they have died. A funeral director in the mountains of West Virginia recounted the story of two unmarried sisters whose brother had passed away. The body was taken to the funeral home where it was embalmed, clothed, and placed in the casket. The sisters requested that the body be transferred to the home for a short period of time before being returned to the funeral home for the wake. When the corpse was returned, the funeral director noticed that the clothing of the deceased was rumpled and unkempt. There was evidence that the body had been moved around in the casket. When questioned, the sisters confessed that they had never had their picture taken with their brother while he was alive. They had removed him from his casket, stood him between them, and had a "family" portrait taken.

FIVE

The Funeral Service

Now when I'm dead and in my coffin,
My pale face turned to the sun;
I want her to come stand around me,
And think the kind things I have done.
—The Callahan Brothers, "She's My Curly
    Headed Baby"

S|ometimes the term *funeral* is used when referring to all the ceremonies or rituals that take place from death until burial. In other instances, it refers to the ceremony (including the songs, scripture, obituary, and sermon) that usually follows the wake or visitation and normally precedes the burial procession. The funeral can be held at the graveside, home, church, or funeral home, in the presence of the body, with the casket open or closed. A "memorial service" is the ceremony that takes place after the body has been removed as either a substitute for, or in addition to, the funeral. The "committal service" is a brief ceremony held at the graveside, cemetery chapel, or crematorium. It may take place after, or in lieu of, the funeral service.

"Humankind, from earliest times, has practiced death ceremonies and procedures in great variety."[1] Death ceremonies and related actions have always been important in satisfying the social and emotional needs of the survivors. First, the funeral, especially when the deceased is displayed, is therapeutic for everyone present. In viewing the corpse, each individual can be sure that the person they once knew is truly dead. It also helps the survivors to openly express their feelings and deal with their grief. Second, the ceremony serves as a rite of passage—just like a baptism, marriage ceremony, initiation, or graduation exercise—commemorating "the deceased's participation as a member of the community and his or her passage from the group by death."[2] Third, the funeral fosters group cohesion. Those present are united in bidding the departed good-bye and providing emotional support for the family. Fourth, the ritual helps to restore the equilibrium that is disturbed when a member is removed from the group. Fifth, the service is a reminder that life is short and the living must give serious consideration to its meaning and values.

The Funeral in Early Societies

The funeral service as we know it today, with a combination of songs, scriptures, obituaries, and sermons taking place in the home, church, or some type of funeral establishment, does not seem to have been a funerary practice among the Greeks, Romans, Egyptians, Hebrews, and early Christians. Habenstein and Lamers report that in Rome, "a funeral oration in the Forum was included in the funeral of those with sufficient prestige to be honored publicly."[3] However, it was certainly not a practice for the common person. As Christianity developed, "the funeral oration honoring those of merit was taken over from non-Christian practice; and after the persecution era, was customarily included in the burial services for leaders or saints."[4]

During medieval times, the Catholic church developed a funeral ceremony based on a belief in purgatory, which included black vestments, black candles, and the tolling of church bells.[5] It consisted of five main stages:

1. A cortege of mourners and clergy carried the corpse to the church, while psalms were sung and incense was used for purification.
2. The coffin was deposited in the church and covered with a black pall. Then followed the Office of the Dead, with the participants constantly repeating "Eternal rest grant unto him, O Lord; and let perpetual light shine upon him."
3. The clergy performed the Requiem Mass.
4. The absolution of the deceased included perfumes, incense, and holy water for the coffin.
5. The burial of the body, with the appropriate prayers, took place in consecrated ground.[6]

After the Reformation, the sermon became an important part of the Protestant funeral:

Manifest on every occasion when the congregation gathered was the desire to provide pious instruction and exhortation. A Protestant funeral was no exception. The reading of Scripture and the singing of hymns, lessons in themselves, were supplemented by a brief discourse on death and resurrection which was given in the home, or in the church or at the grave. For a fee, the minister prepared and delivered a special sermon making particular reference to the life and death of the deceased. Out of this early practice, which joined consideration of the last things—death, judgment, heaven or hell—with the memory of the departed—emerged the Protestant funeral sermon of today.[7]

In Islamic societies, the funeral service, officiated by the family holy man, took place in the mosque or an open space, rather than a cemetery, which was considered too unclean for such a sacred rite.[8]

The Funeral Service in American Society

Funerals, including sermons, were an important part of early American burial practices. Before embalming the funeral had to be performed as soon as possible, usually within twenty-four hours. In the winter, sometimes the body was taken into an unheated back room of the home and frozen until spring when the funeral and burial could be performed. With the advent of embalming, funeral services began to be delayed for several days if necessary.

A few people in America's formative years planned their own funerals. Occasionally, the coffin, grave site, and even the burial shroud were selected before death: "Linen shrouds with drawstrings at the top were woven tight and bleached to a pure white, often to lie for years, yellowing again with age, until they were discarded as no longer usable."[9] Some picked out the songs, scripture, and ministers for their funeral ceremony. In a few instances, the funeral feast was planned and such items as the wine were purchased in advance.

Today, preplanning and prepayment are becoming the norm in the United States. Americans are making arrangements for their funerals, and even paying for everything before their deaths, in an attempt to place less burden on surviving family members. While mourning clothes are no longer as much in vogue as they were in the past, from time to time they are purchased prior to the death of a loved one:

> A touching story was related recently by the proprietor of a dress shop, who told my husband and me that he'd just had a customer desiring "a black dress to wear to a funeral." When the woman had found one she liked, she asked if she might wear it outside to show her husband, who was waiting in the car. After doing this she returned to the shop to pay for the outfit, explaining that the dress was for her husband's funeral. He was suffering from a terminal illness, and since they usually did things together, they had come to pick out her funeral costume.[10]

Letter edged in black that served as an invitation to a funeral in Lexington, Kentucky, April 25, 1887.

In cities until the 1900s, funerals were more intimate than they are today and people didn't attend a funeral uninvited. In New York City in the seventeenth century, an "Inviter to Funerals," dressed in black with long crepe ribbons streaming from his hat, delivered funeral notices, invitations, and mourning cards to those expected to attend. It was considered a breach of good manners not to attend the service if you received an invitation. By the end of the seventeenth century, paid public servants were in charge of delivering invitations.[11]

Messengers on horseback and the tolling of a church bell invited people in early America to a funeral. In the nineteenth century, undertakers accepted the responsibility of notifying friends and neighbors that they were invited to a funeral. "Another custom which grew to fantastic proportions was that of sending gold rings, kid gloves, and various types of mourning jewelry by way of inviting friends to a funeral."[12] Other items given away in great numbers included drapery, door badges, scarves, items of clothing, adult gloves, caps, neckerchiefs, books, and needlework.[13]

In the second half of the nineteenth century, grieving family members notified distant relatives and friends of a death and invited them to the funeral by mailing funeral notices on "various degrees of black-bordered note-paper and envelopes."[14] The recipient knew without opening the envelope that a death had occurred. Black-edged announcements were more prevalent in the city where things were done in a more formal manner. While I encountered stationery edged in black in central Appalachia, it was generally just used for notification purposes, since mountain people didn't need to be invited to a funeral for a relative or friend.

Concomitant with the demise of black-bordered stationery and the rise in popularity of the obituary in the newspaper was the cessation of inviting people to funerals. As the twentieth century progressed, people received the news of a death via the obituary, telephone, and local radio programs announcing deaths and funeral dates. Americans were not notified directly unless they were close friends or relatives. Anyone who wanted to attend the wake or funeral could do so without being formally invited.

Originally, funeral services were held at the the home of the deceased or, less frequently, the grave. Churches eventually supplanted the home, and, later, funeral homes became a convenient place to have the ceremony when they became diversified enough to add a chapel. The nature and location of a funeral service in contemporary America vary with the cultural and religious background of the participants. For example, while the trend has been toward the use of funeral homes for the ceremony, Catholics "are more likely to hold the funeral service in a church, whereas Protestants are as likely to use a funeral home as a church."[15] According to Leming and Dickinson, "approximately 50 percent of the funerals today are held in churches, and the remaining 50 percent are held in funeral homes or cemetery chapels."[16]

In earlier times, funeral services in America usually included a song, prayer, scripture reading, and a sermon. They were dominated by a minister selected by the family. The member of the clergy fulfilled a very important role in providing emotional aid to the family and helping the survivors make preparations for the disposal of the corpse. Funeral ceremonies were long and tiresome:

> Services at the home were invariably long and delivered in a mixed context of religious awe, hope, fear and gloom. After an opening prayer of some four to five minutes at a Protestant funeral, the minister would in many cases read the Twenty-Third Psalm, and possibly short passages from the Seventh Chapter of Revelations. Following this would be the remarks on the mystery of life and death, the suffering on earth as a prelude to a more glorious life to come, and then would come the eulogy in which the character of the deceased would be thoroughly reviewed. Often a short life history would be included, in some cases

delivered by a close friend of the deceased and couched in terms of personal reminiscence. After a closing prayer, and the singing of one or several songs, or possibly the recitation of a favorite piece of verse, the funeral service was completed. The total time consumed was seldom less than an hour.[17]

In the 1800s, the undertaker took over many of the burial tasks. This important role was a combination of the artisan or cabinetmaker, who constructed the coffin, the livery owner, who provided the hearse and horses needed to convey the corpse to the cemetery, and the sexton, who was generally in charge of the bell tolling and grave digging.[18] The undertaker performed a variety of custodial tasks, including supplying the coffin, embalming the corpse, cleansing and dressing the body, providing the folding chairs (when the service was in the home), and supervising the pallbearers, funeral procession, and interment of the body. As the primary funeral location changed from the home of the deceased to the church and funeral home, the service became much shorter, and the undertaker replaced the minister as the dominant figure in the funeral process. Shortly after the turn of the century, the undertaker became the "funeral director."[19]

In America today, the funeral director works with the family to determine the type, time, place, and day of the ceremony. In most instances, it is public, but private funerals have become popular. The service is usually religious, but secular ceremonies are conducted. Today there are also several alternatives to the traditional funeral.[20] First, if the body is donated to science, there may be a traditional funeral followed by transportation of the decedent to a designated medical facility, or the corpse may be transferred to a medical facility with a memorial service to be held at a later date. A funeral service may be conducted with the body present, followed by cremation, or the corpse may be cremated with the expectation that there will be a memorial service in the future. The deceased may be buried immediately, followed by a memorial service. Some families desire graveside ceremonies. Others opt for burial at sea. The deceased also can be interred by the family, a committee, a social organization, or a religious group without the assistance of a funeral home.[21]

The Funeral Service in Central Appalachia

In the past, plans for a funeral had to be made as soon as possible. A few people, particularly the elderly, made their plans in advance.

If death was imminent, and there was enough time, many highlanders felt it was prudent to make plans and take the burden from the family. Today, preplanning is much more prominent in the mountains than it was in the past. For example, a funeral director in eastern Kentucky said that his establishment started preplanning in 1940. In the beginning they had approximately six to ten funerals per year that were planned in advance. In 1983 when we talked, about forty to fifty were preplanned. Elderly people, as in the past, are more likely to preplan than younger people.

Preplanning for contemporary Appalachians includes ascertaining the costs for preparation of the body, selecting the casket and burial clothing, determining the songs, scripture, minister, and pallbearers for the funeral service, and purchasing the burial plot and grave marker. In addition to preplanning, some mountaineers prepay. The money is put into a trust and protected by a state agency. If the person preplanning decides to withdraw the money, it can be done without penalty. Preplanning makes sense financially for many in this area because funerals can be expensive today. Like other Americans, central Appalachians tend to spend a lot of money to indicate how much they care for their deceased loved ones. The more expensive the casket and funeral, the greater their love appears.

Making funeral plans was not always easy to do in early central Appalachia. Prior to embalming, funeral plans had to be made in a hurry, and it wasn't always possible to contact family members who lived a substantial distance from the deceased. Sometimes families couldn't agree about whether the body would be embalmed. My mother told me about members of a family who argued because some didn't want to pay for the preservation. They felt embalming was too expensive.

Rough roads, long distances to travel, primitive modes of transportation, and a lack of adequate communication made it hard to set a time when everybody could be present. The kind of coffin and who would make it, as well as which burial clothing should be used, were important decisions. Occasionally, one person would try to take over and that would irritate other survivors. Sometimes family members could not agree. A funeral director in eastern Tennessee related the story of a funeral where there was a great deal of friction between the second wife of the deceased and the children from his previous marriage.

Barriers such as frozen ground, water, and rock could bring about major changes in funeral plans, and one or more of these factors often resulted in the delay of a funeral for days, weeks, months, or years.

While neighbors were available to provide assistance, the burden of planning a funeral rested primarily with the family. Finding a minister was a problem, especially in the very early years when only circuit riders were available. There were, of course, arguments among family members concerning which minister or ministers should preach the sermon.

Today in the mountains the funeral can be delayed for several days to accommodate those who must travel a long distance, though lengthy delays are seldom necessary. Few people disagree about embalming, and bad roads seldom prevent people from attending the funeral or delay the burial procession. Modern four-wheel-drive vehicles can reach almost any cemetery, ministers are readily available (sometimes families still argue over who will present the message), and grave digging creates few problems since it is usually taken care of by the funeral home or cemetery. If the casket and burial clothes are not selected prior to death through preplanning, there are seldom any major problems (sometimes members of a family may disagree about how much money to spend). Frozen ground, water, and rock no longer deter the digging of the grave or interment of the corpse. While funeral plans are more detailed, the funeral director and minister are available to provide assistance and take a major part of the burden from the family.

THE LOCATION OF THE FUNERAL

A funeral is not, and never has been, a requirement in central Appalachia. The early pioneers, before they built houses or established cemeteries, buried their dead with little or no ritual. Even in contemporary central Appalachia some people are interred without a ceremony. For example, a ninety-year-old east Tennessean in 1983 told me that in the remote section of the mountains where he resided "a lot of times there wasn't a funeral. They just stuck them in the ground and walked away." When there was no minister present, mountain people sometimes practiced "funeralizing," whereby they buried the deceased and then had the funeral months later when a preacher was available.

After the early settlers had cleared their land, constructed homes, and, perhaps, established cemeteries, they frequently conducted a simple graveside service before burial. This practice was especially common when there wasn't enough room in the house or the body needed to be disposed of immediately. Relatives and neighbors (if there were any) gathered around the coffined or uncoffined corpse and had a brief ceremony prior to interment. This service might have been the only one held before burial, or it might have taken place after a ceremony in another location such as the home, church, or funeral home.

Until the early part of the twentieth century, the residence of the deceased was the primary site of the funeral ceremony. The home was the logical location for the funeral since this was where death most often occurred, embalming was performed, and the body was prepared for burial.

During the funeral, the body of the departed was placed in the living room or parlor of the house. Since crowds were generally large, the furniture would be removed from the dwelling, or moved to the side, so that chairs or benches could be placed near the corpse, though many times everyone but the immediate family had to stand during the sermon. A minister in Russell County, Virginia, said that in funerals he had attended in the home, the furniture was removed, chairs and benches were placed in all the rooms, and the minister stood near the deceased to preach the sermon. The crowd was often so large that it would "spill out into the yard with several people clustered together on the porch." He told me that at one funeral there were so many people on the porch that it collapsed. Except for a few onlookers who were "skinned up a little bit," no one was seriously hurt and the funeral continued uninterrupted.

Though it was at times difficult to get the burial container inside, in the winter funerals were held in the house. A woman in North Carolina told me once a coffin was brought into the house through the window because the door was too small. Many times, in the years prior to embalming, the odor from the decomposing body was excessive in the house during the funeral ceremony. Therefore, if it was warm, every effort was made to have the funeral in the yard or on the porch. Trees in the yard and the shelter over the porch provided protection from the sun for the deceased and the survivors, and the funeral was carried out in the fresh air under less cramped conditions. Scalf describes an outdoor funeral in which "the body was carried out into the yard under the big apple tree. The widow sat at the head of the coffin, her children clustered around her."[22] In her *Singing Family of the Cumberlands,* Jean Ritchie depicts a service that was preached in the front yard with "everybody in dark clothes sitting around on chairs and homemade benches set up in a half-circle around the coffin."[23]

As mountain communities began to develop, townspeople established churches and schoolhouses. Churches supplanted the circuit rider and became a permanent fixture in most mountain locales. They were not established in every mountain area, however, especially extremely rural sections, and they were often difficult to reach. When the crowds became too large, churches began replacing homes for funerals. As churches grew in popularity and number, families held funerals there more often. Occasionally schoolhouses and churches shared buildings.[24] School was held during the week and church services were held in the same building on the weekend. In this situation bodies were prepared and taken to the schoolhouse for the funeral.

The firm entrenchment of funeral homes in the mountain culture resulted in the displacement of the church as the primary locale for the funeral. When some establishments started providing a chapel for the convenience of the family, it became more feasible to have the visitation and funeral at the same place. The body was already present, a chapel for religious and nonreligious services was available with ample seating, a piano or organ was provided for musical accompaniment (as well as space for a choir), the atmosphere was more relaxed, and it became expensive and time-consuming to take the body to the church or residence.

While the church is utilized more frequently in some mountain areas than others, approximately 85 to 95 percent of mountain funerals today are held in the funeral home. Services in the residence of the deceased and at the grave (except for the committal service) are rare and more likely to take place in rural sections.

FUNERAL PROTOCOL

The mountainous terrain in central Appalachia isolated people from the kinds of social activities engaged in by mainstream Americans. There were no circuses, carnivals, zoos, or theaters to attend as an escape from the trials and tribulations of daily life. Now and then, events such as barn raisings, quilting bees, and taffy pulls provided a chance for relatives and friends to get together and sing, dance, eat, play games, or just socialize, but these were few and far between. As a result funerals became major social events for mountain people.

Community involvement was as great at funerals as it was in every other phase of the period from death to burial. "Practically everybody for miles around attended the service."[25] It was disrespectful to work on the day of a funeral, so people left their jobs to pay final tribute to the deceased. Davids says that "funerals were actually festivals that brought a thousand—sometimes two thousand—people on foot, on horseback, or by oxen."[26] Buck provides the following portrait of attendance at an early funeral: "Long before the hour for the services had arrived men, as drab and neutral in color as the sodden skies, and women wrapped in shawls of red and blue, began to gather from hither and yon over roads mired to the prohibition even of 'jolt-wagons.' They came on foot or on muddied mules and horses with briar-tangled manes and tails—and having arrived, they waited, shuffling their weary feet against frost-bite and eddying in restless currents."[27]

There are a number of reasons for the large crowds at early funerals. Many people attended because they wanted to pay a final tribute to the deceased and console the family. Services for older people were well attended because of the amount of respect mountaineers had for the elderly. Crowds at funerals for accident victims were large because people were curious about the condition of the body. In the days when travel was difficult, money was scarce, and people saw one another infrequently, funerals served as a reason for a family gathering. Friends and neighbors who seldom interacted had an opportunity to visit and learn the latest gossip. There were those who went to every funeral, whether the deceased was known or not, as others in more densely settled areas might attend a movie or musical show, because they had nothing else to do or look forward to.[28] Some mountain people even attended for the good food that was usually provided before and after the service: "Preacher Tackett figured it would be a high old time with plenty of eating and drinking. He liked funerals almost as much as holding a meeting. Maybe even better."[29]

Funerals were sad occasions for adults, but not for many younger folks who saw a chance to do some "courtin'" or "sparkin.'" This kind of behavior was certainly not positively sanctioned by the grown-ups, especially those who were devout: "Sometimes a boy and his girl sat together in the middle row of the rough wooden benches. It was scandalous for a young couple to attend a funeral together. The congregation especially objected when a girl and boy walked together up to the coffin to view the corpse. A funeral was too solemn for anything like courting."[30]

Crowds at contemporary funerals are smaller than they were in the past. People in the mountains no longer lead a predominantly agrarian existence, and it is difficult to leave their jobs and attend a service during the day. It is easier to go to the wake or visitation and pay their respects. Mourners still socialize, especially at the visitation. Community involvement has decreased, but neighbors and friends continue to bring food and help the grieving family however they can. Courting takes place at the funeral and probably will

Black horse-drawn funeral hearse used in Tazewell, Virginia, in the late 1800s and early 1900s. (Courtesy of Historic Crab Orchard Museum and Pioneer Park, Inc., Tazewell, Va.)

as long as there are young people in central Appalachia, and mountaineers turn out in large numbers for those who died accidentally or violently.

In the years before embalming, the funeral was held around 11 A.M. if possible. This permitted neighbors to get their chores done in time for the service. Also, since funerals sometimes lasted for hours, if the service was started in the morning there was a better chance of completing it before dark so that people could go home, perform the evening chores, and eat supper before going to bed. Today, the time of the ceremony is dependent upon the wishes of the family.

Until recent years, the color associated with death was black. Notification of a death was received on stationary edged in black. Mourning cards were usually black and silver. Women wore black dresses, stockings, skirts, blouses, shoes, and hats, while men wore black suits, shoes, and hats. Many of the mourning clothes were made at home from the wool of black sheep.[31] Gloves and mourning jewelry were black. Even the hearse or whatever was used to transport the body to the grave was black.[32]

The social change affecting other funeral practices also brought about alterations in funeral attire. Today, while there are a few people who adhere to the older traditions, including wearing black, most mourners don't feel they have to wear black.

FUNERAL DUTIES

In the early years in central Appalachia, mountain people couldn't rely on a member of the clergy to conduct funeral services. Until houses of worship were widely established, circuit riders passing through the area offered the only religious instruction. Later, in communities with more than one denomination, family members sometimes attended separate churches and disputes arose over who would conduct the service. Sometimes families compromised and had more than one minister preach, and as a result multiple-minister funerals became popular.[33] Even today when fundamentalist groups are involved, such as the Holiness or Pentecostal churches, the service may include two or more ministers. Multiple-minister funerals are still more common in rural parts of the mountains than in sections that are urban, but even in contiguous areas the practices vary.

When several ministers took part in a funeral, the one in charge was usually the pastor of the church attended by the deceased or the immediate family. Occasionally, the additional members of the clergy were from other churches in the area or friends of the departed. A woman in Madison County, North Carolina, said that in her area, additional ministers were former pastors of the church where the departed had worshiped while he or she was living.

Originally, each minister involved in a funeral would preach a sermon. While this still occurs in some cases, for brevity, generally one preacher delivers the message and the others recite the scripture, offer the prayer, or read the obituary. Usually the number of sermons depends upon the religious affiliation of the deceased. Fundamentalists are more likely to have a ceremony with more than one sermon than nonfundamentalists.

Pastors in most mountain churches today are well educated. Except for some fundamentalist churches where ministers feel "called" to preach and there is more emphasis on ability than education, members of the clergy tend to have a college degree or at least a high school diploma. Because of this, their sermons tend to be more restrained and focused on the scriptures and the ritual of the service. In contrast, preachers in the early mountain churches had a deep devotion to God but very little education. As a result they were perhaps freer to call on their own emotions and the emotions of the loved ones, to draw upon the grief present, and to exercise the strength of their calling. It wasn't until the 1900s that the educational level began to change. In his study of mountain culture in the early 1900s, John C. Campbell found that the level of education for the majority of older mountain preachers was very low: "Most of the older ministers have an extremely limited education; very few have received any scholastic training for their calling. They are usually men of native ability who still have much influence over the older people—influence which they exercise by reason of the fact that they have received what they themselves, and their people as well, believe to be a divine call to preach."[34]

Early mountain preachers served at funerals without pay. They worked on their "little upright farms, or in the blacksmith shop, or at 'public works'"[35] and earned their own living independent of their ministry. Whatever they did at the funeral was out of a sense of neighborliness. If people wanted to make a monetary donation, it was sometimes accepted. Being a member of the clergy today is a full-time job, and a minister is more likely to accept money for services rendered than in the past. However, many still serve out of a desire to be a good neighbor and therefore do not charge for preaching at a funeral.

Until recent years, funerals in central Appalachia varied in length, but were seldom less than sixty minutes. Many lasted for several hours[36] and were sometimes so long that people in attendance had to spend the night (or nights) with a relative or friends until the deceased was interred. The length of the service varied according to the attitude of the minister, the number of ministers, the condition of the corpse, the church denomination, the wishes of the family, and the weather.

Some members of the clergy felt a need to preach a long sermon and often believed it was their duty to make sure the funeral service wasn't too brief. The funeral also provided a chance to influence others and "win souls," so some ministers considered it to their advantage to speak for a long time. Wilma Dykeman describes a minister who, "old and wise in his knowledge that such an audience would not be his again for many another year, took the occasion to speak for an hour and a half."[37] Some ministers got caught up in their sermon and spoke for long periods of time "regardless of whether a bootlegger or church-goer was being buried."[38] An elderly preacher in Russell County, Virginia, who had taken part in many ceremonies, complained that while there was no time frame in the past, recent funerals he had been asked to conduct were limited to about twenty minutes, which was not enough time to "do things properly."

It usually took several hours to conduct a funeral when several ministers were involved. Furman provides an accurate account of multiple-minister funerals when she says that "preachers held forth hour after hour."[39] An elderly couple in Washington County, Tennessee, noted that "when two or more preachers were involved, you needed to take your lunch." Some mountain funerals continue to include more than one member of the clergy, but these services are shorter and occasionally a time limit is imposed. A funeral director in eastern Kentucky reported that funerals today are usually fifteen to thirty minutes in length, though they occasionally last over an hour. He had recently conducted one that continued for four and a half hours. Several ministers participated, and there was two hours of singing and two and a half hours of preaching. The service would have been longer, but some preachers couldn't be there because they had to work. However, they had preached at the wake the night before.

The length of a central Appalachian funeral has always depended to a large degree on the religious affiliation of the deceased or the family. In fundamentalist churches today, while the services are shorter than they were in the past, they are generally longer than those of less fundamentalist groups. A funeral director in southwestern Virginia told me that the average time span for funerals is forty-five minutes for fundamentalists, fifteen to twenty minutes for Methodists, and twenty to twenty-five minutes for Baptists.

Before embalming, services naturally had to be kept as short as possible. Before funeral homes, weather most often affected the length of a funeral service. Obviously, the ceremony was shorter when the weather was cold or inclement. It could be longer if the weather was warm, especially when the service didn't have to be conducted inside a home or church. In the past as well as today, the wishes of the family most often dictate the length. Sometimes members of the clergy or more distant relatives don't want the grieving family to suffer needlessly through a lengthy ceremony.

THE CONTENT OF CENTRAL APPALACHIAN FUNERALS

No two central Appalachian funerals have ever been the same, but most have singing, prayer, an obituary, scripture, and a sermon. At a typical service in the mountains today, first the funeral home attendants enter and close the casket (if it is to be closed during the ceremony), the organist plays or someone sings, a member of the clergy reads the obituary and a scripture and leads a prayer, music plays again, the minister preaches and leads a final prayer, and a final song is sung or played. When the service is completed, the funeral director takes charge. Mourners file past the casket while music plays and then the director prepares for the procession to the cemetery.

Music has always been an integral part of the culture and social events in central Appalachia.[40] The emotional appeal of a sermon was "greatly heightened by the hymns."[41] The early funeral hymns were sometimes sung without musical accompaniment. Many of the old song books didn't contain musical notes, and shape-note singing was performed in several churches. The number of songs at a funeral was largely determined by the number of ministers and the length of the ceremony, though according to Riggleman, "not less than two and sometimes three songs were sung."[42] Obviously, if the service lasted quite a few hours, there would be several hymns.

Typical Appalachian funeral hymns were "old-timey songs," and included such favorites as "Faith of Our Fathers," "Onward Christian Soldiers," "The Old Rugged Cross," "In the Sweet By and By," "Love Lifted Me," "Lord I'm Coming Home," "Shall We Gather at the River," "Precious Memories," and "Life's Railway to Heaven."[43] While family members occasionally made private requests, usually the songs were favorites of the deceased. On rare occasions, individuals sang, but generally groups or entire congregations performed.[44] Performers were not paid for singing or playing an instrument. It was their neighborly duty.

Music is still an important part of the central Appalachian funeral, though the shorter services allow for fewer songs. Occasionally, the family requests instrumental music rather than singing. The old hymns are still popular, and often choirs perform during the service.

Prayer and scripture, two of the most important elements of the funeral service, have changed very little in purpose and content from the past to the present. Prayer provides a means of communicating with God and requesting the deliverance of the deceased from hell.[45] When the departed is a known sinner, the prayer may be directed at those present, asking God to assist them in walking the correct path to righteousness. Traditionally, the minister gives one prayer toward the beginning of the service and one toward the end, but the number can increase with more members of the clergy in attendance. The modern trend, however, is to have one minister offer the prayer and the rest carry out other tasks.

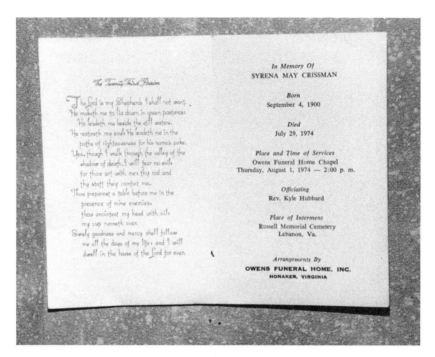

Memorial folder for my grandmother, July 29, 1974.

Since many of the early Appalachian settlers were not able to read the Bible, sometimes scriptures could not be read during the service. When someone present could read, Psalm 23 and John 14 were the most popular. Though the wishes of the family were sometimes taken into consideration, usually the minister chose an appropriate passage to present with the sermon. Primarily, the verses were meant to offer encouragement and inspiration for the survivors.

While there is no way of knowing the extent to which the obituary was used in very early funerals, through the years it did become very popular. A member of the clergy, friend, or relative would read a short biography of the departed, including the birth date, death date, birthplace, and a short genealogical account. This obituary was generally similar to the modern obituary that appears in the newspaper, is presented on radio programs announcing deaths and funerals, and is included in memorial folders available at the funeral.

The obituary wasn't used in all rural areas. A funeral director in western North Carolina told me that while about 50 percent of the funerals he conducts today include a biography of the departed, in the early years it wasn't used because "everybody knew one another." A woman in Dickenson County, Virginia, put it more succinctly when she said that in her church there was never any mention of the deceased because "if you didn't know who was being buried, you shouldn't have been there."

The content of the obituary has changed very little, but it is not used as often today as it was in the past. Some ministers try to steer clear of it if possible. The biography is only used in about 50 percent of contemporary mountain funerals. Whether it is included in a service is primarily dependent on church denomination and the wishes of the family. With the availability of memorial folders, which include biographical data, many people feel that the time in a funeral can be used more constructively.

Funeral services in the mountains, regardless of the denomination, have always been sad occasions. The wake was sometimes a gala affair, but the funeral was not. During the ceremony, the full impact of the loss was felt by the survivors. "There was much weeping and wailing for the deceased by close relatives."[46] The people of the neighborhood or community went to the funeral services and wept with the bereaved family. In Gilmer County, West Virginia, in 1980, an elderly woman said that "the preachers often cried with the members of the congregation."

One author refers to the emotional behavior displayed in mountain funerals as "exaggerated grief."[47] Frequently, even people who previously expressed very little affection for the deceased would "carry on" during the service. To take it hard was the last, final, and best tribute the central Appalachian could pay, and there would be criticism if it was not done.[48] If the loved ones of the departed didn't weep, wail, and carry on, they had not measured up to the expectations of the family and community: "The idea was that if we really loved the dead, then we would show it for all the world to see. Therefore a proper funeral should last at least three hours during which time the wilder and more prolonged the demonstration of grief, the greater the proof of love."[49]

At a funeral, those in attendance often competed with one another to see who could display the greatest amount of grief. They sometimes became so overwrought that they fainted. Female relatives in particular would weep and shout, tell the virtues of the deceased, recall fond incidents, and occasionally throw themselves across the coffin in a fit of hysterical weeping.[50]

The emphasis on the emotional display of the family of the deceased was so great that people would go home and discuss who cried the most. Church members would get together and talk about whether the surviving spouse adequately showed love for the deceased. Sometimes, when people went home after attending a funeral, those who had not gone would ask them to describe the events, especially the behavior of the immediate family: "How did they take it?" "Did they cry a whole lot?" "How did they show their love?"

Some ministers were asked to funerals because of their reputation for preaching sermons with an emotional impact. My mother told me about a preacher who was popular because he always made people cry during the ceremony. If a member of the clergy didn't cause weeping and wailing, the mourners were disappointed. Mountain ministers were so accustomed to preaching "hellfire and brimstone" sermons that they characterized any minister's service, which was more restrained than their own, as "not real religion."[51] Since people attending a funeral were expected to show their emotions, ministers felt obligated to preach a highly emotional sermon. They believed that it was their duty to present a sermon on salvation. It was a good time to "frighten sinners into repentance"[52] since they had a captive audience.

Some of the early ministers who preached emotional sermons viewed them as helpful in facilitating the healing process, as well as a chance to proselytize and fulfill the expectations of the family and friends. Most contemporary psychiatrists, psychologists, grief counselors, funeral directors, members of the clergy, and other experts in the area of thanatology maintain that emotional expression during the wake and funeral is therapeutic. These people believe that the release prevents depression and other mental disorders later.

Some ministers preferred to preach the same message at the services of sinners and repenters alike. Since the sermon was usually directed at the living in an attempt to win souls to Christ, those present were advised to seek salvation before it was too late. Parents were urged to get their lives in order and prepare their children for that heavenly home.[53] Instead of passing judgment on the departed, some members of the clergy informed attendees that only God could judge a person's actions on earth.

Some ministers were reluctant to preach the funeral of a sinner, and there were those who wouldn't perform the service at all if the deceased wasn't a Christian. Some preachers found it difficult to say anything positive about a sinful person. Occasionally, preachers would simply not discuss the deceased at all. Sometimes they covered up the sins of the dead person by focusing on any good deeds or the deceased's benefit to family and neighbors. In some cases, the life of a sinner was used as an example that others should not follow. For instance, an elderly woman in West Virginia told of a funeral in which the preacher elaborated on the transgressions of the departed so his son wouldn't follow in his footsteps. There were usually fewer hymns and less people in attendance at the funeral of someone who led a sinful life.

Janet Holt Giles asserts that "the ritual of noisy and emotional mourning is slowly changing as the Appalachian becomes more and more exposed to other ways."[54] Funerals are still sad, but they are much less emotional. This is due at least in part to the changing focus of ministers. As members of the clergy have become more formally trained, their services have tended to be shorter and less emotional. Instead of singling out sinners for salvation, most pastors today wish to comfort the survivors without playing on their emotions.

When the sermon ended, there was a prayer and song. The time of the final viewing depended upon the wishes of the family. If the coffin remained closed during the services, it was generally opened for a final viewing and the mourners filed past before heading to the burial site. Although the order of filing varied, usually friends and neighbors went first, relatives followed, and the immediate family came next in order of importance, with the most important family member viewing last. Occasionally there was a public or private viewing before the service followed by the closing of the coffin.

Whether the deceased was displayed during the service depended to a large extent on the wishes of the family and the condition of the body. In the past, as well as the present, the coffin was more likely to be left open if the funeral was in the home and closed if it was in the church or funeral home. If the burial receptacle was opened for the last time before the procession to the cemetery, the scene was often extremely emotional. "It was not unusual for some fainting to take place around the coffin."[55] In Wood County, West Virginia, an interviewee told of a funeral in which a survivor tried to drag the corpse out of the coffin. Often mourners had to be restrained. Crying and screaming were usually characteristic of a mountain funeral: "But it is when the casket is opened for the 'last look' that the most emotional scene takes place. Every member of a bereaved family will cry and scream and pray, but the nearest relative, the husband or wife, mother or father, will throw himself on the casket, tear at it, kiss the dead person, plead and pray and moan and sob, even sometimes tear at their own hair or dress. Often they collapse, faint, must be carried out. This is ritual. For days those present will recall it and speak of it, saying approvingly, 'She taken it hard.'"[56]

Influenced by a superstitious belief that kissing or touching the corpse prevented dreaming about the deceased and a realization that the departed could never be seen or felt again, a few mourners when filing past the coffin for the final view would occasionally touch the hand or cheek or actually kiss the deceased. Generally, only members of the immediate family such as the spouse, children, or parents would kiss the corpse. Most mountain people I interviewed considered this practice repulsive, but for some, final contact was important. An elderly man in Berea, Kentucky, told of a funeral in which he saw a woman push a small child into a coffin and say, "Kiss him, you will never see him again." McCall indicates how it could feel to kiss a loved one good-bye: "This here day Ma was in her coffin in front of Four Mile Baptist Church. Ant Nancy asked me to kiss Ma goodby. I did. Not so hot now. Cold cold cold. I can never ever furgit how cold."[57]

After the mourners had filed by the body and left the funeral site, the lid was replaced on the coffin. If the deceased was to be viewed at the cemetery, the lid was simply laid on the coffin. When there was no final viewing, someone permanently attached the lid with nails or screws. In later years, hinges and latches were used.

In contemporary central Appalachia, a prayer and music usually follow the funeral sermon. The deceased is likely viewed before the ceremony while the body lies in state, the casket is usually closed during the service, and the coffin is seldom opened for a final viewing. At the conclusion of a closed-casket service, friends generally leave and the family follows. If there is a viewing, music plays as friends file past first and the closest family members go last. Mourners rarely kiss the deceased or wail and moan. When those in attendance have left, the flowers and casket are taken to the appropriate vehicles, and the burial procession begins.

As with all other traditions associated with death, within the last twenty to thirty years central Appalachian funerals have changed just as they have in the rest of the United States. Instead of the standard funeral with large crowds, some mountaineers now prefer a private service where just the family and, perhaps, a few selected friends are present. Night funerals have become popular since many people can't get off from work during the day to attend a service. Weekend funerals are occurring more frequently, even though they are somewhat more expensive because of extra charges such as overtime for opening and closing the grave. Graveside funerals are preferred by some families. Though cremation and donations to science are rare in the mountains, some families do choose memorial services. The central Appalachian funeral has evolved into a private expression of grief from the social event so common to the settlers of the area. The focus now centers on the family, its wishes, and its feelings. Services are designed to accommodate the living rather than the dead.

SIX

Burial Customs

Lord, I told the undertaker,
"Undertaker, please drive slow,
For this body you are hauling,
Lord, I hate to see her go."
—The Carter Family, "Can the Circle
    Be Unbroken (Bye and Bye)?"

The Burial Procession

T he funeral or burial procession, whereby the deceased is taken to the place of disposal, has been a part of human history since antiquity. Almost every society, past and present, has had to transport the corpse from the site where death occurred to a final resting place. The Egyptians carried the deceased with some of their possessions to the Nile, transported them by funeral barge to the west bank (with two lamenting women on each side of the bier that supported the coffin and mummy), and carried them to the necropolis for burial.[1] The Greeks, dressed in black or dark clothing symbolic of mourning after one day of displaying their grief, formed a procession to accompany the departed to the site of burial or cremation. "It consisted of the corpse on a bier carried by relatives or friends, or, possibly hired 'corpse bearers,' female mourners, fraternity members, either immediately preceding or just behind the corpse, and hired dirge singers."[2] For followers of Islam, after the funeral the open bier was carried by four relatives or friends (which was considered a great honor) to the place of interment. The Hebrews, usually on the evening of death, carried the body on a bier to the place of interment.[3]

The early Christian funeral procession, which was very subdued and reverent, rejected the types of ceremony found in funeral parades common to such civilizations as Rome. Noisy exhibitions of grief were not tolerated and the procession was limited to the corpse, its bearers, and the family and friends of the decedent. If possible, it took place during the day.[4] The procession became more diverse as Christianity developed, especially after the Protestant Reformation.

In early Rome, the libitanarius, a direct ancestor of the contemporary American funeral director, was in charge of much of the burial procession. The libitanarius provided hired mourners and mourning costumes and served as director. While the burial procession of the ordinary citizen was simple, with the family and friends carrying the corpse, it was very elaborate for a wealthy, powerful, or prestigious person:

> At the head of the procession went a band of musicians, followed, at least occasionally, by persons singing dirges in praise of the dead, and by bands of buffoons and jesters, who made merry with the bystanders and imitated even the dead man himself. Then came the imposing part of the display. The wax masks of the *alae* were assumed by actors in the dress appropriate to the time and station of the worthies they represented. . . . Then followed the memorials of the great deeds of the deceased, if he had been a general, as in a triumphal procession, and then the dead man himself, carried with face uncovered on a lofty couch. Then came the family, including freedmen (especially those made free by the testament of their master) and slaves, and next the friends, all in mourning garb, and all freely giving expression to the emotion that we try to suppress on such occasions. Torchbearers attended the train, even by day, as a remembrance of the older custom of burial by night.[5]

THE BURIAL PROCESSION IN CENTRAL APPALACHIA

Unless the funeral service was held at the grave, the mourners proceeded to the burial site following the funeral service. In most cases in early central Appalachia the body was carried by what they only later began calling pallbearers. The term *pallbearer* is derived from the word *pall*, which originated from the pallium, or cloak, with which a Roman soldier would cover the dead on the battlefield. A pall was the cloth placed over the coffin during a religious funeral service. It was owned by the church and stored in the church vestibule with the bier upon which the coffin was placed during the ceremony. Palls were usually black, frequently fringed, generally contained some kind of emblem or herald, and, in the case of well-to-do people, made from expensive material such as velvet. White palls were used for children and women who died in childbirth.[6]

"In early times there were regular bearers and pallbearers, or 'upper' and 'lower' bearers. The latter carried the coffin; the former lifted the pall so that the bearers were not covered by it."[7] With the passage of time, only one set of bearers was needed, since the pall was either omitted entirely, removed before the burial procession, or arranged out of the way of the bearers.

Many times men at a funeral volunteered their services as pall-bearers. However, usually friends and neighbors, selected in advance because of their closeness to the dead person, carried the coffin. Through the years, it became such an honor to be a pallbearer that nephews, cousins, or other specially chosen relatives took an active part in carrying the deceased to the grave. There have been rare occasions, past and present, in which the male children of the deceased carried the body to the burial site. Whether the coffin had to be carried a few feet or several miles, mountain people didn't object. An elderly lady in western North Carolina stated that "the pall-bearers would be more than happy to carry the coffin, no matter how great the distance was."

Since early coffins did not have handles, they were more difficult to carry then than they are today. Usually the pallbearers simply put the casket on their shoulders. Sometimes they inserted wooden boards or ropes underneath and carried the coffin by these. Later they occasionally attached the coffin to poles and put the poles on their shoulders. If the cemetery was not close to the site of the funeral service, two or more sets of four to eight people carried the casket. One set of pallbearers would carry the deceased until they were tired and then another group would take over. The process of switching off would continue until the burial procession reached the grave.

When the cemetery was some distance from the site of the funeral service, horse- or mule-drawn wagons transported the corpse as close to the grave as possible. If the family didn't own one, a neighbor would provide a wagon for the burial procession. Hazards like water, snow, ice, mud, and steep hills sometimes made wagon conveyance impossible. In these cases a sled pulled by a horse or mule was used, but even then sometimes the sled couldn't make it to the cemetery and the body had to be carried part of the way.

When a sled was used, several men had to walk on each side of the coffin to keep it from sliding off. An elderly woman in western North Carolina said that in the 1920s her sister-in-law was brought across a mountain on a sled pulled by a horse. Eight men walked on each side to support the coffin. Quilts were packed around the body to keep it immobile, and when they reached the grave and lifted the lid, the body hadn't "moved around a bit." Gardner provides the following example of the use of a sled: "They loaded Johnnie's coffin on the sled and the journey up the mountain began as soon as the men had finished their meal. The trail was so steep that several of the men had to sit on the coffin to keep it from sliding off the sled. In the late afternoon we reached the graveyard on the very top of the mountain in the shade of some of the most magnificent beeches I have ever seen."[8] Even today, with four-wheel-drive vehicles, some funeral directors told me that they still, though rarely, use a horse and sled to haul a body over steep mountains to a family cemetery.

The first hearses in America were simply "biers on large wheels."[9] In the country, they were open wagons filled with straw to cushion the coffin. Some were about the size of tin peddlers' carts, though they varied widely. By the late nineteenth century, hearses were very ornate and elaborate:

> Later special carriages were constructed with wide and comfortable high seats for top-hatted drivers, and these vehicles became more and more elaborate until in the late nineteenth century their size and decoration rivaled that of contemporary circus wagons only slightly subdued. They had fancy carving along the lines of construction, which was often gilded. Heavy plate glass with beveled edges covered the windows, and the hangings were shirred and draped and ornamented with long tassels. The interiors were carefully finished. In the winter bobsleds replaced wheels, a practice more common in rural areas than in cities.[10]

In the late 1800s when funeral directors oversaw burial, they started using a hearse pulled by a team of horses. A friend or neighbor measured the length of the dead body with one stick and determined the width of the corpse from shoulder to shoulder with the other. The two sticks were taken to the funeral home and were used to construct the casket. The finished coffin was taken by hearse to the home. The embalmed body was dressed and placed in the burial receptacle. Following the wake and funeral service in the home, the hearse carried the body to the grave. Sometimes a wicker "removal" basket was used to carry the corpse from the home to the funeral home, where the body was embalmed, dressed, and placed in the coffin. No corpse ever stayed longer than necessary at the funeral home. The body was always returned to the home in its coffin to await the visitation, funeral, and burial.

Hearses were usually black and pulled by a team of black (though occasionally white) horses. When funeral establishments started providing transportation for the corpse, both the hearse and horses were obtained from a livery stable. After they were firmly established, many funeral homes purchased their own hearses but continued to rent the horses from the livery stable. Mountaineers could rent their own horses and carriages to ride through the procession, but few

Adult removal basket. (Courtesy of Martha Smith Cecil, W. J. Smith and Son Funeral Home, Newport News, Va.)

could afford the expense. Some areas had more than one funeral home but only one team of horses to pull the hearse. In these cases, two funerals could not be held at the same time. Horse-drawn hearses went out of style in the early 1900s when motorized hearses appeared. Horses still came in handy to pull sleds in treacherous weather or terrain.

Before hearses, when corpses were still carried entirely by the pallbearers, the body usually led the procession, followed by the immediate family and then other relatives and friends. Although a few mourners rode on horses or in a carriage, most walked no matter how great the distance. Conveyance by wagon, sled, or horse-drawn hearse did not change the order of the procession. When motorized hearses were introduced, they were usually followed by a procession of other motor vehicles. The order is the same today, with the hearse leading and occasionally immediately followed by a flower wagon, the cars with the immediate family next, and then automobiles containing relatives and friends last. Flags displayed on the cars alert other drivers about the funeral procession.

As more and more mountain people began to purchase automobiles and the highways became crowded with cars, burial processions proved to be hazards that sometimes caused accidents. As a display of respect mountaineers traditionally pull off the road and stop to allow a funeral procession to pass. Today, many people simply slow down when they encounter a procession. Impatient drivers and uncertainty at intersections have forced funeral directors in many areas to enlist police officers to lead the procession and direct traffic. When this cannot be arranged, the funeral director or an assistant leads the cortege with a caution light on the hearse and flags on the cars to indicate that they are part of a burial procession.

Cemeteries

From antiquity to the present, most societies have had a central place to inter their dead. For the Egyptians it was the necropolis (city of the dead), which consisted of the pyramids. A pyramid was designed to be the tomb of a pharaoh or royal person: "In addition to housing the mummy of the deceased, it contained precious objects, foodstuffs, and other materials to ease the deceased's life in the next world. The pyramidal shape presumably assisted the *Ka*, or soul, of the dead person in climbing up the sun's rays to join the gods in the sky. An inspection of the interior of a pyramid reveals a complex maze of numerous passageways and blind alleys to confuse grave robbers."[11]

The early Greeks practiced burial and cremation. The dead were buried in tombs or sepulchers cut in rock or graves similar to those in use today. The tombs were covered with sepulchral iconography. They painstakingly decorated the tombs with ornate inscriptions and carvings.

In Roman society, though bodies were predominantly cremated, the people also constructed tombs for the dead, and everyone, even the slaves, had a burial place, or *loculus*. Since burial was not permitted in the city, the tombs lined the roads leading in and out of Rome. Cremated remains were placed in a columbarium, a subterranean structure containing niches for the urns and marble tablets to identify the remains. Early Roman Christians did not use elaborate tombs, but rather disposed of their corpses in the catacombs on the outskirts of the city.[12]

Among the Hebrews, bodies of the poor were laid on the ground or in a shallow trench and covered with a mound of earth. The rich were buried in natural caves or sepulchers hewn from rock. Similar to family burial in American society, the early Jews interred the dead on the family's land or near the dwelling, and burial was restricted to family members. Burial apart from one's family was a catastrophe.[13]

The Christian church has always prescribed suitable sites for tombs and graves. Very early Christian burials were in family vaults along roads leading from great cities. Early tombs, which were caves or chambers cut out of rock, were naturally very simple. Later ones were more elaborate, though they could not compete with many moslem tombs.[14] Important Moslems have been buried in spectacular tombs. The most celebrated of these is the Taj Mahal, built between 1630 and 1652 in Agra, India. Even the humblest Moslem, though interred without a tomb, is buried facing Mecca.

When the colonists reached America, they faced a brutal life that often ended in premature death for many of them. Most of the early settlers were buried in mass graves that were camouflaged to protect the bodies from the suspected threat of disturbance by Native Americans. People who died on the western trek were buried in unmarked graves. "In pioneer days some bodies were buried quickly and wagons run over the graves to mislead Indians who might desecrate the graves.[15]

The first true cemeteries, whether they were established by the Puritans in New England or the Jamestown Colony in Virginia, were set up by churches. As families began to move, they began burying their dead in family cemeteries. As communities grew larger and time passed, church cemeteries could no longer accommodate all of the dead and occasionally buried corpses on top of each other. Cities set aside land within or outside their limits in an attempt to alleviate space problems and provide a secluded area for bodies infected with yellow fever or cholera.[16]

In nineteenth-century America, the "memorial cemetery" (also referred to as the "memorial garden," "lawn cemetery," "memorial park," and "perpetual-care cemetery") became popular. The land for these burial grounds was chosen for its accessibility and natural beauty. These cemeteries were carefully planned and beautifully landscaped. Reminders of death were removed. For example, upright grave markers were replaced with markers level with the ground and graves were leveled rather than mounded when burial took place. Chidester describes a lawn cemetery established in Cincinnati, Ohio, in 1855:

> Modeled after Central Park in New York City, this new style of cemetery, a large, flat expanse of carefully manicured grass, became the dominant model for American cemeteries. Its main characteristic was

uniformity: Grave mounds were leveled; gravestones were limited in size; grave inscriptions were reduced; and fences or stone boundaries around grave plots were eliminated. Features that had been prominent in earlier cemeteries were removed because they were felt to violate uniformity by emphasizing status distinctions in the city of the dead. But grave mounds, stones, and fences were also eliminated because they obstructed the view of the park and made lawn mowing difficult. Ultimately, however, these features of earlier cemeteries were eliminated because they reminded people of death.[17]

The word *cemetery* derives from the Greek word *koimeterion*, or "sleeping place." This new type of cemetery truly captured the flavor of the original word.

These sleeping places were more exclusive than regular cemeteries, however. Most memorial parks and perpetual-care cemeteries required such things as ground-level headstones and metal or concrete vaults. In addition, most also charged a fee for the burial plot, but this was sometimes subsidized by public funds if the deceased or the family could not afford the cost of interment. These graveyards eventually became known as perpetual-care cemeteries because people purchased burial space with the assurance that the money was put into an endowment fund so that the graves would be taken care of forever.

CENTRAL APPALACHIAN CEMETERIES

Most early American pioneers wanted to find and claim their own land. Central Appalachia, for many, provided a place to settle, raise a family, and spend the rest of their lives. When someone died, it seemed only logical to bury them on family land. Since family ties were extremely strong, the deceased were usually buried near loved ones. For example, a wife would be buried beside her husband, and adult children sometimes preferred to be buried near their parents. The first cemeteries in this part of the country were family cemeteries.

These family cemeteries were almost always on hills or mountains. Guerrant affirms: "I never saw a graveyard in a valley. They bury on the hills and sometimes on the top of mountains."[18] Occasionally, they were a mile or more away, and to reach them was a difficult, exhausting process: "I remember a funeral in the family graveyard on the summit of a barren hill. The climb up the steep slope with the adults was very hard for me. It seemed to me there was a great concourse of people and I thought we would never get there."[19]

Burial on a high place provided some psychological assurance that water would not seep into the grave and disturb the departed. Some mountaineers believed that burial on a hill or mountain meant the deceased was closer to heaven. Since they were buried on high ground facing the east, they would have a better view of the events during the Resurrection. A funeral director in eastern Kentucky told the humorous story of a mountain man who, after carrying the corpse and coffin for a long distance up a steep mountain, announced, "If she doesn't make it to heaven, it ain't my fault. I've already carried her halfway there."

Some mountain people buried their dead on a mountain or hill because they "felt that in death as in life they would want to look over their beloved mountains."[20] To some extent, they believed that though buried in the earth the deceased could still sense the surroundings and even feel emotions: "'He'll rest easy here,'" she told us, "'a lookin' down across the country he loved.'"[21] "We buried her there like a sentry crow overlooking the land below."[22]

Though these cemeteries on high ground satisfied certain psychological needs for earlier central Appalachians, today many of them are inaccessible, isolated, neglected, and forgotten. "In one abandoned cemetery, the trees grow tall and close together near the top of the hill. The spot is dark, gloomy, over-run with weeds. There are no signs of life except for a stray bird or an occasional swarm of mosquitoes."[23]

In December 1990, I climbed to the top of a steep hill in southwestern Virginia to visit a family cemetery I had remembered from my hunting days. The family had been dead for many years. The fence (what there was of it) was rusted and in need of repair, and the entire cemetery was so overgrown with vines, shrubs, and briars that I had great difficulty finding the grave markers. Most of the graves were sunken and there were numerous groundhog holes, trees were growing in several places including a few graves, and the headstones were either leaning or had already fallen on the ground. It was inaccessible by even a four-wheel-drive vehicle and had been neglected for many years. I have found similar examples of this kind of neglect in several family cemeteries throughout central Appalachia.

Some mountain people not only wanted to bury their dead on the top of a hill or mountain, they also wished to inter them beneath a tree if possible. The trees provided shade for the grave, protection from inclement weather, and enhanced the beauty of the deceased's surroundings. They also served as natural markers for graves, as "Bury Me under the Weeping Willow" suggests:

> Oh, bury me under the weeping willow,
> Yes, under the weeping willow tree;

So he may know where I am sleeping,
And perhaps he will weep over me.[24]

Ties to the mountains have always been strong, but out migration has been mandatory for some mountaineers due to a lack of jobs. Many of these migrants continue to maintain contact with loved ones "back home," and when they die, their desire is to be buried in a family cemetery in the mountains.[25] However, the number of out migrants returned to the mountains has declined in recent years. While fond memories of the homeland are maintained in the city, the feeling of home is often transferred to the urban community where the mountaineer resides. A recent study by Obermiller and Rappold indicates that one Appalachian migrant in ten is returned to the region for interment and about half of the decedents sent back are not true migrants but move to the city to receive care from their families. The authors conclude: "Therefore, this 10 percent estimate should be reduced by half because the frail elderly, who may have lived all but the last few months of their lives in the Appalachian region, never had the opportunity to redefine 'home' in the same way as long-term migrants."[26]

Even though they were called family cemeteries they did not exclude nonfamily members. Neighbors were often interred in a separate section of family graveyards. For example, in 1990 while walking through a family cemetery, I found one grave off by itself that contained an "outsider." While traveling through the five-state mountain area, I discovered many such cemeteries where bodies other than those of family members were buried.

When churches were established in the mountains, members of the congregation formed strong, almost familial bonds. Church members helped one another in hard times and rejoiced together in happy times. Because of the closeness of the congregation and because some families did not have their own graveyards, many mountain churches established their own cemeteries. Similar to family cemeteries, they were surrounded by a wooden or wire fence to protect the graves from roaming animals, such as horses and cattle, and located on an elevated site.

Several church burial grounds contained family rows, where only family members could be interred. Occasionally, a mistake was made. I interviewed an elderly woman in western North Carolina who was disturbed because somebody other than a member of her immediate family had been buried in her family's row. She wanted the body exhumed and interred in another section of the graveyard.

As communities in the area developed, many mountain residents no longer owned land or belonged to a church. At some point public or community cemeteries had to be established, where people could be buried when there was no family or church cemetery that would accept their remains. Most of them began charging fees for the plot of land and services they provided. For a price, an individual could purchase a grave plot or entire families could buy a section where members could be interred.[27] Some public cemeteries charged a nominal fee and were subsidized by public funds.

The trend in the modern-day mountains is toward burial in a perpetual-care cemetery. Several funeral directors I interviewed asserted that though most of their burials continue to be in family cemeteries, the number of interments each year in perpetual-care facilities is increasing. Family graveyards are not as prevalent as in the past and many of them are not well cared for. Burial in a church cemetery is not guaranteed, some churches no longer maintain their own graveyards, and many mountaineers do not belong to a church. Central Appalachians are apparently responding to the feeling of security in knowing that their graves will be taken care of forever.

Whether it is a family, church, or public cemetery, each mountain graveyard falls into one of three categories. The traditional cemetery is one in which the upright, or vertical, grave marker is still accepted. Memorial parks permit only grave markers that are level with the ground. The third type accepts both vertical and horizontal grave markers, though the two kinds of markers may be segregated. Usually, it has a section for upright grave stones and one for markers level with the ground. Most family and church cemeteries are traditional. The majority of community or public cemeteries permit a combination of upright and ground-level grave markers, but many allow only the ground-level type.

The Committal Service

When the funeral procession reached the cemetery, the coffin was carried to the grave site, where it was put on the fresh pile of dirt excavated from the grave, a special platform of some kind, or boards or ropes placed across the grave. If a funeral service had not been conducted previously, one would usually be held prior to interment. However, when the funeral service was in the home, church, or funeral establishment, there would be a committal service at the grave (sometimes there was no service, funeral or committal, or it would be held at a later date).

After the coffin was positioned, the mourners gathered around with the immediate family closest to the deceased. When funeral homes became responsible for the burial, folding chairs were provided so that the mourners would be more comfortable. At the committal service the minister seldom preached a lengthy fire-and-brimstone sermon. The service focused on the deceased and committing the body back to the earth from which it came. The prayers and scriptures at this service usually reflected the sentiments in Eccles. 12:7 ("then the dead will return to the earth as it was and the spirit will return to God who gave it") and Gen. 3:19 ("for you are dust, and to dust you shall return").[28] There was usually prayer, a few verses of scripture, and, depending on such variables as the weather and the wishes of the family, a short sermon. Songs were also sometimes provided, but almost always without the accompaniment of a musical instrument.

The length of the committal service depended upon the wishes of the family, the length of the sermon, and the weather. In the summer, the ceremony was invariably short because of the odor from the decaying body. Cold winter weather shortened the service too. The entire committal service was about ten to thirty minutes, though most were fifteen minutes long.

The lid of the coffin was usually removed during the committal service or at the end of the ceremony so that family and friends could take a last look and say good-bye. The burial receptacle was frequently opened so that family members who arrived too late for the funeral would be allowed to view the body. Also, there were instances when friends, neighbors, or relatives could not attend the funeral but were present for the burial. They were sometimes permitted to view the corpse before it was buried. A few mountaineers just wanted to make sure their loved one was "lying comfortably" before the coffin was put into the ground.[29] Since transportation to the grave was difficult, families wanted to reposition the body before burial. The coffin was sometimes dropped or tilted while the pallbearers carried it. The wagon or sled jolted too and bounced the coffin on its journey to the grave. Occasionally, a cloth was placed over the face of the deceased for protection and it had to be removed at the cemetery.

If interment was to take place without a prior funeral service in the home, church, or funeral home, the burial receptacle was usually opened for a viewing. When people began to move from central Appalachia, they maintained their ties to the mountains. After death occurred, the wake and funeral were sometimes held in the area where they died, and the body was then transported to the mountains for burial. Due to curiosity, a desire for one last look, or a need to determine whether the body in the coffin was the loved one, the burial receptacle was opened one last time.

When death resulted from a major accident, mining disaster, debilitating illness, or communicable disease, the coffin was usually not opened. In some cases, removing the lid of the burial container could be like opening Pandora's box. The offensive odor from the decaying body or the scene inside the coffin could make even the strongest stomach queasy: "Someone opened the casket, which the neighbors had constructed for the body. One whole side of her face had fallen off, so they rapidly closed it again and asked me to offer another prayer. I do not remember what I prayed, but I said something."[30]

At the end of the funeral service or the committal ceremony someone occasionally opened the casket so that family members could place personal items inside with the corpse, a tradition that stems back thousands of years. Excavations of prehistoric graves have unearthed grave goods. Early primitive groups as well as the Egyptians, Greeks, and Romans placed a great deal of emphasis on sending loved ones off to the hereafter with objects they possessed during life. Some societies employed extreme measures in an attempt to provide security when a member died:

> The goods accompanying the dead in . . . graves included not only food and drink, but ornaments, weapons, and implements of various kinds. Occasionally the objects were quite large, such as those discovered in the Sumerian city of Ur. Excavators in one of the 5,000-year-old graves found in this city, which is located in modern Iraq, discovered, in addition to the skeleton of a king, a chariot, the remains of a donkey to pull the chariot, various weapons, tools, valuables, and 65 members of the royal court! Apparently the ladies, soldiers, and grooms who made up the entourage had taken a lethal drug, marched to their assigned positions, and died.[31]

Mountain people, past and present, have buried a wide variety of objects in the coffin with a loved one, including jewelry, eyeglasses, tobacco, pipes, money, hats, pocketbooks, combs, guns, knives, toys, and alcoholic beverages. Mourners most commonly placed Bibles and photographs in the casket. A funeral director in southwestern Virginia told me that he put a clock in the casket with a woman. It was a prized possession and she wanted to take it with her to the grave. There were also stuffed animals and photographs in her burial container. Several people told me that they had seen guns positioned in the hands of mountain men before they were interred.

In the days when grave robbery was common, some people were hesitant to leave valuables such as jewelry on the corpse. The jewelry remained on the body until interment; it was removed before the lid was closed for the final time. In many instances today, when the committal service is over and everyone has left the cemetery, the funeral director or an assistant will take the jewelry from the deceased, put it in an envelope, and give it to the closest relative.

Viewing the body at the grave often became more emotional than the scene at the funeral service. Survivors would cry, scream, wave their arms, attempt to drag the corpse from the burial container, and try to prevent the closing of the coffin. Guerrant recalled that he "never witnessed such an exhibition of sorrow, as they clung to the coffin and kissed the cold silent lips."[32] Jean Ritchie provides a vivid description of the emotional aspects of a committal service: "They set the coffin down and made prayer and sang some more, then the time came when they opened up the coffin and we all marched by Grandpa lying there all white. All the women started to scream and wave their arms, looked to me like they were going crazy. All I could do was stand there and watch. I couldn't squeeze out a single tear."[33] The emotional displays dwindled as the grave was filled.

Prior to burial, sometimes the minister or immediate family members sprinkled the coffin with dirt, symbolizing the actual commitment of the body to the earth: "A cold February wind cut across the brow of the hill and the procession of people shivered. A prayer was offered and grains of red clay symbolizing dust-to-dust filtered through Elijah Gudger's fingers onto Sarah Moore's coffin. Then neighbors lowered the cedar box into the raw red earth."[34] A committal service usually ended with a prayer.

In the mountains today, the casket is carried by the pallbearers from the hearse to the open grave, where it remains until burial takes place. The service, which is a committal ceremony, is shorter than it was in the past and a sermon is rare. While everyone crowds around the casket, with the minister and immediate family closest to the corpse, there is prayer, scripture reading, and a dust-to-dust ritual.

There is less likelihood that the casket will be opened for a final viewing, even though embalming has eliminated the odor from the decaying body, transportation has improved and there is no longer a need to open the casket and make sure the body was not disturbed during the transition from the funeral site to the grave, and current restoration and cosmetic techniques make it possible to open the casket even in cases of disfigurement from accidents and debilitating diseases. Caskets are opened at the graveside at the request of family members or when the funeral has been held elsewhere and the body was shipped to the mountains for interment. Personal items are occasionally added to or removed from a casket. A minister I interviewed in southwestern Virginia maintained that social class affects the opening of the casket. In his experience, lower-class people tend to want a final viewing, while middle- and upper-class families don't usually want the casket open at the grave site.

Burial

Throughout human history there have been at least five major alternatives to earth burial: Open-air disposal, water burial, mortuary cannibalism, cremation, and entombment. Today, cryogenic suspension and donation of the corpse to medical science are additional modes of disposing of a dead body.

OPEN-AIR DISPOSAL

In open-air disposal, the dead body is placed on a scaffold, in a tree, or on the ground where it will decay or be consumed by birds or animals. Most groups that employ this technique believe that disposal by earth burial, cremation, and water burial contaminate the earth. When Zoroastrianism became the major religion of Persia in the sixth century B.C., the dead were placed on scaffolds known as high "dakhmas" (towers of silence) where the flesh was devoured by birds of prey. Open-air disposal has also been practiced by some Native American groups and Australian aborigines, and it is still employed by groups such as the Parsee of India.[35]

MORTUARY CANNIBALISM

Mortuary cannibalism is the consuming of all or a portion of a dead body because it unites those who partake in the ceremony with the deceased and endows them with his or her virtues. Archaeological evidence indicates its presence during the Peking and Neanderthal time periods in human history. The Yanomamo Indians of Brazil and Venezuela practice endocannibalism, whereby the crushed remains of the deceased are mixed with banana plantain and eaten during a feast.[36] The Iroquois in North America sometimes ate parts of a body of an enemy who showed bravery.[37] Mortuary cannibalism, at least symbolically, has been practiced as a part of the Christian sacrament of communion, in which the blood and body of Jesus Christ are consumed "in celebration of the redemptive sacrifice of his death."[38]

CREMATION

The utilization of fire to dispose of a dead body dates from antiquity. While the early Jews, Islamic peoples, and Christians were vehemently opposed to cremation, it was a major component of Hindu and Buddhist death procedures. The Greeks and Romans employed disposal by fire at various times in their history, but earth burial was always an alternative. Even when cremating the Romans practiced "os resectum," where everything was cremated but the finger joint, which was buried (a vestige of the custom of earth burial). Cremation is looked upon by many in modern society as a good alternative to other types of disposal. It obviously takes up less space than earth burial and protects the public from possible health hazards.

WATER BURIAL

Burial at sea is a widespread cultural practice. Many Pacific Island societies and Scandinavians regularly dispose of their dead in the water. Death on a long voyage or while serving in the navy, when there is not enough time to ship the corpse home for earth burial, often results in water burial.

ENTOMBMENT

Entombment consists of placing a body, contained in a casket or burial receptacle, in a special building constructed above ground. Abraham's cave, the pyramids, the Taj Mahal, and Lincoln's tomb are examples of entombment in the past; today it has become an answer to the space problems of modern cemeteries. Although you can only dig so far in the ground, for entombment, according to Jessica Mitford, "the sky is literally the limit."[39] Most states and cemeteries regulate the construction of the three major types of tombs: public, family, and individual.

In many areas of America, aboveground disposal is available in a building called a public (or community) mausoleum. This term dates back to 353 B.C., when the widow of King Mausolus of what is now Turkey erected a monument to her husband's memory. The modern public mausoleum contains individual crypts or groups of crypts that can be arranged in a manner similar to cemetery lots. Mitford contends that "10,000 mausoleum spaces to an acre is a most realistic yield. . . . Crypt is stacked upon crypt—six or seven high is currently the vogue—two deep, on either side of a visitors' corridor. The most advantageous size for crypts . . . is 32 inches wide, 25 inches high, and 90 inches long."[40]

In some instances, families may purchase burial plots in a cemetery and build a family mausoleum that may hold as few as one or two bodies or as many as twelve to sixteen. Normally a monument company builds the structure to specification on the cemetery grounds but the family owns the actual building and retains the key. Individuals may also build their own mausoleums that they may share with a spouse or companion. These too are normally built by a monument company but they require the same amount of space as a grave for underground burial.

CRYOGENIC SUSPENSION AND DONATIONS TO MEDICAL SCIENCE

Cryonics or cryogenic suspension is the preservation of a corpse by freezing it to the temperature of solid carbon dioxide. People who accept this mode of disposal believe that the frozen corpse can be thawed in the future when a cure for the terminal illness, such as cancer, that caused death has been found. The process involves "replacing the blood in the body with a glycerol-based substitute, gradually cooling down the body in dry ice over a period of eight to ten hours, and then finally suspending the body upside down in a nitrogen-filled aluminum cannister at a temperature of -196°C."[41]

Some altruistic Americans choose to donate their body to a medical institution. If desired, a funeral service of some kind can be held before the body is transported to its intended destination.

BURIAL IN CENTRAL APPALACHIA

By far the most common form of corpse disposal is earth burial and central Appalachia is no exception. Residents of the area have never practiced open-air disposal, water burial, or mortuary cannibalism. Less than 1 percent of people choose cremation, cryogenic suspension, or donation to science. Mausoleums are being constructed, especially in the more urbanized areas, and a few mountaineers are beginning to purchase crypts so that their bodies can be entombed.

For earth burial in the early days in the mountains, pallbearers normally placed the coffin in the ground. This task usually took at least two ropes and four men. If rope was not available, straps, belts, or the check lines (also called chuck lines or plow lines) from horse harnesses could serve just as well. If the body and coffin were exceedingly heavy, a third rope and additional men were necessary. The coffin was normally placed over the open grave on planks or poles and two men stood on each side. Those on one side passed the rope under the coffin to the men on the other side. The boards or poles were removed and the burial receptacle was slowly lowered until it reached the bottom. The ends of the coffin, and the bottom and sides of the grave, were constructed so the ropes could be easily retrieved without disturbing the corpse, and the grave was filled.

The precarious position of the casket sometimes led to accidents. An elderly woman in western North Carolina told me about a burial in which the "sorry coffin" split into two sections while the corpse was being lowered into the grave. They had to retrieve and repair the coffin, "straighten" the deceased, and start again. In eastern Kentucky, an interviewee related the story of a burial he had attended in which a rope broke and the coffin turned upside down in the grave. He said "they had an awful time getting that rectified." A West Virginian recited the story of a very large man (over four hundred pounds), who was buried in a specially constructed coffin. While placing the body in the container, the embalmers dropped it in sideways and it was stuck. They couldn't get it out, so that was the way the corpse was interred. It took several people to lower the deceased to his final resting place.

Once the coffin was in place, layers of boards were placed on the shelf or bench, about one or two inches above the coffin, to retard the dirt that could accelerate the decay of the burial receptacle and corpse, prevent the coffin from being crushed, and keep animals from disinterring the corpse. Later when vaults, either rough boxes or more elaborate metal or concrete ones, encased the coffin for added protection (the vault was already in the ground when the funeral procession arrived), the lid had to be closed before the grave could be filled. Men at the funeral filled the grave with dirt and mounded the remaining soil so that water would run off the grave and not seep into the ground around the coffin. Flowers, if there were any, were placed upon the mound of dirt or dispersed among the other graves in the cemetery. Sometimes, in the early years, families would remain until the grave was filled. Then they would talk with friends and relatives or work at cleaning some of the graves in the surrounding area. When the burial was completed, friends and neighbors usually prepared a meal for the family.

In contemporary central Appalachia funeral homes or cemeteries almost exclusively take care of the burial. Family and friends usually leave the site while the professionals use mechanical devices to lower the casket into the grave and fill it with dirt. Neighbors and relatives are no longer needed to lower the casket or fill in the grave. As the funeral home system has taken over this part of caring for the dead, mourners have become less involved. When the wake and funeral were held in the home, burial was primarily in a family or church cemetery, and familism and neighborliness were extensive, mountain people attended all the events from the moment of death until interment. Today, it is more difficult, and less vital, for people to leave their jobs and go to the visitation, funeral, *and* burial ceremony. The burial service has evolved into an almost exclusively family-attended event.

SEVEN

Grave Markers and Other Forms of Memorialization

Oft I've wandered in the churchyard;
Tenderly I nursed the flowers.
There beside my mother's tombstone,
I passed many weary hours.
—Vernon Dalhart and Company, "Mother's Grave"

Grave Markers in Other Cultures

H istorical data and archeological evidence indicate that humans have long possessed a need to mark the graves of members of their social group, erect monuments to their dead, and preserve objects belonging to the deceased as a way of remembering them for many years after their deaths. Puckle lists three separate reasons for the erection of monuments to the dead: "First, a belief that the body dwells or sleeps in the place prepared for it. Secondly, to mark the spot where a person of some special attainments has been buried, in which case a suitable inscription is provided, setting forth the claims of the deceased to public recognition for the edification of future generations. Thirdly, the provision of a stone or tablet asking the prayers of co-religionists for a departed soul."[1]

Memorials were an important part of ancient Egyptian society. The tombs and pyramids were constructed as memorials to the deceased, as well as a means of recording the history of the deceased and reminding the living of their own mortality.[2] The walls of tombs were decorated with detailed scenes or panoramas of Egyptian life as it was known to the deceased. This practice of sepulchral iconography was introduced by the Egyptians primarily for royalty. For example, a portrait of King Djoser of the Third Dynasty in Egypt (2686–2613 B.C.) "appeared in the Step Pyramid together with his name and accomplishments, for both commemorative and magic purposes."[3]

The Greeks used eight different types of grave markers: round columns, rectangular slabs, stelae, shrine-shaped stones, huge rectangular stone blocks, marble vases, square or round receptacles for the ashes, and sarcophagi. While they sometimes identified the dead, especially the elite, according to Shushan "the Greeks did not consider the identification of the deceased essential. Their epitaphs, written in verse, reminded the reader of the universality of death."[4] Monuments were used in the commemoration of heroes. In classical Athens, sepulchral iconography included the name and parentage of the dead person and occasionally the word *farewell,* the restrained grief of the living, and the image of the deceased performing a familiar act for the last time.[5]

In early Roman society, an extensive amount of effort was put into identifying the decedent. Above the tomb, a portrait immortalized the deceased and an inscription carried the deceased's name, position, and the names of the relatives responsible for the burial. With this type of sepulchral iconography, the portraits and words were meant to be merely commemorative rather than of any magical value.[6] For those Romans cremated, names were inscribed on tablets over the niches for their remains.

The early Jews, Christians, and Islamic people did not place much emphasis on memorialization and identifying the resting place of the dead. "The Hebrews preferred simple tombs, natural or artificial chambers, unadorned, and even without inscription."[7] As Christianity developed, memorials and identification of the dead, especially powerful figures, became important. Burial in sarcophagi with beautiful iconographic illustrations began in the fourth and fifth centuries A.D.[8] While most of the Islamic peoples may have emphasized simple burials, the rich were sometimes interred in elaborate tombs or mausoleums such as the Taj Mahal.

Grave Markers in Early America

Few grave markers in America predate the 1660s. Before that time, graves were either unmarked or carried wood markers. The first stone markers in America were crude slabs made of imported hard slate.[9] They originally lacked carved designs and contained only minimal inscriptions, such as the initials and age of the deceased, the year of death, and, later, the day and month of death. When grave markers became more ornamental, they included both Christian and non-Christian symbols. These shapes and figures were undoubtedly based on those of earlier civilizations and brought with the first settlers from their homelands.[10]

Non-Christian symbols were a skull and crossbones, death masks, and chubby cherubs. Christian symbols included the hourglass with the sand run out, clasped hands, a finger pointing toward heaven, a harp or lyre with a broken string, the weeping willow tree, Father Time holding his scythe, an open Bible (sometimes with a text carved), angelic forms, lighted or unlighted candles, and, for infants and children, a lamb.[11]

As America grew as a nation, identifying the graves of loved ones became even more important. For Christians, the body of the deceased needed to be protected until Judgment Day. Many Americans wanted to visit the site of interment and place flowers on the grave, meditate, or converse with the departed. Stone carving became a more integral part of marking graves as the funeral business developed. Grave markers became larger and more ornamental with more elaborate inscriptions as stone carving grew into an art. Inscriptions were important. With the advent of perpetual-care cemeteries and the prohibition of the use of upright headstones, markers level with the ground were introduced to satisfy the need to identify a grave.

Grave markers in the United States have been fashioned out of a variety of materials including granite, marble, soapstone, glass, bronze, wood, slate, limestone, and clay, depending on the part of the country where death occurred. Edwards[12] and Schaltenbrand[13] report the use of stoneware and salt-glazed grave markers. Hall encountered several unique ways of identifying a grave, such as seashells, a bedstead, pottery in various forms, medicine bottles, lamps, burned-out light bulbs, spoons, cabinets, and vases.[14] The most common materials used in making grave markers today are granite, bronze, and marble, "with granite markers by far the most common."[15]

Grave Markers in Central Appalachia

The earliest Appalachian pioneers often chose to leave graves unidentified. There was a concern that the Native Americans would disinter and desecrate the body. Frequently, before permanent settlement, there was not enough time for a proper burial and marking the grave. Many early central Appalachians left their graves unmarked because they lacked the skills and inclination to create elaborate grave markers. Because a large number of the early settlers to the area were Christian, when graves were marked two sticks fashioned into a cross were inserted into the ground at the head of the grave. There was no inscription or epitaph. Since wood rotted,

Plain fieldstone used as a grave marker.

after a period of time it was almost impossible to identify who was buried and where the body lay. If several people were buried in the same vicinity, ascertaining which grave belonged to a particular individual could become very confusing.

Fieldstones provided the second most common marker. These rocks of limestone, sandstone, granite, slate, soapstone, and marble were readily available to any mountaineer who wished to denote the location of a loved one. They were placed on the ground at the head of the grave. Occasionally, mountain people used flat rocks, which could be stuck into the ground and remain upright at the head of the grave. In some cases graves were marked with both head- and footstones. A larger rock usually marked the the head of the grave.

Since many central Appalachian pioneers could not read or write, inscriptions were rare. Naturally, this has made it difficult for people today to determine how many bodies are buried in a cemetery, who is interred in a particular place, and the age of the graveyard.

With the passage of time, an increase in literacy, and a desire to iden-tify a grave for future generations, mountaineers began to carve the rocks used as headstones (usually no carving was done on a fieldstone placed at the foot of the grave). Sometimes, only the ini-tials of the deceased were cut into the stone, but occasionally the name, birth date, and death date were carved. A few carvers attempt-ed to shape the stone or make it smoother.

Even today wooden crosses and fieldstones are used to mark graves. Less frequently, mountain people continue to use wooden stakes driv-en into the ground, wooden boards (sometimes with inscriptions), cement headstones, and wooden posts. Commercially produced grave markers were not used in many parts of the mountains until well into the twentieth century. Valued for their esthetic and commemorative characteristics, commercial stones were imported until residents of the area began to work as stonemasons. Now although stone cutting is a major business in the mountains, many residents continue to use the more traditional markers at least partly because commercial markers are too expensive for them to purchase.

A few mountain people purchased tombstones prior to their deaths and even had them placed at the heads of their burial spots so they could be certain their graves would not go unmarked. This happens even more frequently today, since mountaineers have a greater ten-dency to preplan. Usually, however, these graves were temporarily identified with a stick or rock until a commercial stone was purchased in the months following the death. When commercial markers became available, some mountain people purchased headstones and foot-stones. These headstones normally carried the biographical informa-tion, epitaph, and decorative carvings, while the footstones were much smaller and held only the initials of the deceased.

Finding a stone to place at the end of a grave was not a difficult chore in the mountains. Getting a commercial stone to the top of a mountain could be a painstakingly difficult task. In some instances, it was impossible to get one up a treacherous incline. Sometimes it took several men to drag it up the mountain. If possible, a large marker was placed on a sled and pulled to the cemetery by a horse or horses.

Most of the commercial stones placed at the head of a grave in central Appalachia have not withstood the weather and passage of time very well. I encountered numerous stones placed near graves, from the early eighteenth century through the 1940s, that were barely legible. While it varies in quality, the most durable stone is granite. Five-thousand-year-old Egyptian granite carvings show little or no

Headstone for Rhoda Stump dated December 28, 1923.

Footstone for Rhoda Stump.

Metal grave marker in the shape of a mummy coffin in a small cemetery in eastern Tennessee, dated September 13, 1827.

wear, and "in the harsher climate of Northern Europe, granite used in the construction of Gothic edifices is still untouched by time after 1,000 years."[16] Other stones, such as marble, slate, and sandstone, do not withstand the elements as well, as a trip to any older cemetery will reveal.[17]

When a funeral establishment is involved, a metal marker containing biographical information is provided to identify the burial spot until a gravestone can be bought (unless it has been purchased prior to death). While visiting numerous cemeteries in the five-state mountain area of central Appalachia, I found markers containing only a birth date, headstones for a husband and wife with no death dates listed, grave markers listing the birth and death dates for one spouse but only a birth date for the other, and large headstones for an entire family, with death dates listed for some but not all family members.

Grave markers in central Appalachia come in a multiplicity of sizes and shapes. There are a few wooden crosses standing in mountain cemeteries. Fieldstones, which also come in a plethora of shapes and sizes, are still quite numerous in church and family graveyards. Other than these primitive modes of identifying a grave, most burial spots are identified by either rectangular slabs built to stand vertically (upright) at the head of the grave or rectangular (sometimes square) markers made to be placed horizontally, or parallel with the ground, at the head or foot of the interment site.

A few markers for graves have been professionally sculpted in the form of angels and saints, human beings (recumbent, sitting, or standing), animals (lambs, doves), and inanimate objects such as hearts, churches, urns, and crosses. In eastern Tennessee, I recently found a metal marker constructed in the shape of a mummy coffin that was placed horizontally over the grave. Most of the memorials sculpted in the form of beings or specific objects are found in large cemeteries in urban areas. Very few are found in small church or family graveyards in rural areas.

CARVINGS ON GRAVE MARKERS

Carved symbols, insignias, and emblems have appeared on objects used to mark a grave since ancient times. However, except for those rare instances in which a name (or initials) or date were used, central Appalachian pioneers made few attempts to carve anything on a grave marker until professionally cut headstones became available. Some of the professional headstones were plain except for biographical information, but most had objects of some kind carved on them—

usually with a religious theme. The most common theme I have found on central Appalachian grave markers is the "hand of the Lord," which indicates omnipotence and fatherly guidance. A finger pointed upward toward heaven denotes "the path of the spirit's ultimate voyage,"[18] while a hand reaching down through a cloud, with one or two hands reaching upward in an attempt to grasp it, is symbolic of the Heavenly Father gathering a child or children into his fold. Variations on the hand theme are two hands clasped together in a handshake (signifying the last farewell) and hands folded together in prayer. An open or closed Bible is a widely employed carving used to mark the grave of deeply religious people such as ministers. On some headstones, the open Bible contains a short scripture or an inscription of some kind. The dove, a Christian symbol of purity and innocence, often appears holding an olive branch or scroll with words such as "Rest in Peace." The dove and lamb (for innocence and resurrection) are carved on many memorial stones for central Appalachian children.

Objects of veneration and worship, trees and other foliage have frequently been carved on mountain grave markers. Olive branches are popular but the most popular Christian symbol is the weeping willow tree, which signifies grief and sorrow. On many gravestones, the carving depicts the weeping willow tree overhanging the tomb of the deceased. Lilies, ivy, rosettes, tulips, posies, thistles, and leafy clusters were popular and appear in a multitude of different formats.

Other common mountain gravestone carvings are the crown of righteousness (sometimes with a cross inside), angels, a cross, clouds symbolizing the concealment of God from his worshipers, a caduceus indicating the grave of a physician, the image of a cemetery with the gates open, a star signifying guidance for the soul of the deceased, a sheaf of wheat (most often on markers for the elderly), and emblems indicating membership in organizations, such as the Freemasons or the Order of the Eastern Star.

Specialized carvings came later in central Appalachian history. First came biographical identification of the deceased, mostly through initials on the marker. Sometimes an industrious person might carve the entire name or date of death. With the introduction of larger professionally cut gravestones, epitaphs and biographical data became popular in the mountains. Unfortunately, though there have been several books written about epitaphs and inscriptions employed in Europe and America, they have included little information about central Appalachia. I, however, have examined thousands of grave markers in the five-state mountain area dating from the eighteenth

Headstones with the image of a lamb are often placed at the grave of a child in central Appalachia.

Headstone with a memorial portrait of the deceased attached.

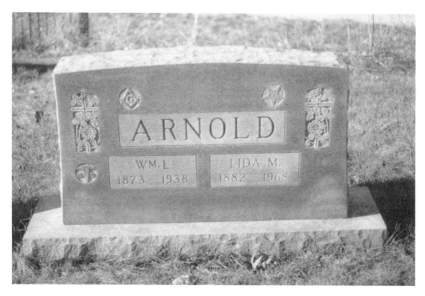

Decorative headstone in eastern Tennessee indicating that the husband was a physician and a Freemason and the wife was a member of the Order of the Eastern Star.

century to the present time. The vast majority of professionally carved headstones since the eighteenth century contain the name of the deceased, the date of birth (month, day, year), and the date of death (month, day, year). Now and then, the age of the deceased at death was carved on the grave marker.

Epitaphs on mountain grave markers usually have a religious theme, and the majority contain only one line. The most common epitaphs that I found are "Gone but not forgotten," "Rest in peace," "In remembrance of," "Asleep in Jesus," "At rest," "From mother's arms to the arms of Jesus," "She died as she lived, a Christian," "In memory of . . . ," "In loving memory," "Love is forever, death is a dream," "Farewell," "Gone to a better land," "We will meet again," and "Precious Lord take my hand." Common epitaphs for children are "Budded on earth to bloom in heaven, "He was the sunshine of our home," "In heaven there is one more angel," "Little ones to him belong," "My beloved daughter," "Our darling one has gone before to greet us on the blissful shore," and "Our darling is now in the grave."

For a parent, popular carvings are "A tender mother and faithful friend," "In heaven there is one more angel," "In loving remembrance of our father," "Our mother has gone home to be with the angels," and "Rest mother, rest in peace." Carvings for a parent or spouse include "Earth has no sorrow that heaven cannot heal," "He is not dead but sleeping," "May she rest in peace," "A voice beloved is stilled," "A place is vacant in our home that never can be filled," "Prepare to meet me in heaven," "Rest ———, rest in quiet sleep, while friends in sorrow o'er thee weep," "Sleep on dear ——— until Jesus comes," "We will meet again," and "Weep not, she is at rest." For mountain men killed in a war, in addition to biographical data, the two most frequently used lines are "He gave his life for his country" and "Who died in the service of his country."

Less common carvings that I discovered on more than one mountain grave marker are "As I am now you're sure to be, prepare thy self to follow me," "Blessed are the dead which die in the Lord," "Blessed are the dead which know God," "Blessed are the pure in heart for they shall see God," "Come unto me ye blessed," "In death we do not part," "Looking unto Jesus," "Love lives on," "Man goeth to his long home," "Nothing between my Savior and I," "No pain, no grief, no anxious fear can reach our loved one sleeping here," "I have fought a good fight, I have finished my cause, I have kept the faith," "The Lord is my shepherd I will not want," and "Thy trial's ended, thy rest is soon." Epitaphs longer than two lines are rare in central Appalachian headstones. One of the longest verses I found is

> My flesh shall slumber in the ground,
> 'Till the last trumpet's joyful sound;
> Then burst the chains with sweet surprise,
> And in my Savior's image rise.

PHOTOGRAPHS ON CENTRAL APPALACHIAN GRAVE MARKERS

Creating the image of a deceased individual on a memorial placed at or near the site of interment has been performed since ancient times. Some early societies used primitive methods to carve or paint the likeness of the decedent on a grave marker. Carved and painted images have been added, on a few occasions, to American memorials. Other attempts at imagery have included sandblasted etchings on black garnet and etchings on metal.

When I was a teenager, while hunting in the mountains of southwestern Virginia, I often passed a small family cemetery containing a headstone that had a photograph of the deceased attached. He had died in 1931 in a mine explosion. This particular marker fascinated me more than any others I had seen. I was surprised that even though the picture had been subjected to all kinds of weather, it wasn't faded and didn't seem to be scratched, torn, or bent, like many of those in the photo album at home.

When I started my research on death, I found a brochure disseminated by the J. A. Dedouch Company of Oak Park, Illinois, which advertised memorial portraits for grave markers. The company was started about 1893 by J. A. Dedouch, an artist and pioneer photographer in the Chicago, Illinois, area. Though photographs on grave markers originated in the middle European countries such as France in the nineteenth century, Dedouch pioneered the work in America.[19] Today there are only very few companies in the United States and Canada that produce monument portraits. In 1990, I talked with Richard Stannard, president of the Dedouch Company and grandson of Dedouch, and toured the facility where the portraits are produced, discussed the production process, and talked about the reasons for their endurance.[20]

An exact reproduction of a photograph sent to the Dedouch Company is taken through a special photographic technique and transferred to an acid-resistant porcelain enamel (or vitreous enamel) body for permanency, with either a copper or stainless steel base (usually copper) for extra strength. The Dedo monument photographs are called ceramic memorial portraits, and each is guaranteed forever under normal conditions. A picture to be copied is sent by the cemetery along with an order form on which the purchaser checks what he or she wants. When ordered, the quantity desired, size number from the catalogue, customer's name or order number, and the manner in which it will be used are indicated. The purchaser denotes whether a bust or full-figure portrait is desired, the portrait is to be vertical or horizontal in shape, a fastener is to be attached, and whether the portrait is to be cemented to a memorial.

If a Jadcrest (designed in 1926 as a frame and cover to eliminate the plainness of the memorial portrait and give it a sense of privacy) is to be included, it must be noted on the order form. It is available in a variety of cover designs and letterings. The buyer also checks whether the portrait is to be black and white, brown and white, or tinted.

After a photographer takes a photograph of the picture sent by the cemetery and develops it, an artist using an airbrush completes the work. Most brown and white (but not black and white) portraits will be tinted or colored. While the early portraits placed on memorials were black and white, approximately 70 percent of those produced today are colored. The coloring is done via instructions from the purchaser. The artist does change the original photograph to make it more appropriate for the memorial portrait but stays within certain guidelines. For example, the artist will not alter hair color and facial expressions, but will remove people, change positions of the deceased, merge two photographs into one portrait, or make people appear to be the same height. Then after the photo is transferred to porcelain and painted (if requested), it is fired in a kiln. It is then overglazed, fired again, and checked. If colors fade or there are defects, repair work is done by the artist and the portrait is taken through the glazing and firing process again.

Each ceramic portrait is provided with a slide or clip that is to be installed by the company providing the decedent's memorial (the Dedouch Company provides the portrait and clip, and installation is performed by the monument provider). A hole is bored into the memorial, the clip is placed in the hole, and lead pellets are punched into the anchor of the clip to lock it into the hole in the stone. A fastener added to the base (or back) of the ceramic portrait then slides into the clip.

These ceramic memorial portraits can be placed on virtually any kind of marker, including traditional upright memorials, flat markers, bronze or stone monuments, headstones, urns, and in mausoleums. Photographs with Jadcrest lift-up or swinging covers may be used on grass-level and medium memorials, while a swinging type is available for large grave markers. Attachment is by expansion anchors or nuts and bolts. The open picture is still the most common, but the covered portrait is popular, especially for ground-level grave markers.

Though I have encountered several portraits on grave markers in central Appalachia, I don't how many there may be. Only 1 percent of memorials across the country have portraits, with most of these in the South, Southwest, and rural areas. Most I have seen are of an individual sitting or standing, a couple, an entire family, and a member of the armed forces in uniform. These range from photos taken when the deceased was young to those taken shortly before death. I have seen some more unusual portraits, including cars, trucks, tractor trailers, motorcycles, stillborn babies, animals (placed on markers in human and animal cemeteries), and a boy dreaming about his dead mother. I found one with a tractor trailer minus the driver. The family didn't have a photo of the deceased, so they used a picture of the truck in which he was killed. Occasionally, a family will wait several years before placing a picture on a grave marker, but generally it is done within a few months after death.

GRAVE HOUSES

In the nineteenth and early twentieth centuries, in addition to burying a loved one on a hill to protect the body from water and digging the grave six feet deep to deter animals from disturbing the corpse, some mountain people, for additional protection, constructed shelters called grave houses over the place where the deceased was interred. John C. Campbell, in the early 1900s, noted that the grave houses he saw were "low latticed houses painted blue and white."[21] Lucy Furman, in *Mothering on Perilous,* described them as "diminutive houses, with latticed sides and roofs of riven oak boards."[22] An elderly woman in eastern Kentucky said that she had seen grave houses "made out of rock with a roof to cover them."

The few grave houses that I found in the mountains were quite diverse. In a large rural cemetery located about thirty to forty miles from Kingsport, Tennessee, I found a small, white frame house with a door and tin roof. It had been constructed by the occupant prior to his death in 1929, and neither the grave nor marker was visible since the floor was concrete. A small family cemetery in Jackson County, Kentucky, contained a large frame building resembling a doll house, with a tin roof, gutters, windows, and a door. Located inside

Grave house in a family cemetery in eastern Kentucky.

Grave shelter in a small family cemetery in eastern Tennessee.

were a solitary mounded grave, a headstone and footstone to identify the deceased (and the location of the body), and flowers. In eastern Tennessee, in a small family cemetery, an elderly mountain man showed me what he called a grave house. It had a tin roof supported by six posts and covered one grave. There was a wrought-iron fence around the grave to deter animals.

The grave houses that I have seen, and those that have been described to me, were erected to cover one grave. They were usually constructed in family cemeteries in rural areas. Most covered little more than the length and width of the burial spot, and all were designed to retard the falling rain, sleet, and snow. The majority were enclosed so that animals could not disturb the corpse. When houses covered the grave, and the marker (if there was one) wasn't visible, some were built with a cross or identifying data placed outside.

Grave houses were constructed almost as soon as the burial was completed: "The day after the burying Old Jared got his crosscut saw, ax, maul, wedge, and frow, and started up the slope in the rear. 'He's aiming to begin on the grave-house,' said Lame John.... An now both were better satisfied—at least the snow and the rain could not fall on Cindy."[23] "That very day, Silas and the neighbor men did not stop until they had made a shelter over the new mound. Four rough posts supported a heavy plank roof."[24] In James Still's *River of Earth,* the mother emphasizes the need for building a grave house as soon as possible to protect her recently interred child: "'You ought to be nailing together a little covering for the baby's grave then,' Mother said. Father fetched walnut planks from the loft and built a gravehouse under the barn shed. It was five feet square with a chestnut shingle roof. During the first lull in the weather, we took it to the Point."[25]

Most of the grave houses constructed in the nineteenth and twentieth centuries have decayed and disappeared or have been torn down. Concrete and metal vaults, along with the growing popularity of the mausoleum, have made them obsolete.

Flowers

The close relationship between flowers and death is not something unique to central Appalachia. While the Jews rejected them in favor of simplicity and the early Christians considered their use to be pagan and a departure from the prohibition of excessive display at a funeral,[26] the Greeks, Romans, and Egyptians used flowers as a part of their death rituals. In early Greek society, "flowers, woven into wreaths, were furnished for the dead by relatives and friends of the deceased."[27] The Romans arranged flowers around the couch where the body lay in state.[28] Among the Egyptians, they were a part of the funeral process, including burial, and were incorporated into the sepulchral scenes in the tombs.[29]

Flowers were not always used in death-related activities just because they were beautiful. Before embalming, their fragrance could cover some of the stench of a decaying body. "Ring around the Rosy," a popular children's game, actually is a vestige of this custom practiced during the bubonic plague epidemic in the Middle Ages.

> Ring around the rosy,
> Pockets full of posy,
> Ashes, ashes,
> All fall down.

"Ring around the rosy" refers to the visible manifestation of the bubonic plague, a rose-colored pox with a ring around it. "Pockets full of posy" means that death was so common that flowers were carried and used to eradicate the odor from a decaying body or bodies. "Ashes, ashes" denotes the use of cremation, which was necessary to dispose of the bodies that no one wanted to touch. "All fall dead" has been replaced by "all fall down."[30]

FLOWERS AT THE FUNERAL

Funeral flowers didn't make their appearance in England or America until after the middle of the nineteenth century, and then they were utilized over the opposition of Christian leaders.[31] Since the Appalachian settlers were heavily influenced by their religious beliefs, they probably did not use flowers until the late 1800s. Many old-timers told me that funerals they attended in the late nineteenth and even early twentieth centuries did not have any flowers. In these cases the family may have considered them inappropriate. When they were used, the family almost always determined their placement, though they generally circled the casket. If the coffin was closed, they were put on the lid. If it was opened, a flower might be placed in the hand or hands of the deceased and the rest were put around the burial receptacle. Today, these practices are still widespread, though the number of flowers at services has increased.

For some mountain people, funeral flowers were, and still are, a waste of time and money. One mountaineer I interviewed argued that sending flowers to a dead person was a "sin." However, just as elsewhere, flowers have served a variety of purposes in central Appalachia. Before embalming they helped cover the odor of the decaying body, as in the Middle Ages. Some people find they soften the harshness of death and add beauty to the dismal funeral service. Flowers are symbolic of the beauty of the soul and can help remind mourners that like a flower the soul is only temporarily on earth. A floral display expresses love for the departed and shows family members that they are not alone in their grief.

Before flower shops became widespread, most mountaineers gathered their own wildflowers for funeral bouquets during the spring and summer. They could easily gather them from the fields, tie the bundles with string or scraps of cloth, and take or send them to the service. Sometimes the ribbon or cloth from these bouquets was kept by the mourner as a memento or sewn into a pillow, quilt, or other needlework. Occasionally, weed flowers and dandelions were used to make a floral arrangement. White flowers symbolizing purity, such as lilies, daisies, wild roses, and apple or peach blossoms were especially popular.

In the fall and winter central Appalachians had to be more creative. Straw flowers, okra pods, milkweed, pussy willows, thistles, cattails, and baby's breath, arranged into bouquets, substituted well. Berries and nuts were occasionally added for embellishment. Crepe paper flowers worked just as well as fresh flowers, and when dipped in paraffin lasted longer too. Some mountain residents fashioned flowers from corn shucks, which were readily available. Greenery, such as laurel, rhododendron, pine, balsam, fern, hemlock, and boxwood made attractive arrangements, especially in the winter. Phipps says that in the winter a "wreath of holly and cedar might be wrapped in ribbon and placed in the home."[32] An elderly woman in North Carolina reported the use of "evergreens and ivy" when it was too cold for wildflowers to grow. Galax leaves, which stay green all winter,[33] were often arranged into funeral wreaths. And like the ancient Egyptians, mountaineers often employed sheaves of wheat. These were generally placed on the closed coffin with a portrait of the deceased as a memorial.

The owner of a floral shop in eastern Kentucky said that when she started her business in the very early 1900s, the primary flowers for an arrangement were carnations and daisies. She remembered staying up all night making twenty sprays of flowers at five dollars each. Today, professional florists need much less time to make a similar, but much more expensive, funeral bouquet. Mountain residents have many more types of flowers to choose from, including realistic artificial and silk flowers. Artificial floral gifts are generally less expensive than those made from fresh or silk flowers.

Today many people choose to donate money to charity in the name of the deceased instead of sending flowers. Still, floral shops are everywhere in central Appalachia and more people are sending more flowers than ever before. Every funeral director I talked with confirmed that the number of flowers purchased for a funeral has increased significantly in the last twenty to thirty years, probably because many people send flowers in lieu of going to the funeral ceremony. The proprietor of a funeral establishment in eastern Tennessee stated that while the average number of flower bouquets at a funeral in the 1940s and 1950s was fifteen to twenty, today it is fifty to seventy-five. In southwest Virginia, a funeral director said that the average number of vases of flowers today is fifty-three.

FLOWERS AT THE GRAVE

In the days when the members of the burial procession walked to the grave, mourners carried the flowers from the funeral service to the cemetery. Until recently a flower ritual ended the funeral in more urbanized areas of the mountains. Flower girls would pick up the flowers, take them outside the building, and form two lines to the hearse. The pallbearers then carried the burial container down the aisle and the flowers were taken to the cemetery. One mountain man told me that people also threw flowers or bundles of wheat onto the coffin after it was lowered into the grave. Similar to the dust-to-dust ceremony where dirt was sprinkled on the coffin, flower petals were sometimes dropped into the open grave.

In the mountains today, the flowers are removed when the funeral ends by either mourners or funeral home employees. If there are enough arrangements they may be placed in a flower wagon and transported to the grave site. Usually, though, the funeral home transports the flowers to the grave after the burial or distributes them among family and friends.

The family has always decided where the floral arrangements should go at the cemetery. In the past they were placed directly on the grave and around the perimeter. In some family cemeteries, live flowers were planted around the edge of the grave and sometimes on the burial mound. According to Bettis and colleagues, "flowers were placed somewhere between the chest and the headstone (sometimes on the headstone dependent on the rules of the cemetery). . . . Only in the instance of a mass of flowers will the flowers be placed at the foot of the grave."[34] The family sometimes placed the excess bouquets on other graves in the cemetery or gave them to friends and relatives.

While flowers have become the major mourning symbol in America,[35] numerous cemeteries have begun to place restrictions on their use: "Most cemeteries have specific requirements concerning decorations, such as flowers, plants, urns, vases, as well as for ground changes or plot improvement. A number of cemeteries require that their own vases or urns be used for crypts and at grave sites, and artificial flowers and wreaths are not permitted; fresh flowers are usually removed after a certain time has elapsed."[36] Since many central Appalachians are still buried in family or church graveyards when they die, few have to deal with this problem. Those that choose public facilities have to decide what to do with all of the arrangements, but they certainly can't put them around the grave of the deceased as in the past.

People don't even put flowers on the grave as much as in the past. In the late 1800s and early 1900s, survivors often visited graves of loved ones and brought flowers. Although greater urbanization and decreasing familism and neighborliness account for some of this behavior, restrictions put in place by cemeteries probably play a strong role. Cemeteries in central Appalachia today are being vandalized. Headstones have been turned over, broken, defaced, and even stolen. Flowers have been stolen or strewn about the cemetery. Vases have been turned over or broken. In an attempt to curb this activity, some cemeteries have increased security and posted closing hours, which may make it harder for vandals to get in but it also makes it harder for relatives to visit their loved ones.

WREATHS

Wreaths made from fresh or dried flowers used to be popular additions to the deceased's residence. Like the black badge hung on the door of the deceased's home by the undertaker in mainstream America in the nineteenth century, the wreath indicated mourning, helped protect the family from unwanted intrusions, and easily identified the house for people coming to pay their respects. Sometimes notices about the death were also hung on the door with the wreath. For two or three days during the mourning period businesses owned by the deceased or the immediate family were generally closed. Wreaths were often placed on those doors too, which helped alert patrons to the death. Today in central Appalachia, however, placing wreaths is rare, though more traditional people still practice this custom.

Artwork

MOURNING JEWELRY

From the eighteenth century to the early 1900s, mourning jewelry was popular in America and central Appalachia. Black mourning brooches, earrings, and rings were worn with, or instead of, mourning clothes. Many brooches, lockets, and even bracelets were made with a miniature daguerreotype or photograph of a deceased person enclosed. A "locket" originally referred to a case containing locks of human hair, and, bizarre as it may seem, some really did.

Collecting hair of the deceased was quite popular in the past. For example, the Greeks would cut the first hair of a child, the beard of a youth, and the tresses of a maiden and offer them to the gods. When a parent died, "the hair of the children, cut off as a token of grief, was placed with the body."[37] In America during the eighteenth and nineteenth centuries, hair work became quite the rage. Hair was considered to be an individual's "crowning glory," and owning a lock of a loved one's hair was very important.[38] Though at first hair was kept to remember the deceased, later it became fashionable to have the hair of loved ones, living or dead. Young lovers would exchange locks of hair, which were plaited and mounted in jewelry. Human hair was used to decorate paintings and photographs, and, in a few instances, it was employed in embroidery and stitching.

In central Appalachia, some people would cut a swath of hair from the corpse and place it in the family Bible along with other memorabilia to be passed on to future generations. Several funeral directors told me that family members, occasionally, still cut a lock of hair from the departed before interment takes place. Jewelry was made from human hair. While it was often commercially made in the rest of America, mountain people usually made their own hair jewelry. Watch chains, bracelets, necklaces, and earrings were constructed from human hair that was woven or braided into beautiful designs. Mourners fashioned ornate patterns with the hair and concealed it behind brooches or pins with portraits of the deceased. Flowers were made from hair and either placed under protective glass or pressed into a book such as the family Bible.

A few mountaineers kept hair albums, with the name and a lock of hair from each member of the family. It is likely that many of the

Mourning brooches such as these were popular in the 1800s.

Mourning brooch containing the hair of the deceased. (Courtesy of the Kentucky Historical Society)

Wreath made from human hair. (Courtesy of the Kentucky Historical Society)

locks of hair contained in the albums were taken long before someone died, since the first hair of a baby was often preserved by the
parents or some family member. The most attractive use of human
hair, in my opinion, was the hair wreath. The mountaineers wove
different colors of hair onto something stiff, such as wire, and created a multiplicity of designs. The weavers probably used hair from
the living and dead members of the family. And unlike some other
traditions, hair work was still made in Appalachia well into the
twentieth century even though it was fashionable in America in the
eighteenth and nineteenth centuries. A museum in Virginia possesses
a wreath that was made in the 1940s from the hair of family members that were deceased. I also found several pieces of hair jewelry
that were made in the early 1900s.

MEMORY QUILTS

Occasionally, mountain women would take remnants of clothes belonging to someone deceased and make a "memory quilt." My sources stated that these quilts did not follow specific patterns but rather
were fashioned by the makers. An elderly mountaineer in eastern
Tennessee recalled his grandmother's best silk dress being used to
make the entire border of a quilt, and a woman in North Carolina
said that she had taken lace from one of her mother's pillows and
made a quilt called "grandmother's fan." The lace was used to make
the fan.

One of the most interesting quilts I've run across is the "graveyard quilt" made in 1839 by Elizabeth Mitchell of Lewis County,
Kentucky. In 1838 she visited the cemetery in Ohio where her two
sons were buried. When she returned, absorbed by her grief, she
made the quilt as a memorial to them.

Made in a star pattern from brown figured calico and plain tan
material, the large quilt represents a graveyard. The Mitchell lot,
located in the center of the cemetery, is eighteen inches square, made
of plain tan, and enclosed by a small brown paling fence. Miniature
trees, with green leaves and pink buds, are growing around the lot
on the inside of the fence. The paling fence appliquéd along the
outside border of the graveyard is much larger than the one surrounding the Mitchell lot and has large rose trees growing around
it. A pathway, which extends from the edge of the graveyard to the
lot, is eighteen inches long and three inches wide and is bordered
on each side by a small paling fence. Over the entrance gate and
along the pathway are rose vines in green and pink.

Outside the large fence that surrounds the graveyard are small

Graveyard quilt. (Courtesy of the Kentucky Historical Society)

brown coffins that have been appliquéd, and some still have papers with family names attached. The original objective was to add coffins when people were born and move coffins when they died. A small coffin was added in 1840, and only four were ever moved to the graveyard.

The quilt is still in good condition, though the lining is stained with age and the walnut dye used in the brown cloth has run in places.[39] The only one of its kind I have been able to find, it is presently a part of the collection of the Kentucky Historical Society in Frankfort, Kentucky.

PHOTOGRAPHS AND PAINTINGS

In addition to those placed on the gravestones, photographs of the decedent served as important keepsakes of the dead. After development, the photographs might be enlarged, framed, and hung on the wall, placed in a photo album, or just kept somewhere in a drawer. In the late nineteenth and early twentieth centuries, a picture of the departed was occasionally placed against a background composed of a sheaf of wheat or a flower wreath, photographed, and kept as a memorial. Photographs also played an important role during the funeral service. If the casket was closed a photograph was often placed on the lid of the coffin. If an affluent person died and the body could not be displayed, a photograph or painting of the deceased was placed on an easel or stand near the coffin. A clip of the decedent's hair might then be arranged so that it looked like it was a part of the photograph. After the funeral the family might frame the photograph and hang it on the wall. If there was no image of the departed, a piece of paper with the name, biographical data, and a clip of hair was placed on the easel near the unopened coffin. The clip of hair was sometimes cut into pieces and presented to the immediate family after the funeral.

Paintings commemorating death were rare in the mountains because few could afford them. Memorial paintings of the deceased were made for the wealthy before photography was introduced. Mourning scenes depicting weeping willow trees, palm branches, sheaves of wheat, angels, grave markers, and lambs were also painted for survivors. In my search for artifacts, I have found only a few lithographs kept by mountain people as mementoes. They usually contained the words "In Memoriam," a graveyard scene (with willow and palm trees, statues, and grave markers), biographical data, a poetic verse, and a portrait of the deceased (if one was available). The general practice was to frame a lithograph and hang it on the wall.

OTHER MEMORIAL PRACTICES

Wearing mourning clothes and keeping stationery edged in black (discussed in earlier chapters) were important forms of memorialization. In America, according to Margaret Coffin, "coffin plates bearing the name of the deceased were sometimes detached and kept as mementoes."[40] Numerous authors have noted that in urban areas of the United States (particularly New England), from the eighteenth to the twentieth centuries, people were invited to a funeral by presenting them with gifts such as gloves, jewelry, scarves, handkerchiefs, and food, and other objects.[41] This custom apparently provided a lasting memory of the departed and encouraged people to attend the funeral.

This practice was rare in Appalachia. Probably because of the intense familism and neighborliness of the area, people did not need to be enticed to attend funerals. I have not uncovered any substantial evidence indicating that central Appalachians collected coffin plates or gave mourning gifts. Most of these people were poor, and their few treasured possessions, such as a favorite ax, gun, quilt, or pocketwatch, were given to surviving relatives or friends.

Many people from the eighteenth century until the early 1900s sent mourning cards to relatives and friends in central Appalachia as a memento of the deceased and to remind the recipient to pray for the soul of the departed. Each card was thick, four-by-six inches in size, black or white (usually black), gilt-edged, and printed in gold. These usually had images on them similar to those used on tombstones. At the top of the card was generally a symbol of the Christian faith, such as two doves holding a scroll containing the words "In loving remembrance of" in their beaks. Below the religious theme, the name of the decedent appeared, frequently encircled by a wreath of ivy and flowers of some kind, the date of death, and age. Beneath the wreath, there might be another scroll with words like "Gone but not forgotten," and then a verse from a hymn, scripture, or poem about sleep or heaven. Another religious symbol, such as as open Bible with a palm branch on each side, normally ended the card. Other forms of memorabilia have replaced mourning cards in Appalachia and across the country. Today memorial folders and obituaries serve to remind the survivors when it is time to pray for the soul of a decedent.

Though mourning gifts and cards had their uses, the Bible, in addition to its importance as a guide book, was perhaps the most common record of the deceased's life and death. This book was used

Mourning card.

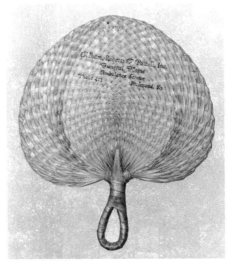

Funeral home fans with advertising were often dispensed for the comfort of mourners.

Envelope edged in black from 1900.

by many literate central Appalachians to record the birth and death dates for each family member and store mementoes of departed loved ones. Biographical and any other important data was entered for each family member. When the person responsible for preserving the Bible (usually the eldest male or female in the extended family network) died, the Bible was passed down to the next generation. Most mountain people I interviewed felt that the Bible, today, is no longer an important site for storing keepsakes of dead relatives or a major source of information about family members.

Other traditions following the funeral besides recording information in the Bible have been discontinued. Church bells are rung less frequently to honor the dead. Ministers no longer provide copies of their funeral sermons to mourners. Changes in behavior, like wearing mourning clothes or remaining unmarried after the death of a spouse for a designated time, are seldom practiced by central Appalachians. They do still remember their dead, but perhaps they do so in more individual ways. Now and then, mountain people place objects on graves at certain times of the year. One mountaineer told me about a man who liked Halloween so much, his wife placed a jack-o'-lantern on his grave each year. Another mentioned a person who was fond of Valentine's Day, so the surviving spouse placed a heart-shaped wreath at the burial spot on that holiday. Toys were sometimes placed on a child's grave. I have found Christmas trees placed on or near a place of interment. One was even decorated.

EIGHT

Funeralizing and Memorial Traditions

When from this world I go,
Leaving forever the scene;
While others are dead, oh, will you then,
See that my grave is kept green.
—The Carter Family, "See That My Grave
Is Kept Green"

T hough religion has long been an important part of central Appalachian culture, many settlers actually moved into the mountains to escape organized religion. Excessive taxation imposed by the Episcopal church led many people to flee the lowlands of Virginia.[1] After moving into the area, mountain people continued to reject the authoritarian structure of Roman Catholicism and Episcopalianism. As a result these two major religions made little or no effort to proselytize there.[2] This disdain for Episcopalianism carried on until at least the early 1900s when Horace Kephart studied mountain life extensively: "Dislike of Episcopalianism is still strong among people who do not know, or pretend not to know, what the word means. 'Any Episcopalians around here?' asked a clergyman at a mountain cabin. 'I don't know,' said the old woman, 'Jim's got the skins of a lot o' varmints up in the loft. Mebbe you can find one up thar.'"[3]

Though the first settlers were primarily Scotch-Irish Presbyterians,[4] the mountain culture was too democratic to support Calvinism and its superiority of the clergy. Further, the Presbyterian church demanded an educated ministry, which the scattered and poor Appalachian population could not support, especially on a regular basis.[5] The Presbyterian church couldn't provide enough ministers to take care of the people in the mountains, and they were left without the assistance of members of the clergy. Large communities "lapsed into irreligion and ignorance."[6]

Organized religion, as most Americans know it, was scarce for many years in the area. The first services were held in open fields, and only later did residents erect crude cabins to serve as churches. Once communities were established, townspeople often built schoolhouses that doubled as churches on Sundays. Even when communities built separate churches, usually there was no one to perform the religious ceremonies and duties.

With the Appalachian population scattered, the mountains difficult to penetrate at certain times of the year, and a scarcity of educated ministers, circuit riders, mainly provided by the Methodist church, became the only feasible way of satisfying the religious needs of mountaineers. "Circuit-riding preachers braved the dangers from wild beasts, unfriendly Indians and the elements"[7] to carry the gospel to people in the remote mountain areas. They traveled on horseback into the mountains "where roads were almost unknown and trails were few and, at times, impassable,"[8] with their earthly possessions in their saddlebags: "The circuit riders were unique figures whose parallel has seldom been seen. Their circuit often covered four or five hundred miles; they lived on their horses and their houses were saddlebags; they never followed wagon trails but preceded them."[9] The best known of these fearless riders was Bishop Francis Asbury, who rode for the Methodist church for nearly thirty years during the eighteenth century.

Because their travel was hard and their territory extensive, circuit riders usually visited an area only once every one to three years.[10] Once arriving, these traveling preachers were lucky to receive respite for the night in a small, crowded, isolated mountain cabin. Some of the wilderness saddlebaggers never received any payment for their services, and the salary for others was only a few dollars a year.[11]

Most mountaineers spent the treacherous fall and winter months without any formal religious instruction. In the spring, when the circuit rider was expected, large communities sometimes organized revivals, or camp meetings.[12] The revival would be held outside in an open space conducive to large crowds. Occasionally, hundreds of people would travel many miles and the service would last for several days. Preaching would be "highly emotional, direct, and fear-filled, as the evangelists sought to convert the sinners to a saving faith."[13]

Wilderness saddlebaggers were expected to perform a multitude of tasks on arrival in a mountain community. In addition to preaching a sermon at every stop, the many fundamentalist residents looked to the circuit rider for baptism. Newborn babies, youths, young adults, and the elderly depended upon the preachers to wash their sins away so that they might be "born again." Marriage ceremonies were often delayed until the circuit rider arrived, though a couple desiring to marry didn't always wait to live together. The circuit rider's visits were so infrequent that cohabitation became legitimized as common-law marriage in some states.[14] Due to the long absence of the circuit rider, "sometimes a baby might without shame be present at the wedding of its own parents."[15] Funerals, too, were delayed until the minister arrived.

Despite the importance of the circuit riders, they could not fulfill all of the religious needs of the mountaineers. Organized religion obviously could not help since the Presbyterian church did not provide trained clergy and the Methodist church supplied only these occasional visiting preachers. As a result, untrained people rose from the ranks to help.[16] With little or no education, these individuals came only with their ability to stir the emotions of their listeners. They worked at their regular occupation during the week and preached on Sunday, and like the circuit riders, they received little or no pay. But unlike the circuit riders, these lay ministers were available for weddings and funerals virtually on demand, and since they knew their congregation intimately, they could become true spiritual guides.

Even with the dominance of Baptist and Methodist churches in central Appalachia today, this tradition of lay ministers strongly affects religious practices. Many mountaineers are fundamentalist and prejudiced against educated, ordained, and salaried preachers. These residents prefer someone "called to preach." Even the more structured religions have been touched by mountain practices. Methodist ministers still ride circuits, but in a different way. Some of these preachers are assigned to geographical areas, or "circuits," and thus serve more than one church. The congregations, however, don't have to wait three years to see their ministers.

Funeralizing

Naturally, with few members of the clergy available, central Appalachians sometimes had to improvise when their loved ones passed away. Some people chose to have their funeral services before they died. Curiosity often led them to be present to hear what others said about them. The dying simply wanted to take advantage of the circuit rider's pass through the area.[17] In some cases, elders or more religious residents were called upon to preach these early funeral sermons.[18] Most of the time, however, mountaineers relied upon "funeralizing" to honor their dead.

According to Kephart, subsequent to his analysis of Appalachian culture: "In all back settlements that I have visited, from Kentucky southward, there is a strange custom as to the funeral sermon, that seems to have no analogue elsewhere. It is not preached until long after the interment."[19] Phipps calls it "the most unusual feature of traditional Appalachian death customs."[20] Referred to by other writers as "unusual," "unique," "ancient," and "strange,"[21] funeralizing entailed burying the dead immediately and holding the funeral service at a more convenient time.

Inclement weather might prevent a formal funeral service from being conducted at the time of death. Snow and rain contributed to already hazardous travel over the rugged terrain, while swollen streams and muddy roads made the mountains almost impassable.[22] Delayed services were sometimes necessary when a minister of the deceased's denomination was not available to preach. In wartime, funeralizing was more convenient than holding a service immediately after a soldier's body was returned home.

Since it was important for all family members to be present at the service, funeralizing better accommodated them: "The burial, of course, takes place immediately after death, but the funeral is 'preached' in the Autumn, when the weather is good, the cultivation of the crops is finished, the water in the creeks is at the lowest, and the kinfolk and friends can gather for a fitting memorial."[23] It was especially hard during the growing season to stop everything and go to a funeral service. Many lay ministers were farmers who couldn't stop their work and officiate at the ceremony: "Silas meant to have her funeral preached in the spring, but Brother Jonathan, whom she had 'named' for that purpose was held back with his hoeing and could not get away."[24]

Funeralizing allowed family members to plan services at their leisure, and as a result they grew from religious occasions into social events. People for miles around attended.[25] Neighbors came prepared with food, and when the service was prolonged, spent the night. As with wakes, regular funerals, and burials, central Appalachians looked upon funeralizing as another social diversion. Most families chose spring and summer for such a festive occasion, but others preferred early fall when the weather was still pleasant and the crops had been harvested.[26] And sometimes since the time span between burial and funeralizing varied from a few days to several years, the dead were practically forgotten. Guerrant reported preaching the funeral of a man who had been dead for fourteen years,[27] and Campbell found a case in which the belated service was preached seventy-five years after burial.[28]

Before the funeralizing, family and friends prepared the body, built the casket, dug the grave, held the wake, and buried the body. At the time of the funeralizing, relatives and friends cleared the grave and donned their mourning clothes. Logs were cut for the family to sit on, while other mourners stood, sat on the ground, or wandered about. The preacher stood and used a makeshift lectern, such as a headstone, tree stump, or board nailed to a tree. If the service was expected to be lengthy, people brought food.

Many times the preacher did not know the deceased. An elderly minister in southwestern Virginia told me that his grandfather, who was a mountain preacher for fifty-seven years, was often asked to participate in a funeralizing for someone he didn't know. Occasionally, residents were able to select the minister they wanted to officiate. For example, the surviving spouse might send a letter to a circuit rider asking him to preside at a funeralizing on his next trip through the area. Later on, funeralizing involved more than one minister.[29] Just like the regular funeral service, every preacher was welcome to join in and be heard.

The funeralizing service included hymn singing (usually without instrumental accompaniment or song books), scripture reading, and prayer. The deceased occasionally selected the hymns, scripture, or even the sermon topic before death. These sermons were much like those at regular funerals, some with hellfire and brimstone and some directed toward the life of the deceased. Most, though, stirred up the emotions of the mourners and forced the family to live through the loss of the loved one all over again. When there were several ministers and the sermons lasted many hours, the ceremony could be exhausting: "The preacher moaned and wept, and wrought up himself and the family over the little twins who had scarcely lived at all, until every woman (and there were but few present who had not lost a little baby) wept aloud, and the children all wept because the mothers did. And the men all wept because these people are emotional and not afraid to show their feelings; so all the congregation wept aloud with him, and the big rough men let the tears stream down their cheeks unchecked."[30]

Since there was no stable ministry, and weddings, baptisms, and funerals could only be conducted when a member of the clergy was in the area, surviving spouses had sometimes already remarried and borne new children when the funeralizing for the dead spouse took place. Huston describes a scene in which a woman had remarried and with a new baby in her arms "was dutifully crying and mourning for her first husband while her present husband sat in the background looking solemn."[31] The minister often so successfully whipped attendees into a frenzy that new spouses would be "weeping and wailing as copiously as the other mourners."[32] Raine describes the behavior of a mountain man and new spouse at the delayed service for his wife, as well as the kinds of dilemmas that could lead to such an unusual situation: "Our friend Felix lost his wife one winter, and the following fall, when Marthy's funeral would naturally have been preached, her brother was away in Ohio. The next year Felix himself was involved at the adjoining county seat in a long drawn-out trial. So when the funeral did finally occur, Felix was sitting in the chief mourner's place with a new wife by his side, and as the preacher rose to the heights of pathetic eloquence, Felix sobbed upon the shoulder of his new wife for the death of Marthy."[33]

Mountain people adapted the best they could to these unusual circumstances. They did not judge harshly remarriage or cohabitation by a surviving spouse before the funeral of a deceased mate. As Janice Holt Giles describes, being alone was undesirable in this area: "A husband or wife may remarry shortly, but no dishonor to the dead is meant. An Appalachian husband is so pampered that he is helpless without a wife to 'do for him.' An Appalachian woman especially with children needs help. One old man told me in sweet confidence, in the presence of his third wife, that he looked forward to living in heaven with all three of his wives."[34]

Funeralizing often had to be brief because most circuit riders had only a day to baptize, perform weddings, and officiate at funerals. Naturally people desired separate ceremonies for loved ones, but sometimes joint services were necessary. These ministers tried to ensure a service for everyone who died. The devotion of the traveling clergy is evident in John C. Campbell's description of a case where a circuit rider spent the night in a home where a baby had died the previous year. Since he had to leave the next day, he climbed the hill to the cemetery and "there in the moonlight preached to the little family group the baby's funeral sermon."[35]

Belated funerals were still being conducted well into the twentieth century, though today they are unnecessary. Inclement weather and inaccessible roads no longer keep mourners or ministers from funerals. And since nearly every community has a resident member of the clergy, funeral services can be scheduled shortly after death. The closest thing to funeralizing in the mountains today is the memorial service, which is held a few days or so after death without the body present.

Memorial Day

Honoring the dead well past the date of burial stems from ancient customs in Europe and Asia. Greeks, Romans, and Druids decorated the graves of loved ones with garlands of flowers. The Chinese Festival of Tombs and the Japanese Festival of Lanterns were special occasions for performing rituals in memory of the dead. In Christianity, religious groups such as Roman Catholics and Episcopalians have long used All Soul's Day to pray for the departed and decorate graves with flowers, wreaths, or candles. People in Italy go to the churchyards on All Soul's Day to place garlands of flowers on graves. Countries such as Rumania, Finland, and Turkey have set aside special days to pay tribute to departed loved ones. The French celebrate May 30 as a legal holiday known as the Day of Ashes, which commemorates the day Napoleon's ashes were transported from St. Helena to Paris.[36]

The exact date and location of the first memorial service honoring the dead in America is uncertain, though it most likely was during the Civil War. In 1863, the women of Columbus, Mississippi, placed flowers on the graves of both Union and Confederate soldiers. On April 26, 1865, Sue Landon Vaughn led some women in Vicksburg, Mississippi, to the cemetery to decorate soldiers' graves. In Winchester, Virginia, on June 6, 1865, several women went to the first cemetery especially established for Southern soldiers and decorated the graves with flowers.

The actions of these Southern women in honoring the dead of both armies impressed people in the North and South. In May 1865, Adjutant General Norton P. Chipman of the Grand Army of the Republic (an organization of Union veterans of the Civil War) suggested to General John A. Logan, who was the commander in chief, that a date be set to decorate the graves of Union soldiers each year. General Logan agreed, and in 1868 May 30 was established as Decoration Day.[37] The Grand Army of the Republic was in charge of Memorial Day each year until the American Legion took over the duties after World War I. Decoration Day did not instantly become a national holiday, nor did the Northern states accept it right away, but in 1869 there were more than three hundred memorial exercises. In 1873 New York became the first state to designate May 30 as a legal holiday and by 1890 all of the Northern states observed it.[38]

Memorial Day is a legal holiday throughout the United States today, with the exception of several of the Southern states that annually celebrate a Confederacy-related anniversary of special significance. Several of the Southern states that observe Confederate Memorial Day also celebrate the national Memorial Day.[39] Alabama and Mississippi use the last Monday in April as Confederate Memorial Day. North and South Carolina celebrate it on May 10. Georgia utilizes April 26, Virginia employs the last Monday in May, and Louisiana observes June 3 as Memorial Day. Tennessee calls June 3 Confederate Decoration Day and Texas celebrates January 19 as Confederate Heroes Day. Originally designated as a day to recognize and honor soldiers killed during the Civil War, Memorial Day now provides an opportunity to pay tribute to all the men and women who gave their lives for their country, whether they are buried in America or a foreign land.[40] Some people use it as a day to decorate the graves of loved ones, whether they died in military service or civilian life.

On June 28, 1968, President Lyndon B. Johnson signed legislation which made the last Monday in May the day to celebrate Memorial Day (which means that it is no longer fixed on the traditional date of May 30) so that Americans could have a three-day weekend. The law became effective in 1971 and applied to the District of Columbia and all federal employees. By 1971 most of the states had changed their date for Memorial Day to the last Monday in May to conform with the federal schedule.[41]

Utilized as a patriotic rather than a religious holiday, Memorial Day is celebrated with speeches, music, and parades in addition to the decoration of graves with flowers. Military posts fly the flag at half-staff from sunrise until noon and at full staff from noon until sunrise. In important ports, tiny boats with flowers are set afloat to honor those buried at sea. At noon there are twenty-one gun salutes at military stations and on ships. Armed forces regulations stipulate that drills and exercises are to be suspended on Memorial Day.

Since World War I, Memorial Day has also been celebrated as Poppy Day. Men and women who served in the armed forces sell small, red artificial poppies to provide help for veterans disabled during military service.

MEMORIAL DAY IN CENTRAL APPALACHIA

While there are some similarities, central Appalachian memorial procedures did not develop from the custom of honoring deceased American veterans on a designated day each year. Instead, they were derived from the practice of funeralizing. The delayed funeral gave mountaineers a chance to go to the graveyard, clean and decorate the graves of those who died without a funeral service, pay their respects to the deceased, worship God, and socialize. When it was no longer necessary to have a belated funeral, the custom had become so important that each family, church, or community established a day of the year when members could get together and carry out basically the same tasks performed at a funeralizing. The main difference was that memorial practices involved the entire cemetery and all the dead who were interred within its boundaries, rather than just the person or persons who were buried without a funeral.

Mountain people used several different terms when referring to the day set aside to care for a cemetery and honor the dead including "Decoration Day," "Memorial Day," "Meeting Day," "May Meeting," "Memorial Meeting," "Memorial Service," "Homecoming," and "Graveyard Meeting." The Primitive Baptists called it the "Annual Meeting"[42] and central Appalachians who held their memorial on July 4 termed it the "crackin' day."[43]

Even in the early 1900s, as Murial Sheppard notes, the national holiday went unobserved in central Appalachia.[44] As in funeralizing, mountaineers picked their own convenient day for memorial services, usually a Sunday between late spring and early fall.

During my interviewing, I found a plethora of dates designated as the time to honor departed loved ones, including the last Sunday in May, the third Sunday in June, the last day of May, the second Sunday in July, the fourth of July, the first Sunday in August, the first Sunday in September, and the thirtieth of May. Some residents of the mountains didn't set a specific date, but waited until the crops were harvested, selected a date, and then notified friends and relatives. With the introduction of radio, newspapers, and the telephone, it became easier to let people know when the memorial ceremony would be conducted.

Usually the weekend prior to the memorial service friends and relatives went to the cemetery to get the graves ready for decoration. Armed with axes, hoes, shovels, picks, mattocks, and scythes, they cut trees, shrubs, weeds, vines, and briars. Occasionally a team of horses and a plow were necessary to remove large obstacles. Tombstones were straightened and cleaned, the fence was repaired, grave houses were repaired and painted, sunken graves were filled, a fresh mound of dirt was placed over each grave, and old flowers were removed. Loretta Lynn, in her *Coal Miner's Daughter*, notes that people would spend days fixing up the grounds, cutting the grass, cleaning the markers, and putting in spring flowers.[45]

Central Appalachians went into the hills to gather mountain laurel (ivy), red rhododendron (red laurel), honeysuckle, sweet peas, daisies, and other flowers in bloom to decorate all of the graves in the cemetery.[46] If fresh flowers were unavailable, paper flowers (occasionally dipped in paraffin for durability) and dried flowers were substituted. When the decoration was completed, the graveyard was a multiplicity of colors. One mountaineer told me the cemetery looked like a flower garden, and Sheppard describes the graveyard as a "blaze of color with nodding blossoms on the low mounds."[47]

Preparing a cemetery for a decoration service was hard work, but there was always time for socializing. Ties to family and friends were strengthened and reaffirmed. Food was prepared and consumed. While the adults worked, the children either helped or entertained themselves. For example, an elderly man in eastern Kentucky said that the young children who couldn't work would swing on grapevines or play games while the cemetery was prepared.

People came on foot, on mules or horses, in jolt wagons, and, in later years, in automobiles to honor the dead. Mourners gathered by the grave for prayer, scripture reading, singing, and a sermon. From a platform erected for the occasion, the minister delivered a passionate sermon ranging from predestination, water baptism, eternal life, and feet washing to conversion of children, restitution, a paid and educated ministry, and women preachers.[48] Listeners were often stirred into outbursts of their own: "The preacher, with much emotion and in a loud voice, intoned, 'Relatives, don't you want to meet your loved one in heaven? If you want to meet him in heaven, change your ways and live with God.' Upon hearing this admonition, some relative would begin crying and wailing. Many people joined the church under the strong emotion."[49]

Services generally lasted all day and sometimes more than twenty-four hours. They were especially lengthy if more than one minister preached. The ministers were frequently of different denominations and tended to compete with one another. The debating sometimes led to "hard feelings" when the service was over.

When the memorial service concluded, the people socialized. Since miles separated many of the attendees, there was always plenty of gossip to catch up on. Horses and mules were traded, and sometimes, out of sight of the crowd, moonshine was drunk.[50] Food was abundant. Memorial Day in the mountains has often been referred to as an "all-day meeting with the dinner on the ground." Though the family holding the service might provide meat, every family came with a basket of food. No household was ever expected to feed the entire flock that gathered for the service.[51] "Each family rivaled in trying to have the most to eat."[52] Everyone shared what they had, even during the service. At the end of the day, those who had several miles to travel were invited to spend the night. The host family provided mattresses on the floor or people slept in the barn, in one of the outbuildings, or under the stars.

Mountaineers seldom gather in the same way for these events today, as the multitude of neglected mountain cemeteries can testify. Though individual memorial days from the spring to the fall are still important in the mountains, family members no longer do most of the work themselves. Graves in perpetual-care cemeteries are maintained by caretakers, and it is easier for family members to hire someone to care for the burial sites in other types of graveyards. Family and friends, though, still travel great distances to personally place flowers on the graves to honor their dead.

Most families hold services in their church on Sunday morning and then people go to the graveyard for a decoration ceremony. However, some families still prefer to have a graveside service with one or more ministers presiding. Most groups still socialize afterward, and some even continue to have dinner on the ground at the cemetery.

Some mountain residents now celebrate the national holiday, and that number will likely increase in the future. Those who do so turn the tasks of honoring the dead over to others. Funeral directors are contacted for names of military veterans who died during the year. The American Legion, Boy Scouts, and other service organizations place flags on the graves of veterans. Though this type of memorial honors the dead, it does so in a way much different from the funeralizing and family involvement of the past.

NINE

Dying, Death, and Central Appalachian Music

Years ago when but a boy singing songs was mother's joy,
When our father dear would leave us all alone.
I can hear her voice so sweet as she sang "When Shall We Meet?"
You'll never miss your mother until she's gone.

—Fiddlin' John Carson, "You Will Never Miss Your Mother
   until She Is Gone"

T he first settlers in central Appalachia possessed a sense of adventure, a desire for isolation, strong ties to family and kin, a devotion to God, and a love of music. Singing accompanied nearly every activity in the mountains, from plowing and milking to spinning and praying. Maude Karpeles reports that while she was collecting songs in the central highlands with Cecil Sharp between 1916 and 1918, "It would often happen that we would hear a voice in the distance and then, following it up, we would find, perhaps, a man singing as he hoed his corn patch, or a girl milking a cow, or a woman nursing her baby."[1]

For residents of the central Appalachian region, two important things that helped make a home were a fire and music.[2] Especially during the long winter months, "there was time after supper to gather before the fireplace to sing and tell stories."[3] Emma Bell Miles in *The Spirit of the Mountains* indicates what life could be like in a mountain cabin at nightfall: "Night falls. Now the red glamour of firelight plays over the main room's rafters, and cotton is brought out and laid on the warm hearth for all unoccupied fingers to pick it, casting out the seeds. This is the social hour, when there is time for discussion and pleasant raillery and the barbaric jangle of a banjo or the less pleasing whine of a fiddle. At eight o'clock, however, it is time for bed."[4]

Since there were few recreational outlets such as theaters, bowling alleys, circuses, radio, and television in most parts of the mountains until well into the twentieth century, music served as an emotional outlet. It was the main source of enjoyment for people of all ages. Instead of listening to the radio or watching television in the evening, or attending a movie on Saturday night, members of the family engaged in musical activities.

Social events where mountaineers gathered to help with raising a house or barn, shucking corn, stringing beans, or making molasses usually ended with music and dancing.[5] As mountain society developed, Saturday night square dances with local musicians became popular. Singing was also expected during religious services, including church or revival meetings, wakes, funerals, graveside ceremonies, and funeralizing.

Many of the songs and ballads in central Appalachian society were brought by settlers from Scotland, Ireland, Germany, England, and Wales, "where they had long been sung as an expression of the souls of a rugged people."[6] These songs were most often broadside ballads that were printed on one side of a sheet of paper and sold on the streets. Some highlanders kept these in a ballad, or "ballit," box and handed them down to future generations: "Mrs. Rena kept a 'ballit' box. It wasn't a fancy one, rather it was a lap-sized cardboard box she had whipstitched along one edge for a hinge. It was in this box that she kept the 'ballits' or words written down of 'the lovesongs or mountain songs, old people's songs'—the songs she had learned through the years."[7]

Since a large portion of the central highlanders couldn't read or write, most had to rely on their own memories to pass songs down to their children and grandchildren. Collectors such as Cecil Sharp and Maude Karpeles, Patrick Gainer, and Bradley Kincaid found diverse versions of popular ballads such as "Barbara Allen" and "The House Carpenter" because, as Sharp and Karpeles note, "owing to their isolation, the mountain people had been preserved from commercialized music and songs they had inherited from their forefathers had been evolved according to the taste of the singers themselves without any extraneous influence."[8]

Early central Appalachians could not rely on musical instruments to help pass down these songs either since there were few households lucky enough to possess a fiddle or guitar. Most mountaineers sang without musical accompaniment "in accordance with the older traditional method of singing, both in England and in America."[9] After the five-string banjo was invented by Joel Walker Sweeney in 1831,[10] it was sometimes used to support the singing of an individual or group. But even by the early 1900s, only one of 1,600 songs collected by Sharp and Karpeles was performed with instrumental accompaniment.

After the Civil War, shape-note singing was introduced in many parts of central Appalachia from Harrisonburg, Virginia. The new technique, which did not require the use of instrumental accompaniment, involved reading the notes on the basis of their peculiar shape rather than their position on the staff.[11] This was particularly helpful for residents who could neither read nor write. This new way to teach songs became so popular that some communities hired itinerant singing teachers, also called "singing masters," to teach at "subscription schools," which were supported by voluntary enrollment of families in the area.[12]

Shape-note singing became a social activity. "Almost everyone in the community learned to read music and sing hymns in four-part harmony."[13] It was convenient because everyone who knew how could sing along whether they read music or not. Shape-note singing was used in regular church services and revival meetings. At singing conventions, church choirs often competed against one another using hymnals with shaped notes.

Shape-note singing was popular until well into the twentieth century when other traditional forms and styles of mountain music began dying out. Though people still sing and play in the old way at fiddlers' conventions, folk festivals, and gospel sings, central Appalachian music has changed dramatically since the time of the early settlers.

Once people began moving out of the area to find work or enter military service, they began encountering other kinds of music. If they returned home, they brought the new music with them and introduced family and friends to it. By the middle of the twentieth century, when radios became affordable to most mountain folk, music from the outside world was easily accessible. Families gathered around on Saturday nights to listen to the Grand Ole Opry broadcast from WSM in Nashville or the National Barn Dance transmitted from WLS in Chicago. Numerous other stations such as Wheeling, West Virginia's WWVA, Bristol, Virginia's WCYB, Knoxville's WNOX, and Cincinnati's WLW were popular among mountaineers. These transmitted favorite commercial recordings of "hillbilly" music, such as hits by Jimmie Rodgers and the Carter Family, across the area.

Television delivered the death blow to traditional central Appalachian music. Now people watch singing on television rather than performing it with family and friends. Today most mountaineers prefer country music over hillbilly music or ballads. "Barbara Allen" and "Pretty Polly" have been replaced with such popular contemporary recordings as Clint Black's "Walkin' Away," McBride and the Ride's "Can I Count on You?" and Randy Travis's "Heroes and Friends."

The Mountains as Home

Central Appalachians had songs for every mood. In his introduction to volume 2 of Bradley Kincaid's *Favorite Old-Time Songs and Mountain Ballads,* John F. Smith provides a description of the different types of central Appalachian music:

> There are love songs for those whose affections have been centered upon some loved one; cradle songs for the mother who rocks her child while she attends to some household duty; skipping and dancing songs employed by the young folks who will be merry in the midst of toil; merry songs for those whose hearts become light at times and who love to express their gladness in melody; plaintive songs for those who have experienced sorrow, and religious songs for those who love to express their adoration for sacred things in music.[14]

Many of these songs centered on what was important to residents and what was familiar and commonplace in their lives. Subsequent to the first recordings of "hillbilly" music in 1922 and 1923, mountaineers began to enjoy commercially recorded songs and instrumentals, as well as the traditional music of their ancestors. The songs of Mississippi's Jimmie Rodgers were as popular as those of southwest Virginia's Carter Family. Commercial recordings such as "Wildwood Flower" and "Frankie and Johnnie" became as fashionable as traditional ballads like "Barbara Allen" and "Pretty Polly."

Love of home is reflected in songs from Fiddlin' John Carson's "The Little Old Log Cabin in the Lane" to the Statler Brothers' "Maple Street Memories" to Joe Diffie's "Home." Few highlanders would deny the beauty of their land, and the Carter Family captured the appeal of the mountains in "'Mid the Green Fields of Virginia," "My Old Cottage Home," "My Clinch Mountain Home," and "Homestead on the Farm."

Home, of course, is more than just the area, it is the house you grew up in. People usually carry sentimental memories about this place no matter where they go. Such recordings as the Callahan Brothers' "Little Poplar Log House on the Hill," Rutherford and

Foster's "Cabin with the Roses at the Door," and Fiddlin' John Carson's "The Little Old Log Cabin in the Lane" capture these memories of childhood. Probably the most cogent portrayal is Joe Diffie's "Home":

> Home was a swimming hole and a fishing pole
> And the feel of a muddy road between my toes.
> Home was a back porch swing where I would sit
> And mom would sing "Amazing Grace" while she hung out the
> clothes.
> Home was an easy chair, with my daddy there,
> And the smell of Sunday supper on the stove.
> My footsteps carry me away,
> But in my mind I'm always going home.[15]

The mountain refugee, in song, yearns to return home. "'Mid the Green Fields of Virginia" depicts such a desire to revisit the homestead where the parents have died:

> 'Mid the green fields of Virginia, in the vale of Shenandoah,
> There's an ivy covered homestead that I love;
> With its quaint old-fashioned chimney and its simple home-like air,
> 'Twas the home of my dear parents now above.[16]

For those incarcerated, this desire can be especially strong and home can mean freedom. The convict in the Blue Sky Boys' "The Prisoner's Dream" wants to return to a lover, while the prisoner in Vernon Dalhart's "The Governor's Pardon" hopes his mother can obtain a pardon so that he can go home. Home is a place of comfort, and in "Someday I'll Wander Back Again" by Foster and Young, the drifter wants to return to the old homestead to die. Typically, mountaineers want to die at home:

> Oh, the dear old cabin, my own cabin,
> It's my home on my own native shore.
> I would yield my latest sigh, I have lived and I will die,
> In the cabin with the roses at the door.[17]

Mountain sojourners may want to go home, but for many it seems like a pipe dream. In Si Kahn and Kathy Kahn's "Blue Ridge Mountain Refugee," a migrant working in a factory in the city laments never seeing home again, while the singer in Billy Edd Wheeler's "Ain't Goin' Home Soon" hasn't been home in a long time and exclaims: "I ain't goin' soon, no I ain't goin' back soon."[18] Some highlanders may have strong ties to the mountains and want to return, but others, such as Sarah Ogan Gunning, have "Dreadful Memories" of their life in central Appalachia:

> Dreadful memories, how they linger,
> How they ever flood my soul,
> How the workers and their children
> Died from hunger and from cold.
>
> Hungry fathers, wearied mothers
> Living in those dreadful shacks,
> Little children cold and hungry
> With no clothing on their backs.[19]

It is difficult, if not impossible, to separate love of home from love of parents. Family ties are strong in the mountains, so when highlanders leave home, they continually wonder about Mom and Dad:

> I wonder how the old folks are at home;
> I wonder if they miss me while I roam;
> I wonder if they pray for the boy that went away
> And left his kind old parents all alone.
>
> I hear the cattle lowing in the lane,
> And see again the fields of golden grain;
> I almost hear them sigh as they bade their boy "goodbye";
> I wonder how the old folks are at home.[20]

For the central Appalachian migrant, home is where parents live. I have realized that no matter where I travel, or how many houses I own, home is always where my parents reside in Virginia. When it comes time for my vacation, friends and colleagues are informed that I am going "home."

There are few traditional songs about Mother, but Mother's love is a major theme in commercial recordings. The attitudes of most central Appalachians are accurately portrayed when Foster and Young note that "we can only have one mother" and Vernon Dalhart says that she is "a boy's best friend." In songs well-liked among mountain people, Mother is generally the moral agent of the family. In songs such as "I Believe It for My Mother Told Me So," "Hymns My Mother Sang," and "My Mother's Beautiful Hands," her word is accepted as truth, she teaches her children the value of prayer, and she is the caretaker in times of affliction.

Similar to the female parent in central Appalachian society, the mother in popular mountain lyrics is willing to give her life for her child. It is the mother who generally attempts to get her child out of jail or prison (e.g., "I'm Here to Get My Baby Out of Jail"), regardless of the cost. She is there when her child dies. In "Little Bessie," the mother sits with her dying child, and in Bradley Kincaid's "The Fatal Derby Day," she watches as her son is killed in a horse race. When children leave home (e.g., "The Ship that Never Returned"), Mother bids them good-bye, never knowing if they will come back.

Sentimental songs speak of strong ties to mothers even at the brink of death. Sons dying away from home request someone to "take the news to mother." The dying cowboy in Carl T. Sprague's "When the Work's All Done This Fall" asks his friends to take his belongings and wages to his mother. Dying mothers evoke special sentiment, as in "The Lightning Express," where the son tries to get home to his mother before she dies. Many mountaineers, like the singer in Kelly Harrell's "I Have No Loving Mother Now," feel helpless without their mothers' love and desire to join them in heaven (e.g., The Delmore Brothers' "I Long to See My Mother" and "Shake Hands with Mother" by Mainer's Mountaineers).

Although most commercial recordings made after 1922 portray kind, gentle, and loving mothers, some of the traditional songs gathered by collectors such as Cecil Sharp and Maude Karpeles, Patrick Gainer, Herbert Shellans, and Bradley Kincaid picture her as cruel and heartless. In "The Cruel Mother," also known as "Down by the Greenwood Sidee," she stabs and kills her two children. Their ghosts later return and inform her that she will soon die. The wife and mother in "The House Carpenter" (known in earlier times as "James Harris" and "The Daemon Lover") leaves her child and husband and runs away to sea with a former lover. However, in the end she gets her just deserts:

> She had not been on sea three weeks,
> I'm sure it was not four,
> Till they sprang a leak in the bottom of the ship
> And she sank to rise no more.[21]

Except for a few songs, such as Holly Dunn's "Daddy's Hands," Gene Autry and Jimmy Long's "Silver Haired Daddy of Mine," and Jimmie Rodgers's "Daddy and Home," there have been few adequate tributes to fathers. The vagabond in "Silver Haired Daddy of Mine" offers a tribute to his father but also apologizes, now that his father is getting old and "dear mother is waiting in Heaven," for causing him pain and sorrow.[22] In "Daddy and Home," recently recorded by Tanya Tucker, the wandering child wants to return to "fading" Dad:

Your hair has turned to silver,
I know you're fading too;
Daddy, dear old daddy,
I'm coming back to you.[23]

A few composers depict fathers as loving, kind, and gentle, such as the Blue Sky Boys in "There'll Come a Time," Vernon Dalhart in "The Dream of the Miner's Child," Blind Alfred Reed in "Explosion in the Fairmount Mines," and Holly Dunn in "Daddy's Hands."

Many of the songs characterize fathers as hardened, wayward, or weak alcoholics or criminals. In the Blue Sky Boy's "The East Bound Train," the mother is sewing to make a living for the family, while "poor dear old blind father is in prison almost dead."[24] The lyrics in Blind Alfred Reed's "The Prayer of the Drunkard's Little Girl" indicate that the family was once happy until Daddy started drinking. There is, however, a happy ending. The family is in a state of upheaval and the mother is dying, but when the father stops drinking and returns to the fold, equilibrium is restored:

"Dear ones I've come back, I'm not drinking today,
Please don't be afraid, do not cry."
And then a sweet voice from the Lord seemed to say,
"Your mama will live, she'll not die."[25]

True to the theme found in many songs about Father, the girl in Jimmie Davis's "Nobody's Darlin' but Mine" proclaims: "My mother is dead and in Heaven, my daddy has gone down below."[26]

Despite strong familism in songs sung in central Appalachia, lyrics rarely focus on sibling love and support. The Carter Family, in "Motherless Children," maintain that while the brother and sister cannot take the place of Mother, siblings do furnish family support when necessary. In the Dixon Brothers' "Answer to Maple on the Hill, Part 1," the sister sits through the death watch and listens to her sibling's wish to be buried beneath the maple on the hill beside a former lover. The sister also takes part in the death watch in "Little Rosewood Casket." She reads the letters from her dying sister's former lover and is present when she dies. When the wayward man is sent off to prison in "In the Hills of Roane County," his sister bids him a tearful good-bye. It is the sister who is supportive of Charles Guiteau after he murders the president of the United States. The sister and brother both show up to say a last farewell when Henry Clay Beattie is to be executed.

Sibling rivalry pervades some of the songs played and sung by central Appalachians, particularly the murder ballads, but most lyrics emphasize family solidarity. Families can remain intact even after death. In songs such as "The Dying Girl's Farewell" (Ernest V. Stoneman's version), one family member requests that the rest focus their attention on the "home in glory" so they can all be together "on that celestial shore."[27]

Sometimes, of course, families can't be kept together. Some of the saddest lyrics in commercially recorded music focus on orphans. Composers paint parentless children as poor, hungry, sad, innocent, and alone. In "The Village School" by Nelstone's Hawaiians, the orphans lack love and care, which makes them feel isolated and perform poorly in school. The Carter Family's "Motherless Children" delivers a warning similar to the one in "We Can Only Have One Mother"—when Mother is dead, no one can take her place. Brother and sister will provide insufficient care, and friends will "turn their back on you."[28]

Songs such as Jimmie Rodgers' "A Drunkard's Child" and Bradley Kincaid's "Two Little Orphans" moralize about the fate of the children. The home in "A Drunkard's Child" was happy until the father started drinking and gambling and the mother died of a broken heart. The child wanders about seeking food and shelter, people drive her away from their doors, and she dies from cold and hunger. The "Two Little Orphans" become parentless when the father is lost at sea and the mother succumbs to death. They seek refuge at a church where the sexton finds them the next morning:

> The sexton came early to ring the church bell,
> He found them all covered snow white,
> The angels made room for two children to dwell
> In heaven with mama tonight.[29]

Orphans in some songs wish for death to release them from their lives of hunger and suffering. There is little doubt that the children in the much-recorded "Row Us over the Tide" want to die. In Kelly Harrell's version, the gambling father has forsaken his family, the mother is dead, and the children want to join her. In the Blue Sky Boys' adaptation of the song, "papa, mama, and sister are gone," the two remaining children want to be with them in heaven, and their wish is granted:

> Jesus who died for the rich and the poor,
> Answered the little one's cry;
> Took them to Heaven to sorrow no more,
> Rowed them over the Tide.[30]

Death and Dying in Song

Death, commonplace in mountain life and so often on the minds of residents, naturally manifested itself in the popular music of the area. Ballads of visions and premonitions were favored by mountaineers. "Lady Gay," a well-known ballad in central Appalachian society, is the story of a woman who sends her children away to school. They die while away from the mother, and later, perhaps because of guilt or grief, she has a vision in which she encounters them for a final time. The young girl in "Explosion in the Fairmount Mines" and "The Dream of the Miner's Child" has a premonition of impending doom in the coal mines, begs her father to refrain from going to work, and asks him to tell all his friends that there will be an explosion. The mother in G. B. Grayson and Henry Whitter's "He Is Coming to Us Dead" predicts her son's death when he goes off to war. The father, while waiting at the train station to receive his son's corpse, declares, "She said this's the way that he'd come back, when he joined the boys in blue."[31]

Many singers predict their own deaths. The girl in Vernon Dalhart's "The Dying Girl's Message" tells her mother to wipe the cool drops from her forehead, which she insists are "death marks."[32] The dying hobo in Burnett and Rutherford's "Little Stream of Whiskey" and Jimmie Rodgers's "Hobo Bill's Last Ride," the lover in Jimmie Davis's "Nobody's Darlin' but Mine," the former lover in Bradley Kincaid's "Little Rosewood Casket," and the little boy in "Fatal Flower Song" by Nelstone's Hawaiians realize that they are dying, and most of them have final requests. One of the most poignant requests is found in the words of the dying lover in "Maple on the Hill":

Don't forget me, little darling, when they've laid me down to die;
Just one little wish, darling, grant I pray.
As you linger there in sadness, you are thinking of the past,
Let your teardrops kiss the flowers on my grave.[33]

Many of these dying singers have people with them at the end. While the sister performs the death watch in "Little Rosewood Casket" and the Dixon Brothers' "Answer to Maple on the Hill, Part 1" and the mother and father carry out the task in Ernest Stoneman's version of "The Dying Girl's Farewell," the mother generally sits by the bedside of a dying child in mountain music. In the Everly Brothers' "Put My Little Shoes Away" she maintains the vigil by the side of her child, and in "Little Bessie" and "The Dying Girl's Farewell" the daughter bids her mother a tearful good-bye. Loved ones often must listen to visions of the dying. The little girl in "The Dying Girl's Farewell" tells her mother that she is going to heaven to be with Jesus "on eternity's shore."[34] In a later verse she says:

> Oh, look mother, and see that wonderful sight;
> Those beautiful angels are dressed in pure white.
> They are coming, I know, to bear me above,
> For Jesus in Heaven, that city of love.[35]

Similarly, Little Bessie, while her mother sits by her death bed, hears a voice calling her name:

> Just before the lamps were lighted,
> Just before the children came,
> While the room was very quiet,
> I heard someone call my name.
>
> Come up here, my little Bessie,
> Come up here and live with me,
> Where little children never suffer
> Through the long eternity.[36]

Visions of death haunt the incarcerated in song too. Most of them hope to escape their fate in the electric chair or noose and long for freedom. The prisoners in such songs as the Blue Sky Boys' "The Prisoner's Dream," Cliff Carlisle and Wilbur Ball's "Birmingham Jail Two," and Vernon Dalhart's "The Convict and the Rose" sit behind bars and dream of the women they left behind. In "The Prisoner's Song," an early country music classic, the convict sings:

> Now, if I had wings like an angel,
> Over these prison walls I would fly;
> And I'd fly to the arms of my poor darlin'
> And there I'd be willing to die.[37]

Many, despite their dreams, like John Hardy, Charles Guiteau, Henry Clay Beattie, and Charles Burger, are executed. While the prisoners in some lyrics, such as in Vernon Dalhart's "Behind These Gray Walls," give up hope and wait "till the great Master calls,"[38] others, including the singer in Grayson and Whitter's "Dark Road Is a Hard Road to Travel," continue to hope that "where there's a will, there's a way."[39] Mothers most often try to free their sons from prison, and sometimes they end up paying the price for their efforts. In "I'm Here to Get My Baby out of Jail," a mother promises the warden that she will pawn her jewelry, wash his clothes, and scrub his floors if he will release her son. The son is released and the mother dies in his arms:

> Two iron gates swung wide apart,
> She held her darling to her heart,
> She kissed her baby boy and she died, but smiling,
> In the arms of her dear boy, there she died.[40]

Even the free have last wishes recorded in song. Bradley Kincaid's "Bury Me out on the Prairie" includes a request to have the grave covered over with "boulders of granite huge and round."[41] Some dying people ask that a dove (or wings of a dove) be placed on the coffin or grave to show the world they died for love. In "Fair Ellen," the dying man asks that one woman be placed in his arms and another at his feet. Some desire their graves dug deep (the McMichen-Layne String Orchestra's "Rake and Rambling Boy" and Bradley Kincaid's "Bury Me out on the Prairie"), wide and deep (the Blue Sky Boys' "The Butcher's Boy," Bradley Kincaid's "Fair Ellen," and "The Farmer's Boy," and "Sweet William" collected by Herbert Shellans), long and narrow (Bradley Kincaid's "Barbara Allen"), or deep and narrow (Bradley Kincaid's "Barbara Allen").

Few lyrics in common central Appalachian music depict preparation of the body or dressing the corpse, though many bodies in cowboy songs, such as "Bury Me out on the Prairie," "In the Streets of Laredo," and Jimmie Rodgers's "Cowhand's Last Ride," are wrapped in blankets, old cowhide, or white linen. When the girl's body is found in Burnett and Rutherford's "Willie Moore," it is carried by weeping friends to the parents' room and dressed in a "shroud, snowy white."[42]

I could find no songs adequately describing the construction of a coffin and few that depicted burial receptacles at all except to declare "he is coming to us in a casket." In a song by Aunt Idy Harper and the Coon Creek Girls, "The Old Apple Tree" is used to construct a casket. Bradley Kincaid mentions the coffin, pall, and pallbearers in "In the Streets of Laredo." "Parents, Warning" describes two lovers buried in a double coffin:

> A double coffin was directed,
> To which these two true lovers were laid;
> They were laid in the arms of each other,
> And then were laid in the silent grave.[43]

By the time most of these songs begin the graves have already been dug, and in murder ballads this means trouble. In "Pretty Polly," the victim senses that the hole in the ground is for her and the murderer exclaims, "You're guessin' about right, / I dug on your grave the biggest part of last night." In the final verse he states:

> Oh, I threw the dirt around her
> And turned to go home.
> And left Pretty Polly
> With the birds to weep and mourn.[44]

Loved ones bury the dead at sea (Dock Boggs's "False Hearted Lover Blues"), in a meadow (Dock Boggs's "Country Blues" and Bradley Kincaid's "Darling Corie"), on a prairie (the Carter Family's "Cowboy Jack" and Bradley Kincaid's "Bury Me out on the Prairie"), under a tree (the Carter Family's "Bury Me under the Weeping Willow," Martin and Roberts's "Bury Me 'neath the Weeping Willow," and Bradley Kincaid's "Fair Ellen"), under a loved one's doorstep (Dock Boggs's "Old Rub Alcohol Blues"), in the sand (Jimmie Rodgers's "Cowhand's Last Ride"), or in a graveyard ("Broken Engagement" collected by Herbert Shellans and Bradley Kincaid's "Barbara Allen" and "In the Streets of Laredo"). But in the Carolina Tar Heels's "Rude and Rambling Man" the singer doesn't want to be buried, he just wants his bones soaked in alcohol.

A few songs, for example the Carter Family's "Can the Circle Be Unbroken?" (more commonly known as "Will the Circle Be Unbroken?"), convey the feelings of mourners as the deceased is buried: "But I could not hide my sorrow when they laid her in the grave."[45] These songs rarely mention funeral processions, though "Can the Circle Be Unbroken?" contains a brief reference and in Bradley Kincaid's version Barbara Allen looks down the road and sees the funeral cortege with Sweet William's body. The funeral procession in "In the Streets of Laredo" includes pallbearers, music, and flowers: "We beat the drum slowly and played the fife lowly, / And bitterly wept as we bore him along."[46]

Sometimes the body is viewed for a final time. Barbara Allen asks the pallbearers to set down the coffin so she can look upon Sweet William, and the singer of "Broken Engagement" paints the scene for the parted lovers:

> They have buried her in a lonely graveyard
> At the hour of half past eight.
> Long he stood and looked upon her,
> Oh, for well he knew her fate.[47]

"George Collins" by Roy Harvey and the North Carolina Ramblers offers an eerie example of the final viewing:

> Set down the coffin, take off the lid
> Lay back the linen so fine;

And let me kiss his cold pale cheeks
For I know he'll never kiss mine.[48]

As in mountain culture, the graves of the dead are honored in song too. Songs such as "Gathering Flowers for the Master's Bouquet" and "Sweet Flowers" reflect the comfort and beauty flowers extend to mourners. The dying often plead to have flowers sown on their graves, be buried under violets blue, or have their coffins decorated with flowers. The song "See That My Grave Is Kept Green" suggests the desire of many to be remembered after death and not be buried in a cemetery like the one in the Dixon Brothers' "Answer to Maple on the Hill, Part 1": "There's two graves beneath the maple. / One is old and caving in, / And the other one has recently been filled."[49] Most hope their loved ones will be faithful like the son in Vernon Dalhart's "Mother's Grave" and continue to visit and care for their burial places, perhaps even leaving burial objects, as in Dock Boggs's "Lost Love Blues":

> Keep all the little tokens
> I have so fondly gave.
> Just grant to me my last request
> Take them with you to your grave.[50]

Having a marker would probably help people remember where someone is buried, so the dying person in song, as the hero does in the Carolina Tar Heels' "Rude and Rambling Man," wants "a marble stone at my head and feet." Unfortunately, like the cowboy in "When the Work's All Done This Fall," a multitude of highlanders have been buried with only wooden boards to mark their graves.

Many mountaineers believe in a life after death, which has to be prepared for just as death does. Religious songs often question religious status. "Are You Washed in the Blood?" "Don't You Want to Go to That Land?" and the Monroe Brothers' "What Would You Give in Exchange (for Your Soul)?" ask if mountaineers are ready for what is to come. Cogent warnings and suggestions for action punctuate "Keep on the Firing Line," "Turn Your Radio On," "Walk That Lonesome Valley" by Mainer's Mountaineers, Bradley Kincaid's "There's a Red Light Ahead," "Life Is like a Mountain Railroad" ("Life's Railway to Heaven"), the Monroe Brothers' "The Old Crossroads," and the Blue Sky Boys' "Take Up Thy Cross." In "The Dying Girl's Farewell," the mother is asked to warn the rest of the family:

> Go tell brother and sister, and father, too,
> For to follow the Savior in all that they do.

> For life will be over, trials are fair,
> We will all be united in Heaven up there.[51]

As the Chuck Wagon Gang's "Jesus Hold My Hand" and the Blue Sky Boys' "I Need the Prayers (of Those I Love)" illustrate, life for believers isn't always easy, but as these titles show, being saved can be glorious: "I'll Have a New Life," "There'll Be Joy, Joy, Joy," "I Mean to Live for Jesus," "I'm Going Home to Die No More" (by the Cumberland Ridge Runners), and "I'm S-A-V-E-D" (by the Georgia Yellow Hammers). For Christians, heaven means equality for all: "The whites and the colored folks, the Gentiles and the Jews, / We'll praise the Lord together and there'll be no drinking booze."[52]

Transportation to heaven may be by chariot ("Swing Low, Sweet Chariot"), boat ("Row Us over the Tide"), ship (the Carter Family's "Gospel Ship"), train (the Delmore Brothers' "Gospel Cannon Ball" or the Carter Family's "Little Black Train"), or a cloud of bright angels (the Carter Family's "This Is like Heaven to Me"). Of course, there is always the chance that a decedent may be headed on Frank Hutchison's "Hell Bound Train."

Judgment Day is described in several songs including "For the Day is A-Breakin' in My Soul," "Hallelujah! There's a Rainbow in the Sky" by Vernon Dalhart and Adelyne Hood, Bill Cox's "We'll Sow Righteous Seed," the Carter Family's "On the Sea of Galilee," and "Great Speckled Bird" by Roy Acuff and his Crazy Tennesseans:

> When he cometh descending from Heaven,
> On the clouds as He writes in His word;
> I'll be joyfully carried to meet him,
> On the wings of that great speckled bird.[53]

"I'll Have a New Life" collected by Herbert Shellans in Fancy Gap, Virginia, provides an even more graphic portrayal of the resurrection:

> Graves are burstin', saints a-shoutin',
> Heavenly beauty all around;
>
> I'll have a new body, praise the Lord,
> I'll have a new life.[54]

Heaven in song is a concrete, tangible place where people look just like they do on earth. At the entrance are the pearly gates, and according to a song by Ernest V. Stoneman and his Dixie Mountaineers, the righteous will go "Sweeping through the Gates." The dead will encounter streets of gold and no pain, sorrow, suffering, poverty, struggling, or inequality. One may "Bathe in That Beautiful Pool" (Dock Walsh), search for loved ones (the Cumberland Ridge Runners' "I

Dreamed I Searched Heaven for You"), or interact with relatives ("For the Day is A-Breakin' in My Soul"). Heaven is a place where "We'll Never Grow Old" according to a song by Smith's Sacred Singers. In "We Read of a Place That's Called Heaven" it's beautiful:

> The Angels so sweetly are singing,
> Up there by the beautiful sea;
> Sweet chords from their gold harps are ringing,
> How beautiful Heaven must be.[55]

For some, heaven is the ultimate vacation spot:

> There the weather will always be perfect,
> Not a cloud shall sweep over the sky;
> And no earthquake or cyclone shall threaten
> You are invited to go along.[56]

Love and Death

Some of the saddest ballads chronicle the loss of a lover, such as "Little Rosewood Casket," "Nobody's Darlin' but Mine," and Roy Acuff and his Smoky Mountain Boys' "The Precious Jewel." George Collins goes home one winter night and dies, leaving his sweet little Nell to mourn. In "Asleep at the Switch," the switch operator leaves his wife to care for the family. Old Dan Tucker succumbs to old age (in Bradley Kincaid's version), leaving a wife and sixteen children. When the wife in Vern Gosdin's "The Garden" dies, her husband laments: "It's just beyond me why God took her from me."[57] Bereaved lovers are left in the aftermath of drownings ("Asleep in the Briny Deep" and "Willie Moore"), exposure to the elements of nature ("Young Charlotte"), and overexertion ("John Henry").

Usually women in song, such as the one in Jimmie Rodgers's "Soldier's Sweetheart," hear the news that a loved one has died, although a few songs, for example "Put Me in Your Pocket," tell the story of a veteran who returns to find a sweetheart has died. Cowboys tend to die away from home and the women they love ("The Dying Cowboy"), though some ("Cowboy Jack") find their lovers have succumbed to death. Executions take loved ones in Vernon Dalhart's "The Convict and the Rose" and the Carter Family's "John Hardy Was a Desperate Little Man," leaving family behind to mourn.

Love often leads to suicide in these ballads. In "Katie Dear," the young lovers kill themselves when her parents refuse to accept her marriage to the man she loves:

> So he picked up that silver dagger
> And plunged it through his troubled heart,
> Saying "goodbye Katie, goodbye darling,
> Tis now forever we must part."

> So she picked up that bloody dagger
> And plunged it through her lily white breast,
> Saying "goodbye papa, goodbye mama,
> I'll die for the one that I love best."[58]

The woman in "The Butcher's Boy" (also known as "The Railroad Boy") hangs herself when the young man she loves rejects her for another. In Buell Kazee's adaptation of the song, when her father cuts her down, he finds the following request:

> Go dig my grave both wide and deep,
> Place a marble slab at my head and feet;
> And over my coffin place a snow white dove
> To warn this world that I died for love.[59]

Dinah in Bradley Kincaid's song poisons herself when her father tries to force her to marry someone she doesn't love. He does, however, regret his decision when he finds her body:

> He fell down beside her and felt of her heart,
> Crying, "from my dear Dinah I never will part";
> He kissed the cold corpse ten thousand times o'er,
> And called her his Dinah, but she was no more.[60]

"The Fatal Wedding," recorded by several artists including Bradley Kincaid and Vernon Dalhart, relates the story of a wedding that is interrupted by the bridegroom's wife carrying their dead child. The prospective bride, her parents, and the outcast wife leave the husband alone in the church where he takes his own life: "No wedding feast was spread that night, two graves were made next day; one for the little baby, and in one the father lay."[61]

The best-known ballad in central Appalachian society is probably "Barbara Allen" or "Barbara Ellen." Collected throughout the mountains and recorded by a multitude of artists, it is the tale of suicide because of a broken heart. Sweet William and Barbara are lovers, but at one of the local drinking establishments he pays too much attention to the other women and slights his true love. She rejects him and he becomes ill. When he dies, Barbara realizes the extent of his love, recognizes that she could have saved him, and then dies from remorse:

> O mother, o mother, go make my bed,
> Go make it soft and narrow,

Pretty William has died for pure, pure love
And I shall die for sorrow.

O father, o father, go dig my grave,
Go dig it deep and narrow,
Pretty William has died for me to-day
And I shall die tomorrow.[62]

True love wins out in the end, and they are together—at least symbolically:

A rose grew up from William's grave,
From Barbara Ellen's a brier.
They grew and they grew to the top of the church
Till they could not grow any higher.

They grew and they grew to the top of the church
Till they could not grow any higher;
And there they tied in a true love's knot,
And the rose wrapped round the brier.[63]

Murder Ballads

Death in central Appalachia, even in song, was not always so easy or so poetic. In perhaps the largest group of ballads, murderers take the lives of mountaineers. As is common in ballads, the reasons for murder are unclear in "Little Marion Parker," the Everly Brothers' "Down in the Willow Garden," Molly O'Day's "Poor Ellen Smith," and "Little Mary Phagan." Although most versions of "Pretty Polly" do not reveal the reason for her death, Bradley Kincaid hints that she was pregnant and the father of the unborn child didn't want to marry her. Indeed, lovers do much of the killing in these songs. Jonathan Lewis apparently murders Naomi Wise (the song is sometimes called "Ommie Wise") because he doesn't want to run away with her and be married, but the young girl in "Banks of the Ohio" and "Knoxville Girl" is murdered when she refuses to marry her murderer. One of the goriest killings in musical literature is perpetrated by the rejected lover in "Knoxville Girl":

I fell in love with a Knoxville girl, with dark and rolling eyes,
I promised her I'd marry her if me she'd ne'er deny.

I called her at her sister's house, about nine o'clock at night,
And little did that fair girl think I owned her in a fright.

I said to her "Let's take a walk and view the meadows gay,
That we might have a little talk and plan our wedding day."

We walked along, we talked along, till we came to level ground.

There I picked up an edgewood stick and I knocked that fair girl down.

She fell upon her bended knee. "Oh Lord, have mercy!" she cried.
"Oh, Willie, dear, don't murder me here. I'm not prepared to die."

Not minding one word she said, I beat her more and more.
I beat her till the ground around stood in a bloody gore.

I took her by her long yellow hair, I dragged her round and round.
I dragged her to still waters deep that flows through Knoxville town.[64]

"Old Rachel" in the Frank Hutchison song is evidently killed because she talks too much. In gruesome murder ballads such as "Pearl Bryan," "Little Mattie Groves" (gathered in central Appalachia under numerous titles), and the Blue Sky Boys' "Fair-Eyed Ellen," jealousy is the primary motive.

Although there are fewer songs about women killing men, in most instances, as the lyrics to "Young Heneree" or "Young Hunting" (recorded by Dick Justice in 1932 as "Henry Lee"), "Farewell Lovely Polly," and Jimmie Rodgers's classic "Frankie and Johnnie" indicate, they usually do so out of jealousy. Johnny Randal (or "Lord Randal" or "John Randolph"), in the version collected by Patrick Gainer, is poisoned by his lover. In "Leaving Home," by Charlie Poole and the North Carolina Ramblers, sweethearts get into a quarrel, the man threatens to leave, and the woman shoots him:

> Send for your rubber-tired hearses,
> Send for your rubber-tired hacks,
> Carry little Johnnie to the graveyard,
> I shot him in the back.[65]

Sibling rivalry often leads to death in murder ballads. The older sister in "The Two Sisters" (also known as "The Sister's Murder" and "The Twa Sisters") drowns her younger sister out of jealousy. In "The Two Brothers" (also collected in the mountains as "Our Young Son John" and "The Twa Brothers"), the brothers have an argument and one is fatally stabbed by the other. While some versions of the song suggest that the stabbing is an accident, others attribute it to jealousy.

Mountain men in songs often kill to protect their sisters. When the sister elopes with her lover after being promised to another in "The Seven Sons" (also known as "Earl Brand" and "The Douglas Tragedy"), her seven brothers and father follow her in hot pursuit. The father and brothers are killed, the groom is fatally wounded, and the bride dies from sorrow and grief. In "The Banks of Yarrow" (sometimes called "The Braes of Yarrow"), a murder ballad collected by Patrick Gainer in Gassaway, West Virginia, the brothers meet and kill their brother-in-law.

Brothers didn't always protect their sisters in mountain music. According to Patrick Gainer, young family members had to ask permission of parents and older siblings before they could marry.[66] Naturally, these young lovers didn't always ask first. In "The Bride's Murder" (also "The Cruel Brother"), the prospective bridegroom seeks the permission of everyone but his intended's older brother. After the wedding, the brother murders his sister:

> He had a knife both sharp and stout,
> And with it he cut her fair white throat.
> The blood ran down upon her breast,
> She knew that hour would be her last.[67]

There are at least two different versions of "Edward" (or "The Father's Murder"). The lyrics collected by Cecil Sharp and Maude Karpeles indicate that the brother kills his sister's husband in an argument, but in the version Patrick Gainer reproduces, the boy kills his father so that his mother can inherit the property and money.[68]

Some of the most colorful murder ballads recount the deeds and deaths of infamous outlaws such as Jesse James, Cole Younger, and John Hardy. Kinnie Waggoner's exploits have been told and retold in poems, songs, and on phonograph records in only slightly exaggerated form. A native of Scott County, Virginia, he operated throughout central Appalachia and the South in the early 1900s as a substitute mail carrier, dog trainer, circus trick-shot artist, prison escape artist, thief, bank robber, murderer, and one of the South's most colorful bad men.[69]

One of the most sensational episodes in the era of the clan wars occurred on March 14, 1912, when members of the Allen clan led by Claude Allen entered the courtroom in Hillsville, Virginia, where Floyd Allen was on trial. They shot to death the judge, the commonwealth attorney, the sheriff, two jurors, and a witness. Both Floyd Allen and his son Claude were sentenced to die in the electric chair. Shortly thereafter, Claude Allen was portrayed in song as a victim of the state who would leave behind "a pretty sweetheart," "mother weepin'," and "friends in bitter tears":

> How sad, how sad, to think of killin'
> A man all in his youthful years,
> A-leaving his old mother weepin'
> And all his friends in bitter tears.[70]

Few tales of cunning and murder in central Appalachia rival the story of Frankie Silvers, who has the distinction of being the first woman hanged in North Carolina. Goaded by jealousy, she killed her husband in the winter of 1831, chopped the body into pieces, and cremated his remains in the fireplace. At that time in North Carolina, bodies of the executed were turned over to medical students for dissection, and there were several demands for Silvers's remains because a woman's corpse was hard to obtain. However, her father buried the body in a secret place that was never found.

Silvers wrote a poem in her last days of imprisonment and read it on the scaffold before she was executed on July 12, 1833. In the poem, which was later set to music, she recounts her crime:

> The jealous thought that first gave strife
> To make me take my husband's life.
> For days and months I spent my time
> Thinking how to commit this crime.
> And on a dark and doleful night
> I put his body out of sight;
> With flames I tried him to consume
> But time would not admit it done.[71]

In the last verse, she seems to question her fate:

> Great God! How shall I be forgiven?
> Not fit for earth, not fit for Heaven.
> But little time to pray for God
> For now I try that awful road.[72]

Perhaps the most tragic ballads relate murders of children. The unwed mother of "Down by the Greenwood Sidee" kills her children at birth. Mary Hamilton, in a song of the same name, throws her illegitimate child into the sea. "Bolakin," a song collected in West Virginia by Patrick Gainer, is the story of a stonemason who kills the lord's child when he does not receive payment for building a castle:

> Bolakin came to the castle gate,
> Where he saw the lord's child at play.
> He seized the child by the neck,
> And carried him away.

> They found the child's body by the road,
> His life had been taken away.
> But Bolakin was never seen again,
> He's alive to this day, they say.[73]

Nelstone's Hawaiians recorded "Fatal Flower Song" in 1930, which is also known in mountain society as "The Duke's Daughter," "Little Son Hugh," "Sir Hugh," and "The Jew's Daughter." This twist on child murders narrates the story of a girl who entices a young boy to come into her house and then tortures and kills him.

Two of the most noteworthy ballads written about the murder of children are "Little Marian Parker" and "Little Mary Phagan." "Little Marian Parker" is a tragic tale of kidnapping and murder in California in the early 1900s. Musical versions of the story were written by several composers, including Carson J. Robison and Andrew Jenkins, and recorded by artists such as Al Craver. Mary Phagan was killed in 1913 while collecting her pay at the National Pencil Factory. Leo Frank was accused of the murder, sent to jail, and later lynched by some of the citizens of Marietta, Georgia. The versions of the song recorded by Al Craver and Rosa Lee Carson end with the sentencing of Frank:

> Judge Roan passed the sentence,
> You bet he passed it well;
> Solicitor Hugh M. Dorsey
> Sent Leo Frank to . . .[74]

In 1982, new evidence indicated that the janitor at the pencil factory killed her for her pay of $1.20.[75]

A few ballads recount even more famous murders. Charlie Poole and the North Carolina Ramblers' version of "White House Blues" relates the story of the 1901 assassination of President William McKinley: "Doc come a-running, took off his specs. / Said, 'Mr. McKinley, better pass in your checks, / You're bound to die, bound to die.'"[76] "Charles Guiteau" depicts the hanging of the disappointed office-seeker who killed President James A. Garfield on July 2, 1881. The song is reported to be the work of Guiteau himself:

> My name is Charles Guiteau, my name I'll never deny,
> To leave my aged parents to sorrow and to die;
> But little did I think, while in my youthful bloom,
> I would be carried to the scaffold to meet my fatal doom.[77]

In 1949, Bascom Lamar Lunsford recorded a series of songs about the assassination of presidents for the Library of Congress's Archives of Folk Song, including "Charles Guiteau," "Mr. Garfield" (describing the final hours of President Garfield), "Czolgosz" (a variation of "White House Blues"), and "Booth Killed Lincoln."[78]

Multiple killings are rare in murder ballads, but when a North

Carolina tobacco farmer named Charlie Lawson went berserk on Christmas day 1929 and killed his wife, six children, and himself, the incident was sensationalized in "The Murder of the Lawson Family." Written by Walter "Kid" Smith and recorded for Columbia by the Carolina Buddies, the fifth verse speculates on Lawson's last words:

> "And now farewell to friends at home;
> I'll see you all no more,
> Into my breast I'll fire one shot
> And my troubles will be o'er."[79]

Work and Death

WAR

Patriotic mountaineers have fought in every major war from the American Revolution to Operation Desert Storm. Ballads have been written about every war and the soldiers who served their country. However, contemporary central Appalachians tend to remember modern classics such as "God Bless the U.S.A." and "Americana" and forget the older works including Elton Britt's World War II song "There's a Star Spangled Banner Waving Somewhere."

"The Rebel Soldier" relates the story of a Confederate soldier and the death he has seen. "St. Clair's Retreat" describes the defeat of the U.S. Army under the command of General Arthur St. Clair in 1791 in a battle against the Miami Indians. "The Soldier's Poor Little Boy" recounts the fate of an orphaned son, while the hero of "The Drummer Boy of Waterloo" bids his mother good-bye as he marches off to battle and death. While many women are left behind when men go off to fight, the girl in "The Cruel War" dresses in men's clothing and goes to war with her lover. The final words of the dying soldier are reflected in songs such as "Brother Green" and "The Ballad of the Rebel Soldier." Many mountaineers ended up like the fighter in G. B. Grayson and Henry Whitter's "He Is Coming to Us Dead."

Thousands of mountain men have been willing to go to war, fight, and die for their country, but few have been prepared to accept the kinds of treatment received by Vietnam and World War I veterans when they returned to America. "The Forgotten Soldier Boy" is a good example of the feelings of many mountaineers who have returned and been forgotten by their country and government:

I saw my buddies dying and some shell-shocked and torn,
Although we never faltered at the Battle of the Marne.
Then we were told when we left home we'd be heroes of the land,
Though we came back and found no one would lend a helping
hand.[80]

RAILROADS

Mountain people loved the thrill of the railroad during its heyday in the early 1900s. They listened to outsiders such as Jimmie Rodgers, as well as native mountaineers like Roy Harvey and the Carter Family, when they sung the exciting songs about railroading. Numerous train songs with death as the primary theme were recorded in the 1920s and 1930s.

Prior to the arrival of the airplane in America, the train was the primary mode of travel and transporting merchandise. Sometimes travel by rail is depicted in railroads songs as fun and adventure.[81] However, for the little boy in "The Lightning Express" who needs to reach home as soon as possible before his mother dies and the child riding "The East Bound Train" to seek a pardon for the father in prison, the train offers urgent and necessary transportation. And sometimes that travel is grim, as in "He Is Coming to Us Dead," when the father waits for the train bringing the body of his son home for burial.

Railroad workers, like members of other professions, have their cultural heroes, fictional and nonfictional. In addition to heroes of the rail, such as Billy Richardson and Casey Jones, who died in the line of duty, two particular characters well known in American folklore are Railroad Bill and John Henry. While Railroad Bill was a notorious badman, John Henry became the hero of workers. In folk song, John Henry attempts to prevent the use of machinery over human labor in the building of the Big Bend Tunnel in West Virginia. He enters into a contest with a steam drill and wins, but dies with his hammer in his hand.

Devotion of railroad workers makes them go beyond the call of duty. In Ernest V. Stoneman's "Asleep at the Switch," the switch operator leaves his ailing son and goes off to work. He dies on duty, apparently from a heart attack due to stress, and a major train wreck is avoided through the actions of his daughter who arrives to inform him that the crisis with his son has passed. The engineer in Jimmie Rodgers's "The Mystery of Number Nine" goes to work and finds his engine cold. The stoker's daughter reports that her father died on the way to work. Even though the engineer's child is dying in the Vernon Dalhart song of the same name, duty calls him to work. The dangerous life of brake operators is illustrated in Bradley Kincaid's "True and Trembling Brakeman." When the brake operator falls between the cars of a freight train and is dying, he asks his sister to carry a warning to his brother:

> "Sister, when you see my brother,
> These few words I send to him;
> Never, never venture braking,
> If he does, his life will end."[82]

Many of the early songs chronicle train wrecks and the bravery of engineers, who were accorded the respect reserved for captains going down with their ships. Recordings such as "The Wreck of the Southern Old Ninety-seven," "The Wreck of the Virginian Train No. Three," "Altoona Freight Wreck," "The New Market Wreck," "The Wreck on the C and O," "Old Number Three (Billy Richardson's Last Ride)," "The Wreck of the 1256 (on the Main Line of the C and O)," "The Wreck of the Royal Palm Express," "Jim Blake" (or "Jim Blake's Message"), "Casey Jones," and "The Wreck of No. Four and the Death of John Daily," so popular in central Appalachia, recount these tragic tales. The railroad workers usually leave loved ones behind to grieve. Engineers kiss their wives good-bye before dying in a wreck (the Arizona Wranglers' version of "The Wreck of Ninety-seven" and George Reneau's "The New Market Wreck"). Jim Blake is hurrying to get home to his ailing wife when he dies in a crash.

COAL MINING

The dangers of mining made their way into songs in the mountains shortly after the industry became big business for central Appalachia. Ballads such as "Dark as a Dungeon" and "Sixteen Tons" describe working conditions in coal mines. The mining wars and violent unionization movement are reflected in songs such as Sarah Ogan Gunning's "I am a Girl of Constant Sorrow," Aunt Molly Jackson's "I Am a Union Woman," and Florence Reece's "Which Side Are You On?":

> If you go up to Harlan County
> There is no neutral there,
> You'll either be a union man
> Or a thug for J. H. Blair.[83]

The violence and danger created heroes who were immortalized in song from the fictional Big Bad John (in Jimmy Dean's song) to real-life men such as Harry Simms ("The Murder of Harry Simms" by Jim Garland). One of the most outstanding figures during the early unionization movement was Mother Jones. In his classic recording of "The Death of Mother Jones," Gene Autry describes her as follows:

> She was fearless of every danger,
> She hated that which was wrong;
> She never gave up fighting
> Until her breath was gone.[84]

Disasters claimed the lives of many miners. Premonitions of death color "The Dream of the Miner's Child" and "Explosion in the Fairmount Mine." "The Hyden Disaster," "Mannington Mine Disaster," "The Coal Creek Explosion," and "West Virginia Mine Disaster" recount the needless loss of life in mining tragedies. "Shut Up in the Coal Creek Mine" reflects the final thoughts of men trapped in a mine:

> Our lamps are burning dimly,
> Our food is almost gone.
> Death's grasp is sure but awful,
> Soon we'll be carried home.
>
> Goodbye, dear wives and children,
> May you be treated kind.
> For now our time has come to die,
> Shut up in the Coal Creek mine.[85]

Most of these dead miners, such as those "Shut Up in the Coal Creek Mine" leave wives at home to grieve for them and care for surviving family members. In songs such as "Jenny's Gone Away," the widow has to leave the mountains to make a living for her family in the city.

Changes in Central Appalachian Music

Though older mountaineers listened to sorrowful songs about dying lovers, miners, railroad workers, accidents ("The Death of Floyd Collins"), catastrophes (Ernest V. Stoneman's "The Titanic"), violence (Martin and Roberts's "The Marion Massacre"), industrial accidents, and work-related illness, contemporary residents have neglected this traditional music. Beginning in the 1920s, people turned away from the songs of their ancestors to listen to those on the radio and on phonograph records. After the 1940s, country and western became the preferred form of music, with drinking and cheating replacing death as the central theme. Today most mountaineers prefer country music, but many listen to rock and roll, rhythm and blues, and classical music. Though death is no longer the prevailing theme, the relationship between ecology and death has become an important issue in the music of central Appalachia. Mountaineers have joined mainstream America in placing an emphasis on the importance of preserving the environment and protecting life.

TEN

Mining Disasters and Death

Eleven of us were 'prisoned,
And two dear ones have died.
Nine more are left to suffer
And die in the Coal Creek Mine.
—Dick Bell (Green Bailey), "Shut Up in
the Coal Creek Mine"

F or the first mountain settlers, farming was the dominant mode of making a living and remained so for most central Appalachians until the nineteenth century. This subsistence work was hard, so people looked for ways to improve their lives whenever and however possible. When coal was recognized as an important fuel and then discovered in the hills, many central Appalachians looked upon it as a godsend. This find offered opportunities beyond most farmers' dreams for steady pay and security for their families. Thousands fled to the mines to take advantage of the riches they imagined lay there. The industry brought economic changes into the hills, growing communities, increased technology, and an influx of new settlers. Miners returning home to their families brought with them new ideas, new songs, and new perspectives that made central Appalachians emerge from their isolation and reinterpret their lives to include this whole new world. Mining eventually helped bring the area into the twentieth century and indelibly altered the people and the culture until it finally became inseparably associated with central Appalachia.

Unfortunately, what had seemed so good did not come free. Farming and other occupations could be hazardous at times, but coal miners took their lives into their hands from the moment they entered the hole in the ground until the day's work was completed. Since the first mine catastrophe in the Black Heath pit near Richmond, Virginia, on March 18, 1839,[1] thousands of miners have been killed or injured in mine-related accidents.

A huge number of mountaineers who left their family farms ended up in "coal camps." These housing communities set up by many of the coal companies contained identical single-family dwellings in addition to boarding houses. The mine owners also provided churches, schools, and company stores where miners, for exorbitant prices, could purchase goods with scrip, a form of monetary wage received on pay day in lieu of U.S. currency. The company also deducted the costs of electricity and coal for heating from their employees' paychecks each month.

Most of the coal camps were not well maintained, and living conditions in many were atrocious. Howard Lee refers to the residences as "cheap frame shanties that in many instances were unfit for use as cow barns,"[2] and Erikson provides an equally disturbing description: "The worst of the camps were filthy and polluted, a degrading scene of air turned rancid by surface privies, hogs wallowing in the muddy streets, swarms of flies creating a great democracy of germs, mounds of decomposing garbage scattered everywhere, and raw sewage making a foul paste of the streams passing through the settlements."[3]

In 1946, the secretary of the interior, as coal mines administrator, asked the Bureau of Medicine and Surgery of the U.S. Navy to study housing and sanitary conditions in coal mining areas. In April 1947 the bureau documented the health hazards:

> Ninety-five percent of the houses are built of wood, finished outside with weather board, usually nailed direct to the frame with no sheathing. Roofs are of composition paper. Wood sheathing forms the inside finish. The houses usually rest on posts with no cellars. . . . The state of disrepair at times runs beyond the power of verbal description or even of photographic illustration since neither words nor pictures can portray the atmosphere of abandon dejection or reproduce the smells. Old, unpainted board and batten houses, batten gone or going and boards fast following, roofs broken, porches staggering, steps sagging, a riot of rubbish, and a medley of odors. . . . There is the ever present back-yard privy, with its foul stench. . . . Many of these ill-smelling backhouses, perched beside roads, along alleys, and over streams, leave their human waste exposed, permeate the air with nauseating odors, and spread disease and death. . . . Then there is the camp dirt—a mixture of coal dust, dust from the dirt roads, smoke from the burning "bone pile," which blend into a kind of grime that saturates the atmosphere, penetrates houses and even clothing, and sticks tenaciously to human bodies.[4]

Not only native Appalachians subjected themselves to the misery of coal mining, though in the late 1800s the workers were almost exclusively white men from the mountain area. After 1900, a large number of the miners were African Americans or immigrants from Europe, including Austrians, Poles, Hungarians, Russians, Italians, Czechoslovakians, Yugoslavians, and Turks. Some African Americans had stayed on to mine coal after working for the railroads but most outside workers were recruited by mine owners to supplement the insufficient number of mountain laborers. Though they worked together, during off hours these miners lived segregated lives. Each group had its own church, school, and housing area, and seldom socialized with any other group.

The miners did die together, however. Although people associate coal mining deaths with native central Appalachians, in actuality more foreign-born than native-born miners died in major disasters. For example, according to statistics compiled by the Monongah Mines Relief Committee, in the Monongah explosion in West Virginia on December 6, 1907 (the worst in American history), 74 Americans, 11 African Americans, 15 Austrians, 52 Hungarians, 171 Italians, 31 Russians, and 5 Turks perished.[5] Lacy Dillon provides further evidence from his discussion of mining accidents in West Virginia: "At Monongah the percent of foreigners ran nearly 80 percent, while at Benwood, 1924, only about 10 men of the 119 who died were American born. Black men were in heavy percentage killed in the state's southern mines, but small in numbers in northern counties. Elk Garden (1911) had no blacks, while First Lick Branch had mostly blacks in the list of victims. Algoma, 1902, were all black but two."[6]

The Hazards of Coal Mining

Early coal mining was a difficult and dangerous occupation. It was "almost a solitary contest between man and mountains."[7] A Miner entered the shaft with a manually operated breast auger, pick and shovel, tamping bar, long iron needle, open-flame lamp (powered by whale oil, lard oil, or carbide), cap of soft canvas and leather, black powder, and round tin dinner pail. Each worker set timbers to support the roof of the mine, drilled and shot the coal, and shoveled it into a bucket, wagon, or car, which was then conveyed to the surface. In large mines the wagon or car loaded with coal was pulled from the mine by a horse or mule. When the coal reached the surface, it was shoveled into railroad cars and transported to its destination. Kai Erikson, in *Everything in Its Path*, provides a description of coal mining in the early 1900s in Buffalo Creek, West Virginia:

A man would begin the process of removing coal by cutting a narrow shelf at the base of the seam, a task usually accomplished by swinging a pick while lying on one's side, and then he would drive a deep hole into the face of the seam with the auger, a five- or six-foot drill looking like an oversize brace and bit with a breastplate at one end. He would pour powder into a paper cartridge, crimping the ends as if he were rolling a sausage, and shove that package into the hole with the needle, an iron bar five or six feet long and the width of a pencil. The hole was filled with damp dirt or clay and packed tightly with the tamper after a fuse had been inserted. And when all that had been done, the miner lighted the fuse, hurried to safe ground, and listened while the cartridge exploded and shattered a ton or so of coal from the face of the seam. The final step of the process was to shovel the coal onto waiting cars and push them along the hollow shaft to the main passageway, where mules hauled them to the surface.[8]

METHANE GAS

Perhaps the greatest hazard coal miners have ever had to face is methane gas. It is an odorless, colorless, lighter than air, volatile, flammable gas that has been a factor in almost every major mine explosion. Methane forms an explosive mixture known as firedamp when mixed with certain proportions of air. Mines naturally accumulate methane gas, but certain conditions can influence the amount of gas seepage. A slate fall or explosion to loosen the coal can open a seam that allows an excessive amount of methane buildup, but changes in barometric pressure pose the greatest threat. Mining conditions are "most dangerous during weather changes, when low barometric pressures allow gas to escape from coal seams in greater quantities than normal."[9] Many mountain residents in mining areas refer to autumn as "the explosion season."[10]

For over a hundred years, the primary instrument for detecting methane gas has been the Davy lamp, invented in 1815 by the British chemist Sir Humphry Davy. Davy covered a regular open-flame lamp with a wire gauze screen, which allows methane to reach the flame and burn but prevents the flame from exploding the gas outside. The fire boss and other experts can tell the extent of the gas present by observing the height and color of the flame. The flame burns blue rather than yellow when dangerous levels of methane are in the shaft. Methane in levels of 1 to 4.5 percent of the air can explode when coal dust is present. Without coal dust methane can explode at amounts of 5 to 14 percent.

In early mining, canaries, and occasionally other animals, were sometimes used as methane monitors. If they died, miners assumed

Miner's safety lamp used in the detection of methane gas.

the gas was present. Some mining operations hired "suicidal specialists known as 'cannoneers,' whose mission was to crawl along the tunnel floor under a wet canvas before a shift, igniting 'puffs' of mine gas near the roof with an upraised candle.[11] While the gas is odorless and colorless, there has been at least one claim that it is audible: "[Splashdam] was one of the hottest mines that ever was blown with gas. You [could] hear the gas just like bees. I crawled in there [one time], laid down flat on my belly, [put] a carbide light up in it and let it blow out. Fire burned right over my back, scorched my eyebrows off. It's a wonder we hadn't all been killed."[12] Some miners still use flame safety lamps to measure methane levels, but mining technology has introduced other instruments such as methanometers and methane monitors, which are approved by the Mine Enforcement and Safety Administration.[13]

Only fresh air could dispel or dissipate the methane gas in a mine. A shaft, or vertical hole, was sunk into the mountain, and a large fan impelled the air into passageways through doors, ducts, or curtains called brattices. Brattice cloth (a heavy type of burlap) was purchased in rolls wide enough to reach from the ceiling of a mine tunnel to the floor and strung in such a manner that it served as a partition separating the passageway into an upcast and downcast chamber. The methane gas, which was lighter than air, was forced from the downcast chamber into the upcast chamber by fresh air, where it was diluted, retarded, and pushed to the outside of the mine so that the inside atmosphere was less than the legal limit of gas for tolerable working conditions.

Cloth miner's cap with carbide lamp attached.

Unfortunately, the forced-air system was never foolproof. Fans or brattices could be impaired by a rock slide, slate fall, or explosion. Damage to brattices or failure to close the air-lock doors used to regulate the air in a mine could result in a short-circuit of the air supply system.[14] A forced-air system could do more harm than good if a fire already existed in a mine. As was the case in the Farmington, West Virginia, disaster in 1968, it might fan the flames and cause the deaths of more people.

The dominant variable in mine fires and explosions until the complete changeover to battery-powered electric cap lamps was the open-flame lamp worn on the front of miners' caps. It was usually powered by carbide. The two-inch acetylene flame was produced by striking flint, in basically the same way the modern cigarette lighter is ignited. When the open flame made contact with methane gas, the miner almost certainly perished.

Since its establishment in 1910, the Bureau of Mines has tested and approved safe battery-operated lamps to be used in underground mining, but in 1941 about half the miners were still using carbide lights,[15] and some workers continued to use them for several more years.

Naturally other factors could trigger a mine fire or explosion. In the past, miners could strike matches or smoke cigarettes anywhere they pleased (a practice not permitted today). Fuses (eventually supplanted by electrical detonation) used to discharge black powder or dynamite were safety hazards, and the resulting explosion could also ignite the gas. Inexperienced or careless miners, after drilling a hole, occasionally did a poor job of tamping the black powder or dynamite and produced a "blow out shot," where fire blew out the end of the hole. Eventually, mining operations hired explosive experts called "shot firers" or "shot foremen" to tamp and ignite the charges after the miner had drilled the hole. Even the later introduction of electrical devices could not prevent stray sparks from metal scraping against metal or curb fires altogether.

COAL DUST

In the first three decades of the twentieth century, when most of the tragic mine disasters took place, coal dust was almost always a major factor in the explosions. As with methane, open-flame lamps, sparks, or matches could ignite the dust. While there was always some dust in a working mine, certain activities could increase the amount or produce more hazardous types. "Shooting on the solid" could pulverize the coal into a flour-like carbon "bug" dust that was highly explosive. Some miners increased the charge they inserted into the hole so that more coal blew free: "Eventually, it got so tight that they put on what they call the 'shot foreman.' You'd drill your holes, have to furnish the powder, then this man would come and he'd shoot your coal for you so it wouldn't be shot too hard. Well, here's what I'd do: I'd drill my holes and then I slipped me a stick of dynamite right in the back of that hole, He didn't find that, so he'd tamp his [dynamite] right in on it. You had to learn to be shifty."[16] Although the extra charge produced more coal and made work easier for the miners, it also sometimes produced more dust.

Some mines in the first part of the 1900s used a sprinkling system, since wet dust was less likely to explode. Later other companies introduced rock dusting, which "involves rendering coal dust inert with 65 percent crushed limestone,"[17] to make the coal dust less volatile. Modern methods of allaying the dangers of discharging coal dust in underground mining are more sophisticated than they were in the first three decades of this century and safety rules are more strictly enforced, but the danger of an explosion is always present.

Most of the major mine disasters in central Appalachian history have resulted from the discharge of methane *and* coal dust. When both detonate the velocity of the explosion often accelerates from the site of the ignition to the outside of the mine. Lacy Dillon says that the combination explosion at Eccles, West Virginia, on April 28, 1914 (which killed 187 miners), "nearly blew the mines inside out."[18] The result was gruesome: "To describe the outside discharge is beyond the imagination. At the shaft mouth out came everything such as parts of humans, mine cars, mine timbers, bits of metal, rocks, and pieces of mules."[19]

BLACKDAMP AND AFTERDAMP

Many coal miners survived a mine disaster only to die from suffocation or asphyxiation. In the aftermath of an explosion, numerous men died from inhaling carbon monoxide or carbon dioxide gas, which produced quick suffocation. Both gases are primarily the result of a fire or explosion (although they can be released from the coal) and are incapable of supporting life or flame. Another gas that is sometimes the product of an explosion and can create death through asphyxiation is a combination of carbon monoxide and nitrous oxide: "The other asphyxiation is CO gas mixed with nitrous oxide (laughing gas) that intoxicates the victim and puts him into a stupor. He dies easily, sometimes smiling or in a reclining or sitting position. Men have been found dead while eating with food in hand near the mouth. Boys were found dead after the Stuart explosion as if they were playing a game of some kind."[20]

The terms *blackdamp* (a mixture of carbon dioxide and nitrogen) and *afterdamp* (carbon monoxide) are used when the air in a mine becomes oxygen deficient to the extent that the workers can be asphyxiated or suffocate. The gases are propelled rapidly through the passageways of a mine following the detonation of methane gas or coal dust. In some disasters, such as the Detroit mine explosion in West Virginia on January 18, 1906, the "victims realized their situations and made no attempts at survival."[21] Occasionally, miners tried to outrun the pursuing gas, but few were successful. Those trapped in the Jamison (Farmington) no. 8 catastrophe in West Virginia on January 14, 1926, used the hay for feeding the horses and mules to make a barricade. The bales of hay were stacked in the opening of the tunnel and any small holes were plugged with straw and mud.[22] These desperate measures sometimes worked, but rescue had to be quick before the available oxygen supply was exhausted.

As late as 1925 when the Barrackville explosion took place in West Virginia, canaries were still used to test for blackdamp before rescuers entered the mine. At that time, the bird was taken cautiously into the suspected area where it "gasped a time or two and paid the sacrifice on the alter of industry."[23] Today stain-type toxic gas detectors, carbon monoxide meters, and hydrocarbon alarms can detect both blackdamp and afterdamp. The lethal gases then had to be dispelled in the same fashion as methane. Fresh air had to be forced into the tunnels to drive out the blackdamp and afterdamp before rescue efforts could be attempted. The dangers to rescuers were lessened when oxygen masks were introduced.

OTHER HAZARDS

Toxic gases and coal dust were not the only factors in coal mining deaths. When electricity was first installed in mines, a lack of regard for safety often resulted in electrocution when a worker came in contact with a "live" wire. There was, and still is, the inevitable rock slide or slate fall that could kill or disable. Perhaps the greatest indirect, nonviolent cause of early death was a "progressive, gasping, breathlessness associated with prolonged inhalation of fine coal dust, a condition known (from autopsy observations) as 'black lung' or pneumoconiosis." The problem has not been eliminated, for modern mining machines churn up "greater and greater clouds of dust."[24] There is no way to tell how many workers died from black lung.

On February 26, 1972, a makeshift slag or "gob" dam owned by the Buffalo Mining Company collapsed, releasing 132 million gallons of debris-filled muddy water. It annihilated the community of Buffalo Creek, killing 125 individuals and leaving 4,000 people homeless.[25] Even seemingly positive changes in the industry cost huge numbers of lives. During the mining wars in the early 1900s, when workers were beginning to unionize, hundreds of mountaineers were disabled or killed as they fought the coal operators. Such places as "Bloody Harlan," Kentucky, Matewan, West Virginia (site of the "Matewan massacre"), and Blair Mountain, West Virginia (scene of the Battle of Blair Mountain), became bloodbaths in the bitter struggle.

Rescue Efforts

Hundreds of people rushed to the scene of a coal mine disaster. Some came to offer help or just to say they were there and recount their experiences for years to come. Some were close enough to hear the explosion or feel the earth tremble, while others came from long distances when they heard the news. Since these accidents always drew national attention reporters traveled to the scene to convey the news. Doctors were needed to care for survivors; morticians were needed to care for the dead. Occasionally the crowds were so large or uncontrollable that law enforcement officers had to isolate the mine site and keep a constant vigil to maintain order.

As soon as they received the news, relatives hurried to a disaster area to wait to hear about their loved ones and hope for a miracle. Usually in a state of near hysteria, they wailed, shrieked, shouted, and prayed. One woman at the scene of the Monongah, West Virginia, accident "pulled her hair out by the handful," and another "disfigured her face with her fingernails, screaming frantically in the meantime."[26] Men as well as women wept openly for their kin imprisoned in the mine. Family members stood in all kinds of weather, including freezing rain, awaiting some kind of information—good or bad.

The cost to each family that lost a loved one was extremely high, since most workers provided the sole source of income and security for their families. Many miners left behind a wife and several children, while numerous families lost more than one member. For example, in West Virginia's Detroit mining calamity, one family mourned the death of three brothers, another was deprived of a father and son, and two families each interred two brothers. One woman buried her husband and four brothers. These huge losses occurred in almost every major mine disaster in central Appalachian history.

The most important people at the scene of a mine explosion were, of course, members of the rescue team. It was a special kind of person who entered the danger zone, with its multiplicity of hazards, to emancipate any workers that might be alive and retrieve the bodies of the dead. Unlike today, in the early years when most mining catastrophes took place there were no trained rescuers. Members of rescue teams were usually employees of other mines. They were generally skilled miners and aware of the dangers they could encounter. In contemporary central Appalachia, mining companies have personnel trained in the art of entering a mine to save lives and recover the remains of the deceased.

Workers involved in rescue efforts after a disaster had to face a multitude of problems. A number of different perils could feasibly await them in the mine. A fire could still be burning or might easily be rekindled. A buildup of methane gas and coal dust could be ignited by the carbide lamps. Asphyxiation from the deadly blackdamp or afterdamp was always a possibility, not to mention slate falls, rock slides, and roof falls. Later rescuers had to watch for live wires to avoid electrocution. These hazards tested the skill and courage of the workers, but for many, finding the dead proved to be the greatest trial.

Mine disasters usually left the dead almost completely unrecognizable. The intense heat generated in a fire frequently left the victims virtually cremated, and even when the bodies were mostly intact they were difficult to identify and transport to the surface. Equally horrifying was discovering miners asphyxiated by toxic gas. Sometimes the dead miners appeared to be merely sleeping but those who suffocated from blackdamp or afterdamp were contorted in pain from gasping for their last breath.

The force of an explosion, especially one that was a combination of methane gas and coal dust, was often so great that it turned objects in its path into projectiles. The Detroit accident provides a good example of the power of an explosion: "A mule and Shetland pony were tied about 150 feet inside the drift when the blast came. They were blown to the outside and in projectile fashion over the mountainside to the tracks below. Observers of the day claimed that these beasts were so broken and mangled that their species were only distinguishable by the differences in their hooves."[27]

Miners caught in the direct path of an explosion were hurled against the walls and tossed about as though they were toothpicks. Clothing was torn to shreds and bodies were badly mangled and impossible to identify. When miners provided their own detonators and black powder or dynamite, explosions were even more destructive. Some of the workers carried explosives with them or stashed them close by. When the gas or coal dust was ignited, these explosives were detonated, literally blowing the unfortunate miner to bits.

People could die horribly even without fire or explosions because of the constant threat of a roof or slate fall. Most central Appalachian coal is supported by a layer of slate, sometimes two or three feet thick, lying on a smaller layer of sandstone. The slate adheres weakly to the sandstone and can easily break loose and fall on the workers below. To deal with this problem, mine timbers were used to support the ceiling until steel roof bolts were introduced.[28]

Slate or roof falls usually kill or maim miners below. A childhood friend of mine died in a roof fall, and his body was so completely destroyed that it was impossible, even with cosmetic restoration, to display his body during the wake and funeral. I talked with elderly ex-miners who described the gruesome process of removing a flattened corpse from under fallen slate with crowbars, jacks, and shovels. Harry Caudill tells the following story: "An aged Negro once related to me how he and two of his 'buddies' loaded the pancake-flat remains of a foreman and two miners into a coal car for removal to the outside. Their bodies, he said, were ground into the floor and the miners scraped them loose with their huge coal shovels. As he put it, 'We had to jest shovel 'em up.'"[29]

Animals died in mine accidents too. Prior to the use of motorized machinery, mules, horses, and Shetland ponies pulled the mine cars and performed other tasks too difficult for the miners. These animals were stabled in the mine so in times of disaster they were caught up in the explosion and injured or killed. Sometimes their bodies had to be removed before rescue efforts could be continued so that there would be fresh air free from decay and contamination. They were generally carried to a convenient place outside the mine and cremated or left to rot. Lacy Dillon, in *They Died in the Darkness*, relates the story of a man who, after the First Eccles mining calamity, informed the mining company that he would remove the fifty-seven mules left decaying in the mine for a fee of fifty dollars per mule and one gallon of moonshine whiskey daily to settle his men's stomachs after the day's work was completed. Supposedly, the company accepted the deal.[30]

More care was taken with the corpses of the miners. Most commonly the bodies were carried to the surface on stretchers, though sometimes the remains were loaded onto a wagon or mine car and pulled to the outside by a mule, horse, pony, or motorized vehicle. Some bodies were wrapped in sheets and carried out by two or more rescue workers. In a few mines, coffins were lowered into the shafts. The corpses were identified (if possible), prepared for burial, and placed in the coffins, which were then conveyed to the surface.

The most nauseating problem was the odor from the decaying bodies. The putrefaction was sometimes so intense that the rescuers had to work in teams, with as many as seven or eight men carrying a dead body. The odor often drifted to towns and villages miles away. The men involved in recovery efforts found it difficult to remove the stench when their job was completed:

> The wife of a mine foreman [after the First Eccles accident in West Virginia on April 28, 1914] told in later years that she did not see her husband for two weeks while recovery men searched for bodies. The day he came home—they lived in the coal camp—he yelled to her to get washtubs, put them in an outbuilding, and fill them with hot water. He could not get near the house or her since he had the strong odor of dead humans on him too strongly for an ordinary sense to bear. She stated that for days, no matter how much bathing he did, he still bore the obnoxious odor.[31]

The cool water that collected in the mines sometimes retarded or delayed putrefaction:

> A deep mine such as Eccles far below creek bed level catches an enormous flow from water seams between the strata. In this case, the pumps were destroyed allowing water to collect especially in the lower levels. When recovery men searched for bodies, they probed every water hole. The corpses as a rule were found submerged in the black water mixed with coal and slate and in some cases under the slate fall. Bodies that were in drier levels were swollen, had turned black, and a few days afterwards putrefied. The task of removing them was terrible. Many had swollen until their clothes were bursting. In some cases, those found submerged in water were not decayed or swollen badly, but were preserved by the cool water.[32]

Identifying the Dead

The identification of men killed in an accident while mining coal was important. Family members wished to claim their loved one, provide a decent funeral and burial, and mark the grave. Unfortunately, identification was occasionally impossible because of extensive damage to the body. Even intact corpses might be identified only by distinguishing characteristics, such as skin or hair color. Body parts were sometimes assembled on the basis of skin color, belt buckles, musculature of the extremities, or hair color. Many men were buried in unmarked graves because they were not recognizable. Some workers, of course, didn't want to be recognized. These miners moved to central Appalachia to lose their identity, occasionally working under assumed names and interacting with others as little as possible. They were buried in unmarked graves. An enormous number of mine employees who lost their lives were African Americans or immigrants recruited for work. Many were unmarried or left families behind, expecting to make some money and send for them later. No one could claim or identify these bodies either.

Especially when coffins were hoisted down into the mines, the dead were identified inside before the remains were removed. However, most of the time workers took the bodies to a large building near the entrance of the mine, such as a machine shop, blacksmith shop, warehouse, or the company store. Preparation of the bodies for burial was sometimes carried out before family or friends arrived. These corpses were arranged in a row, in or near the coffins, prior to viewing by the family. No one but relatives and participants in the identification process were allowed to see the dead.

In early mine accidents many of the dead were buried in un-marked graves because they could not be identified, and in fact some-times mine owners didn't even know how many workers were in the shafts. Since then the mining industry has worked to develop adequate identification systems. Some states have passed legislation; for example, West Virginia requires a tag system: "Today, it is a state law that any miner who reports for work is issued a stainless steel tag the size of a silver dollar with his number and name thereon, and a duplicate is left in the lamp house on a tag board, and the building is not set where it can be blown away nor is it made of flammable material."[33]

Familism, Neighborliness, and the Death Watch

Mine accidents didn't always mean instant death for workers trapped inside. Many miners were seriously hurt and taken home to die in the presence of loved ones. Family and neighbors then cared for these injured workers and watched over them as they died.

After death their bodies were most often washed, dressed, and readied for the coffin by family and friends. After embalming be-gan, undertakers cared for the bodies of miners in the same way as other decedents. In mine disasters, however, most corpses were pre-pared on the spot before the families claimed the bodies.

Mine workers washed, embalmed (when the process was avail-able), and dressed the corpses, placed them in coffins, and turned them over to the families. Occasionally, all the rescuers could do was douse the corpses with a disinfectant or astringent to suppress the odor and prevent the transmission of disease, put them in coffins, and hoist them to the surface for a quick burial. Some miners car-ried formaldehyde to suppress the odor. Unidentifiable body parts ended up in coffins that were not opened later for viewing. Occa-sionally, the parts of miners were "mixed in each other's caskets since the pieces were not always recognizable."[34]

Undertakers and their assistants from surrounding areas gener-ally supplied assistance to care for the huge number of casualties. If the bodies were not prepared in the mine they were taken to a large building nearby that served as a morgue or, if possible, transported to the funeral home, where they were washed, embalmed, and dressed before release to the families. In cases where decomposition was too extreme for washing and dressing, the undertaker disinfected the body and placed it in a casket as soon as possible.

By the late 1920s bodies of miners were embalmed if at all possible. After West Virginia's Yukon mine disaster on May 22, 1928, the bodies were embalmed at the accident site:

> May 24 dawned pretty and the bodies were laid outside the machine shop so that the two morticians from War, a town one mile above Susanna, could prepare the bodies. Some onlookers watched them open the veins of the corpses, drain off their blood in small vessels before pumping the embalming fluid into their bodies. The blood was taken to a spot near a slate pile and poured into small pits dug by helpers and then covered with dirt and shale. The morticians in turn washed the bodies as much as could be washed over with burnt flesh, and dressed them in suits or suitable attire for burial. The coffins were not on hand immediately but soon arrived on the baggage coach of the "short dog" passenger train. After all the bodies were prepared and coffined, they were carried by miners and helpers down the railroad track to the company store where relatives could claim them and have them shipped to their destinations.[35]

The coffins of deceased miners were generally constructed by a neighbor or someone in the mining community. Usually made of cheap wood such as white pine and occasionally covered with black cloth, the burial receptacles were brought to the accident site and arranged in a row to await their occupants.[36] Sometimes they were lined before construction, sometimes while rescue efforts were in progress, and sometimes there wasn't enough time to insert a lining before interment. Later, of course, nearly all coffins were professionally constructed, and some large mining companies kept them on hand. In the event of a large accident, however, the company acquired more from other mines. Occasionally, they were transported by train as close to the accident site as possible and then hauled by a horse and wagon the rest of the way.

Mining companies usually furnished the coffins for accident victims, although families of miners that died from other causes were stuck with all of the funeral expenses. Some miners paid into a burial fund, which helped allay some of the costs, though survivors ran the risk of encountering the "coffin racket":

> A practice of the operators, closely related to the burial fund, was what the miners called the "coffin racket." Most of the early operators in southern West Virginia carried a stock of cheap, pine-box coffins. They were covered with black cloth, lined with muslin, and probably cost about $20 or $25 dollars each. When needed, they furnished one of these boxes to a bereaved family, and charged as much as $200 against the burial fund. One former mine superintendent told me that on one occasion, "when the burial fund was flush," he supplied a coffin that

cost $30, and the mine owners required him to charge $300 against the burial fund.[37]

Friends and neighbors of the family normally dug the graves, though the mining company or the community provided freshly dug burial spots for miners with no relatives. In some instances, whether there was a disaster or fatal mishap that took the life of one person, other miners dug graves out a sense of responsibility or as a tribute to the deceased.

Most families held wakes for their dead unless the bodies were too badly decomposed. Then simple graveside services sufficed. The funeral directors I talked with in central Appalachia maintained that there is no difference between the funeral for someone killed in a coal mine today and any other service. This was also true, in most instances, for fatal mining accidents in the past. The funeral was generally held in the home or church, with the family and friends present to pay their last respects. With huge accidents, however, entire communities were affected. George Korson in *Coal Dust on the Fiddle* reports that after the Monongah mine explosion, "for several days the undertaker's black wagon toiled up and down Monongah's narrow muddy streets, making so many stops that there was hardly a gate in the camp without its gruesome sign of death."[38]

Home funerals could become extremely crowded when entire communities turned out to pay their respects. Joint funerals for all miners killed were sometimes held in churches or the village square, which alleviated some of the congestion and offered the community a better opportunity to mourn all of the dead.[39] Ministers from all faiths descended to assist and made every effort to avoid conflicting funeral services. These ministers provided a variety of services for the families in addition to preaching at the funeral. They offered comfort, support, and in most cases broke the news of their loved one's death. Rex Lucas, in his extensive study of a contemporary mining accident, reported that mine officials notified the member of the clergy listed by the miner. The religious leader then contacted the family and informed them of the demise of their loved one.[40]

Except when bodies could not be recovered or when, as in the disaster in Farmington, West Virginia, in 1968, the mine was sealed with the trapped workers inside, the dead were interred in the ground with a simple ceremony. Most survivors wanted their loved ones buried in the family graveyard or near relatives in a community or church cemetery. Some counties assumed the responsibility of burying miners with no next of kin, though they segregated African-American graves from those of white Americans and occasionally buried more than one miner in a grave. Many mining organizations provided a company cemetery for the interment of its employees, whether they died from a fatal accident or natural causes.

Unfortunately, as with other small graveyards, many of these company cemeteries have been deserted and have fallen into ruin. When the coal was depleted and the company moved out, the graveyards were forgotten and left to disappear. A good example is the one known as "Little Egypt," where the remains of many of the victims of the Jed, West Virginia, explosion on March 26, 1912, were interred:

> Today, if you ask about the graveyard where they were so hastily buried, you'll be told that it's not possible to find any graves. . . . The graves were never tended to, and the identification tags fell off the markers—if there was ever any put there—from the stakes driven into the ground as a headpiece. . . . For a time, only the clay showed where the graves were, and then the brush and brambles, which grow so profusely in the moist mountain climate, obliterated the last evidences of a graveyard. . . . The people living nearby needed garden space. They cut the saplings, the briers, the so-called trash, and burned it above the bones of the unfortunates. Some hapless Ukrainian or Muscovite from the steepes of Russia, or a Sicilian lies now below a potato patch, or a Big Boy tomato vine.[41]

Coal Mining and Death in Contemporary Central Appalachia

Luckily, as with most other things in central Appalachia, the coal mining industry has changed dramatically. A disaster like the one at Monongah, West Virginia, will probably never happen again. While an occasional death may occur as a result of a freak accident or a violation of safety standards, the emphasis on safety and the use of sophisticated technology significantly diminish the possibility of any major catastrophe. Methane detectors, roof bolting machines, coal dust control mechanisms, modes of detecting the presence of carbon monoxide and carbon dioxide, and modern machinery utilized in excavating the coal make mining relatively safe. Today's miner need not face the hazards of afterdamp, blackdamp, excessive methane and coal dust, rock falls, slate falls, or searching for the bodies of the dead as in the first three decades of the twentieth century.[42]

Summary

Now when I die, good woman don't you wear no black.
Now when I die, good woman don't you wear no black.
For if you do, my ghost will come a-creepin' back.
—Tom Clarence Ashley and Guinn Foster, "Haunted Road Blues"

In the early years of mountain settlement, familism and neighborliness took over when families were in need, particularly when someone was dying. Neighbors and kin provided home remedies and later made every effort to either bring a doctor to the home or take the ailing individual to medical care. Neighbors did the chores and provided food so that close family members could concentrate on their loved one. Some neighbors even took part in the death watch, where care was provided for a dying person until he or she either expired or improved.

To a slightly lesser degree, central Appalachians still practice neighborliness and familism. While providing assistance to a dying individual and the family, neighbors and kinfolk continue to take part in a death watch, but not as often as in the past. The principle scene of the vigil has changed from the home to the hospital, and usually the immediate family, nurse, or doctor are present at death. As in previous years, participants look for signs of impending death such as premonitions, visions, and the death rattle.

Prior to embalming, friends and relatives were notified and helped prepare the corpse for burial. They thoroughly cleaned the body and combed the hair. A shroud or regular clothing, usually black, was placed on the corpse, and it was put in a coffin or casket for burial. Embalming and the rise of the funeral industry has revolutionized this practice. Family and friends no longer worry about whether their loved one will be buried alive nor do they need to prepare the body for interment. Instead, a licensed practitioner prepares and preserves the body in the funeral home. Families are able to schedule wakes and funerals at their convenience since corpses no longer need to be disposed of as soon as possible to prevent disease and undesirable odors. Relatives and friends now have time to travel long distances and still attend the wake and the funeral.

Early wakes were mixtures of diverse practices brought to the area by migrants. Before embalming they lasted only through the night of death with burial the following day, though friends and relatives usually sat up the entire time with the deceased. Some wakes were quiet and solemn, while others were fun-filled with jokes, dancing, and singing. When embalming and funeral establishments penetrated the mountains, the wake moved from the home to the church and, more commonly today, the funeral home. Today the wake is mainly an opportunity for friends to pay their respects to the dead and to the family and to view the deceased for a final time. Instead of an all-night affair, the typical visitation is usually held in the evening for about three hours.

The wake and the funeral have developed into two distinct mourning rituals. Today the funeral is mostly a private affair for the family, but in early central Appalachia both were considered social events and were well attended. Since social activities were scarce, many mountain people looked upon wakes and funerals as opportunities to visit with friends and relatives they hadn't seen in a long time and to provide food and care for the grieving. The funeral followed the day after the wake in the home or at the cemetery. Most mountaineers wore black and truly demonstrated their mourning by weeping and wailing during the hellfire-and-brimstone service. These emotional services lasted over an hour, sometimes conducted by several different preachers. Circuit riders or traveling members of the clergy officiated at some of the earliest funerals, but their scarce numbers led mountaineers who felt the call to step forward to preside. In addition, since these traveling ministers could not always be counted on to be available at the time of death, a delayed form of funeral, known as funeralizing, became popular, which allowed mountaineers to show their respect for loved ones, sometimes years later, even when a formal funeral could not be held at the time of death.

Funerals today are less emotional than in the past but otherwise have changed little in content. Most have prayer, music (instrumental or vocal), an obituary (used less frequently today), scripture reading, and a sermon. When the ceremony is concluded, mourners still file by the casket (although it is more likely to be closed than it was in the past), with the closest relatives generally leaving last. Today, however, the type of service ranges from private, night, and weekend funerals to graveside and memorial services.

In the early years the funeral culminated in a procession to the place of interment, normally a church or family cemetery. As friends and relatives followed behind, pallbearers carried the corpse to the grave or loaded the coffin onto a wagon, sled, or hearse for transportation. These burial grounds were often on hills to provide better protection for the bodies from the elements, so travel to the grave was often treacherous. Today a hearse or four-wheel-drive vehicle leads the procession of cars to the graveyard, which is almost always easily accessible. Law enforcement officers sometimes direct traffic for the funeral cortege but in many cases the hearse announces the oncoming procession with flashing lights and flags. Mountain people often show their respect for the long line of flagged cars by stopping or slowing down.

Early central Appalachians were buried without coffins or caskets. However, permanent settlement and reverence for the dead led residents to construct containers to protect their dead. These early mummy-shaped coffins were usually made from wood by a neighbor or friend and lined with quilts, cheap cotton material, or whatever was at hand or inexpensive. The highlanders then dug the grave so that the cheap coffin was at least partially protected from the earth. Eventually, as communities grew, coffin making developed into a profession and funeral homes provided coffins or caskets as one of their services. The wooden rough box was then introduced as a crude burial vault. In the 1900s durable, attractive metal caskets replaced wooden coffins as the most popular form of burial container and remain the most popular today. Many cemeteries now require metal and concrete vaults since they are stronger than other types and slow to decay.

In the past, male members of mountain communities typically dug the graves in family and church cemeteries, and they did so out of a sense of duty, an attempt to relieve the burden of the family, a display of respect for the deceased, and a chance to engage in social intercourse. In addition to making their way to the graveyard, which was often nearly inaccessible, and deciding where to dig, these men often had to penetrate frozen ground, excavate rock, and eliminate water seepage using only hand tools, such as picks and shovels. As the funeral industry grew, public and perpetual-care cemeteries increased in popularity while many family and church graveyards fell into disuse. Today, friends and neighbors only occasionally dig graves. Professionals employed by the funeral home or the cemetery use backhoes and mechanized equipment to remove the dirt from the burial spot.

Before the casket is lowered into the ground, some ministers provide a committal service, which at least partially resembles the earlier graveside funerals. A short, fairly unemotional ceremony, with the casket closed in most cases, precedes final interment. Highlanders still occasionally place objects in the coffin, but they no longer watch as neighbors and friends lower the casket into the ground. Today employees of the funeral home or cemetery use lowering devices after mourners have left to bury the dead.

Although the first graves in central Appalachia were not marked, later settlers used wooden sticks (often in the form of a cross) and fieldstones to identify burial spots. Some mountaineers crudely chiseled identification data into the rock until stone carving developed as an art in mountain culture. These stone memorials carved from granite and marble provided a better way to mark a grave and are now available in a variety of sizes, shapes, and colors. Loved ones can specify long inscriptions or epitaphs or request symbols, insignias, and emblems on these markers. In the past upright headstones and some footstones characterized traditional graveyards, but today many public and perpetual-care cemeteries require ground-level markers. Though they are limited in size and shape, they too can be engraved to meet the wishes of the grieving family.

Earth burial remains the predominant mode of interment in central Appalachia, though people throughout the world practice various forms of disposal, including open-air burial, mortuary cannibalism, cremation, water burial, entombment, cryogenic suspension, and donation to medical science. Very few mountaineers have ever been cremated, and rarely do they donate their bodies to medical science. To my knowledge, no resident has ever chosen open-air disposal, mortuary cannibalism, water burial, or cryogenic suspension. Today mausoleums are being constructed in some areas, and a few highlanders are taking advantage of the chance to spend eternity above ground.

After the funeral and burial, mourners looked for ways to remember their dead. In the past, family members kept objects belonging to the loved one, made jewelry from the hair of the deceased, took photographs of the body, built grave houses to protect the burial site, placed favorite objects on the grave, sent mourning cards, wore black, and tolled bells. Grave markers were important memorials, and some mountaineers still attach photographs of the decedent to the marker. Placing flowers on the grave is still popular, but many cemeteries restrict the kind and number of floral arrangements. Wreaths on doors of businesses and residences seldom announce a death in contemporary central Appalachia, and black is no longer required or expected mourning attire. A few mountaineers continue to keep the ribbons from flower arrangements and use the family Bible to preserve mementoes of a departed loved one.

Memorial Day evolved into a specific and concrete way to remember the dead. Its commemoration in contemporary central Appalachia resembles the national observation to a greater degree than it did in previous years, but many families, kinship groups, churches, and communities still gather on their own established days to honor the dead. Although earlier residents took the opportunity to clean graves and beautify the cemetery, today employees of the graveyard usually take care of these tasks. Mourners come from across the country to bring flowers to the grave, and some still bring food, though contemporary repasts seldom resemble the old "dinner on the ground." Memorial Day, however it is commemorated, would not be complete without a ceremony either at the church or in the cemetery.

Death perhaps became such an important part of central Appalachian culture because it was so commonplace, so ever present, so imminent. They dealt with what life handed them by respecting death, commemorating it, singing about it. Still, they did their best to improve their circumstances. Unfortunately one of the most promising opportunities turned out to be one of the most deadly. When coal mining was introduced in the mountains, many residents left their farms to seek employment in the mines. In the early years, death was a constant companion for these underground workers. Methane gas, coal dust, open-flame lamps, unstable black powder, blackdamp, afterdamp, roof falls, electrocution, and black lung made work treacherous.

Mostly the bodies of miners killed on the job were transported home for burial in a family or church cemetery, though corpses of miners with no known families frequently were interred in company graveyards. In major mine disasters, there was little time to observe common burial rituals. Workers frequently identified and prepared the bodies underground before placing them in coffins and transporting them to the surface. Families then usually collected their dead and buried them in their family or church cemeteries. Later undertakers frequently performed their services inside the mine or transported the corpses to their place of business for quick preservation before the bodies were released to the families. No matter where they died, the dead were revered by central Appalachians. Miners working to support their families, soldiers fighting overseas, and emigrants to other parts of the country still received the same visitations, the same funerals, the same burials, and the same memorializations as central Appalachians who spent their whole lives in the mountains.

Changes in Death and Dying Attitudes and Practices

Central Appalachians no longer look on death or treat dying in the same manner as their ancestors. Though slow to change, the residents of the area no longer react much differently from those in the rest of the United States when a loved one dies. After each interview conducted in central Appalachia, I asked the respondent why he or she felt that attitudes and practices related to death and dying had changed. More than half the interviewees indicated that the changes were related to alterations in family relationships.

As I noted earlier, twentieth-century mountain culture has been characterized by diminishing family cohesion and solidarity. While husbands and wives worked together to support their families in the early years, in the mid-1900s they began to go in separate directions to seek employment. These workers often went to factories in the Northeast and Midwest, where they came in contact with different ideas and practices and brought them back home. Residents of the mountains could no longer remain isolated from the rest of the world. Soldiers too brought back tales from abroad and newcomers to the mountains arrived with their own culture. Residents of the central highlands began to absorb an enormous amount of information about attitudes and behavior patterns of people in other parts of the United States and gradually assimilated them into their own culture. For example, the use of metal caskets and embalming in the mountains resulted from interaction with people outside the boundaries of central Appalachia.

This migration pattern was instrumental in altering mountain society. Mountaineers, especially those working far from home, had to become more independent, and as a result they also became less altruistic and less concerned with their families. Family members stopped working and playing together like they did in the past and some even became estranged from one another. For example, an elderly woman in Gilmer County, West Virginia, told me that she knew brothers and sisters who hadn't seen one another in twenty or thirty years.

Once mountain families stopped living close to one another and mobility increased, many traditions older residents adhered to vanished. Church bells could no longer convey news of a death to everyone who needed to know. Sisters were no longer a short ride from their dying brothers. Family members simply couldn't provide care for their dying loved ones any longer. When your parent died it was easier to pay a funeral establishment to prepare the body, supervise the wake and funeral, perform the burial, and take care of the details. Survivors commenced burying their dead in public or perpetual-care cemeteries where employees would care for the graves since they couldn't. These changes don't mean that familism is no longer apparent in central Appalachia, it still definitely is part of the culture, but they do signal its waning influence.

Like familism, diminishing neighborliness has dramatically changed how mountaineers deal with death. Almost every person I interviewed declared that members of mountain communities are not as close today as they once were. My interviewees lamented that their neighbors are less likely than their ancestors to perform the chores when someone is ailing or dead, participate in a death watch, prepare the body and build a burial receptacle, dig the grave, attend the funeral and committal service, and bury the dead. In addition, many felt that neighbors are in "such a big hurry" that they don't stop to help a family deal with its grief when a relative expires. They noted that while early highlanders would stop their work and provide whatever support the family needed, modern-day mountain dwellers hesitate to leave their jobs to attend a funeral or burial service. A woman in western North Carolina said that today "neighbors attend a visitation for a couple of hours and then completely abandon the family."

Lack of neighborliness perhaps reflects the larger movement toward greater anonymity in the area. As central Appalachia entered the twentieth century, it became more urbanized, population increased, and interaction between community members decreased. Further, urbanization resulted in greater goods and services available and better technology. Family members and neighbors not only didn't have the time to care personally for their dying and dead relatives, they also didn't have to do it all themselves anymore. Doctors, nurses, and medical centers replaced home care for the ill and dying. The funeral industry spread into mountain communities, and funeral directors and their assistants began to take over virtually every task once performed by the family. Families found it easier, both mentally and physically, to pay professionals for these services.

Until recently, home was the only place central Appalachians died. Today hospitals, nursing homes, and hospices allow people the freedom to live their lives without worrying about caring for their dying family members. Naturally, this rise of the total institution has dramatically changed the entire atmosphere of dying. The family can concentrate on its own needs rather than the needs of the dying family member. And once someone dies, the family can send the body directly from the hospital to the funeral home, where trained professionals can continue the care.

This easy transition led to changes in how mountaineers honored their dead as well. Preparation of the body shifted from the residence of the deceased to the embalming room. The wake became known as the visitation, moved from the residence to the church and funeral home, and shortened since it was no longer necessary to perform an all-night vigil. When crowds became too large for the home, the primary site of the funeral was transferred to the church and funeral home chapel. Family and church burial grounds were replaced by community cemeteries since many residents of urban areas didn't own land on which they could be buried, have a family with a graveyard, or belong to a church that had a cemetery. Professionals also had technology at their disposal that a mountain family could not begin to take advantage of. Embalming, metal caskets, concrete and metal vaults, mechanized lowering devices, machines to dig graves, and other forms of technological advancement have made it substantially easier to bury the dead.

The Future

The future holds continued change for mountaineers. Based on my extensive interviewing, an examination of the literature, and an analysis of trends within the funeral industry and mountain society, I predict that traditional ways will eventually die out. Care for the dying will certainly shift almost completely from the home to total institutions. Hospitals are already available in most rural areas, and these will become larger and better equipped as dependence on their services increases. While most early highlanders would never have considered relinquishing the care of their elderly and incapacitated to outsiders, the dependence on extended-care facilities such as nursing homes and hospices is escalating.

Reliance on technology will characterize disposal of the dead as well. More and more mountaineers will explore better and alternative ways to preserve themselves. I suspect a few will even choose cryogenic suspension. Caskets will become even more elaborate (if that's possible) as people focus more on the aesthetics of death rather than on the process. I have little doubt that casket manufacturers will attempt to further extend the durability of coffins and burial vaults.

Perhaps forms of burial will see the most change. As people get farther away from their earliest ancestors in the area more and more family cemeteries will be deserted. Similarly, church graveyards will see less use while perpetual-care cemeteries will undoubtedly increase in popularity, as will mausoleums. More mountaineers will choose cremation as the amount of available burial space decreases or they consider preservation of their bodies less crucial.

Honoring the dead will become less important and take less time. Most likely, the wake or visitation will remain short and change very little in structure. Funerals are already short, but they will probably become even shorter and concentrate on the needs of the survivors. More people will contribute money to charity in the name of the deceased rather than send flowers. Mountaineers will, at least in obvious ways, honor the dead less often since yearly memorial services will likely decline as well.

Overall, central Appalachia will lose its characteristic isolation, its family-centered ways, its tradition. Urbanization, acculturation, and technology, even with their positive influences, have wrought far-reaching and sometimes unwelcome transformations to the culture of the area. Familism, neighborliness, and caring for the dead and dying were not simply quaint practices for these people, but rather important parts of life that gave mountaineers their identity. Before too much longer, residents will find themselves to be not much different from the rest of the country, in life or in death.

Notes

Introduction

1. L. A. DeSpelder and A. L. Strickland, *The Last Dance: Encountering Death and Dying*, 2d ed. (Palo Alto, Calif.: Mayfield, 1987), 17.
2. Ibid., 9.
3. J. B. Kamerman, *Death in the Midst of Life* (Englewood Cliffs, N.J.: Prentice Hall, 1988), 3.
4. Ibid., 2.
5. DeSpelder and Strickland, *The Last Dance*, 499.
6. S. Stoddard, *The Hospice Movement* (New York: Vintage Books, 1978).
7. D. Sudnow, *Passing On: The Social Organization of Dying* (Englewood Cliffs, N.J.: Prentice Hall, 1967).
8. R. J. Kastenbaum, *Death, Society, and Human Experience* (New York: Macmillan, 1991), 4.
9. E. Kubler-Ross, *On Death and Dying* (New York: Macmillan, 1969); J. Mitford, *The American Way of Death* (New York: Simon and Schuster, 1963); R. W. Habenstein and W. M. Lamers, *The History of American Funeral Directing* (Milwaukee: Bulfin Printers, 1962).
10. DeSpelder and Strickland, *The Last Dance*, 36.
11. Kamerman, *Death in the Midst of Life*, 4.
12. S. G. Wilcox and M. Sutton, *Understanding Death and Dying: An Interdisciplinary Approach*, 3d ed. (Palo Alto, Calif.: Mayfield, 1985).
13. J. C. Campbell, *The Southern Highlander and His Homeland* (New York: Russell Sage Foundation, 1921), 10.
14. J. Gaventa, *Power and Powerlessness: Quiescence and Rebellion in an Appalachian Valley* (Urbana: University of Illinois Press, 1980), 33.
15. J. E. Weller, *Yesterday's People* (Lexington: University of Kentucky Press, 1966), 9.
16. H. B. Lee, *Bloodletting in Appalachia* (Parsons, W.Va.: McClain, 1969), ix.
17. See "Why Study Appalachia?" in *Appalachia: Social Context Past and Present*, ed. B. Ergood and B. E. Kuhre (Dubuque: Kendall/Hunt, 1976), 7, for support of this contention.
18. R. R. Widner, "The Four Appalachias," in *Appalachia: Its People, Heritage, and Problems*, ed. F. S. Riddel (Dubuque: Kendall/Hunt, 1974), 1.
19. Ibid., 8.
20. H. M. Caudill, *Night Comes to the Cumberlands* (Boston: Little, Brown, 1963), 5–9.

21. P. W. Gainer, *Folk Songs from the West Virginia Hills* (Grantsville, W.Va.: Seneca Books, 1975), xv; Widner, "The Four Appalachias," 2.

22. P. L. Jewell, "Early Family Settlers and Settlements of Southern Appalachia," in *Appalachia: Family Tradition in Transition,* ed. E. M. Essin III (Johnson City: East Tennessee State University Advisory Council, 1975), 28.

23. Caudill, *Night Comes to the Cumberlands,* 6.

24. Ibid., 29.

25. A. P. Hannum, *Look Back with Love: A Recollection of the Blue Ridge* (New York: Vanguard, 1969), 19.

26. P. M. Fink, "Religion in America," in *Appalachia: Family Tradition in Transition,* ed. Essin, 36–37.

27. Caudill, *Night Comes to the Cumberlands,* 13.

28. Weller, *Yesterday's People,* 10.

29. Ibid., 11.

30. R. Gazaway, *The Longest Mile* (Baltimore: Penguin Books, 1974), 63.

31. B. Ergood, "Toward a Definition of Appalachia," in *Appalachia: Social Context Past and Present,* ed. Ergood and Kuhre, 37.

32. C. N. Buck, *The Code of the Mountains* (New York: W. J. Watt, 1915), 69.

Chapter 1: Familism, Neighborliness, and the Death Watch

The epigraph is from the Blue Sky Boys, "Little Bessie." Recorded on Jan. 25, 1938, in Charlotte, N.C., originally issued on Bluebird B-8017 and Montgomery Ward M-7470, and reissued on Bluebird AXM2-5525. © Berwick Music Corp. Used by permission.

1. T. Parsons, *The Social System* (Glencoe, Ill.: Free Press, 1951); W. Ogburn and M. F. Nimkoff, *Technology and the Changing Family* (Boston: Houghton Mifflin, 1955).

2. J. K. Crissman and A. P. Buteau, "Actual Family Size and Desired Family Size: A Comparison of Central Appalachian and Non–Central Appalachian Residents in an Urban Environment," in *Building Family Strengths: A Time of Change,* ed. J. G. King and L. Sydorenko (Jonesboro: Arkansas State University, 1989), 93–103; K. Keniston, "The Myth of Family Independence," in *Marriage and the Family in a Changing Society,* ed. J. M. Henslin, 2d ed. (New York: Free Press, 1985), 27–33; J. J. Kronenfeld and M. L. Whicker, "Feminist Movements and Changes in Sex Roles: The Influence of Technology," *Sociological Focus* 19, no. 1 (1986): 47–58; S. A. Levitan and R. S. Belous, "Trends in Fertility," in *Marriage and the Family in a Changing Society,* ed. Henslin, 77–84; Parsons, *The Social System;* T. Parsons, "The American Family: Its Relations to Personality and to Social Structure," in *Family, Socialization, and Interaction Process,* ed. T. Parsons and R. F. Bales (Glencoe, Ill.: Free Press, 1955), 3–34.

3. R. K. Kelley, *Courtship, Marriage, and the Family* (New York: Harcourt, Brace, and World, 1969); L. Zakuta, "Equality in North American Marriage," in *Marriage and the Family in a Changing Society,* ed. Henslin, 67–76.

4. J. K. Crissman, "The Impact of the Urban Milieu on the Appalachian Family Type," in *Too Few Tomorrows: Urban Appalachians in the 1980's,* ed. P. J. Obermiller and W. W. Philliber (Boone, N.C.: Appalachian Consortium Press, 1987), 81–88; J. K. Crissman, "Family Type and Familism in Contemporary Appalachia," *Southern Rural Sociology* 6 (1989): 29–44; Parsons, "American Family," 3–34; T. Parsons, "Conclusion: Levels of Culture Generality and the Process of Differentiation," in *Family, Socialization, and Interaction Process,* ed. Parsons and Bales, 353–96; M. Zelditch, Jr., "Role Differentiation in the Nuclear Family: A Comparative Study," in *Family, Socialization, and Interaction Process,* ed. Parsons and Bales, 307–52.

5. Crissman, "Family Type," 29–44; K. Melville, *Marriage and the Family Today* (New York: Random House, 1983); Parsons, "American Family," 3–34; A. Skolnick, *The Intimate Environment: Exploring Marriage and the Family,* 2d ed. (Boston: Little, Brown, 1978).

6. G. A. Theodorson and A. G. Theodorson, *Modern Dictionary of Sociology* (New York: Thomas Y. Crowell, 1969), 146.

7. R. O. Blood and D. M. Wolfe, *Husbands and Wives: The Dynamics of Married Living* (New York: Free Press, 1960); C. C. Zimmerman, *Family and Civilization* (New York: Harper and Brothers, 1948).

8. M. McKee and I. Robertson, *Social Problems* (New York: Random House, 1975); Melville, *Marriage and the Family Today;* Skolnick, *The Intimate Environment;* J. H. Turner, *Sociology: The Science of Human Organization,* 2d ed. (Chicago: Nelson-Hall, 1985).

9. Parsons, "American Family," 3–34. Sociologists generally distinguish between two types of family in American society. The nuclear family consists of the husband, wife, and their own or adopted children (if any). There are exceptions such as the broken nuclear family (by divorce, death, or separation) and the incomplete nuclear family. The extended family consists of at least three generations living together and functioning as an economic unit.

10. D. R. Blisten, "Three Major Types of Family Organization: Comparisons and Contrasts," in *Sociological Essays and Research,* ed. C. H. Anderson (Homewood, Ill.: Dorsey Press, 1974), 335.

11. E. Durkheim, *The Division of Labor in Society,* trans. George Simpson (New York: Free Press, 1947).

12. R. Collins and M. Makowsky, *The Discovery of Society,* 2d ed. (New York: Random House, 1978).

13. W. G. Frost, "Our Contemporary Ancestors in the Southern Mountains," *Atlantic Monthly,* Mar. 1899, 311–19; G. E. Vincent, "The Retarded Frontier," *American Journal of Sociology* 4, no. 1 (1898): 1–20.

14. H. Kephart, *Our Southern Highlanders* (Knoxville: University of Tennessee Press, 1980), 18.

15. E. T. Breathitt, "Urban and Rural America," *Appalachia: A Journal of the Appalachian Regional Commission* 1 (June–July 1968): 88–89; M. V. Carter and G. L. Osborne, "Appalachia in the Information Age: A New Chance for Change?" *The Rural Sociologist* 7, no. 1 (1987): 38–43; H. M. Caudill, "Jaded

Old Land of Bright New Promise," in *Appalachia in the Sixties: Decade of Reawakening*, ed. D. S. Walls and J. B. Stephenson (Lexington: University of Kentucky Press, 1972), 240–46; O. B. Graff, "The Needs of Education," in *The Southern Appalachian Region: A Survey*, ed. T. R. Ford (Lexington: University of Kentucky Press, 1962), 188–200; K. W. Lee, "Fair Elections in West Virginia," in *Appalachia in the Sixties*, ed. Walls and Stephenson, 164–76; P. Schrag, "The School and Politics," in *Appalachia in the Sixties*, ed. Walls and Stephenson, 219–23; R. Straus, "Health Barriers," *Appalachia: A Journal of the Appalachian Regional Commission* 1 (Apr. 1968): 21.

16. Vincent, "Retarded Frontier," 4.

17. Kephart, *Our Southern Highlanders*, 385.

18. K. Kahn, *Hillbilly Women* (Garden City, N.Y.: Doubleday, 1973).

19. T. A. Arcury and J. D. Porter, "Household Composition in Appalachian Kentucky in 1900," *Journal of Family History* 10, no. 2 (1985): 183–95.

20. Vincent, "Retarded Frontier," 4.

21. V. C. Jones, *The Hatfields and the McCoys* (Atlanta: Mockingbird Books, 1976), 4.

22. Kephart, *Our Southern Highlanders*, 387.

23. Caudill, *Night Comes to the Cumberlands*, 49.

24. Ibid.

25. Ibid.; Jones, *Hatfields*.

26. Jones, *Hatfields*, 1.

27. V. M. Slone, *What My Heart Wants to Tell* (Washington, D.C.: New Republic Books, 1979).

28. B. L. Burman, *Children of Noah: Glimpses of Unknown America* (New York: Julian Messner, 1951); R. M. Day, "Pride and Poverty: An Impressionistic View of the Family in the Cumberlands of Appalachia," in *Appalachia: Family Traditions in Transition*, ed. Essin, 71–80; J. B. Stephenson, *Shiloh: A Mountain Community* (Lexington: University of Kentucky Press, 1968).

29. J. S. Brown and H. K. Schwarzweller, "The Appalachian Family," in *Appalachia: Its People, Heritage, and Problems*, ed. Riddel, 69.

30. G. L. Hicks, "Kinship and Sex Roles," in *Appalachia: Social Context Past and Present*, ed. Ergood and Kuhre, 210–19; L. Shackelford and B. Weinberg, *Our Appalachia* (New York: Hill and Wang, 1977); C. Marshall, *Christy* (New York: McGraw-Hill, 1967).

31. J. H. Giles, *Forty Acres and No Mules*, 2d ed. (Boston: Houghton Mifflin, 1967); L. Jones, "Appalachian Values," in *Voices from the Hills: Selected Readings in Southern Appalachia*, ed. R. J. Higgs and A. N. Manning (New York: Frederick Unger, 1975), 507–17.

32. J. Stuart, *Taps for Private Tussie* (Atlanta: Mockingbird Books, 1975).

33. Weller, *Yesterday's People*.

34. Brown and Schwarzweller, "The Appalachian Family."

35. Day, "Pride and Poverty"; Gazaway, *The Longest Mile*.

36. Weller, *Yesterday's People*.

37. P. L. Heller and G. M. Quesada, "Rural Familism: An Interregional

Analysis," *Rural Sociology* 42 (Summer 1977): 220–40; P. L. Heller et al., "Familism in Rural and Urban America: Critique and Reconceptualization of a Construct," *Rural Sociology* 46 (Fall 1981): 446–64.

38. J. K. Crissman and T. G. Jelen, "Familistic Tendencies of Central Appalachian Migrants in an Urban Environment," paper presented at the annual meeting of the Illinois Sociological Association, Chicago, October 1987; Crissman, "Family Type," 29–44.

39. J. Fetterman, *Stinking Creek* (New York: E. P. Dutton, 1967), 23.

40. C. Reeder and J. Reeder, *Shenandoah Heritage: The Story of the People before the Park* (Washington, D.C.: Potomac Appalachian Trail Club, 1978), 19.

41. D. Dunn, *Cades Cove: The Life and Death of a Southern Appalachian Community* (Knoxville: University of Tennessee Press, 1988), 186.

42. K. T. Erikson, *Everything in Its Path* (New York: Simon and Schuster, 1976), 114.

43. Shackelford and Weinberg, *Our Appalachia*, 19.

44. Ibid., 19–20.

45. Campbell, *The Southern Highlander*, 197.

46. D. F. Hirt, "Semi-retained Rural Society on the Appalachian Family-Life during the Post–World War II Period," in *Appalachia: Family Traditions in Transition*, ed. Essin, 56–57.

47. J. W. Raine, *The Land of Saddlebags: A Study of the Mountain People of Appalachia* (New York: Council of Women for Home Missions and Missionary Education Movement of the United States and Canada, 1924), 88.

48. Fetterman, *Stinking Creek*, 47.

49. W. L. Montell, *Ghosts along the Cumberland: Deathlore in the Kentucky Foothills* (Knoxville: University of Tennessee Press, 1975).

50. W. D. Campbell, *Brother to a Dragonfly* (New York: Seabury Press, 1977), 148.

51. L. R. Aiken, *Dying, Death, and Bereavement* (Boston: Allyn and Bacon, 1985), 96.

52. E. S. Sanderson, *County Scott and Its Mountain Folk* (Huntsville, Tenn.: Esther Sharp Sanderson, 1958), 61.

53. J. F. Day, *Bloody Ground* (Garden City, N.Y.: Doubleday, Doran, 1941), 38.

54. Raine, *Land of Saddlebags*, 86.

55. Campbell, *The Southern Highlander*, 197.

56. H. P. Scalf, "The Death and Burial of 'Boney Bill' Scalf," *Appalachian Heritage* 2, no. 2 (1974): 58.

57. P. Ariés, *Western Attitudes toward Death*, trans. Patricia M. Ranum (Baltimore: Johns Hopkins University Press, 1974).

58. R. S. Walker, *Lookout: The Story of a Mountain* (Kingsport, Tenn.: Southern, 1941), 187.

59. J. Thomas, *Devil's Ditties* (Chicago: W. Wilbur Hatfield, 1931), 19.

60. C. G. Strub and L. G. "Darke" Frederick, *The Principles and Practice of Embalming*, 4th ed. (Dallas: L. G. Frederick, 1967), 55.

Chapter 2: Preparation of the Body

1. DeSpelder and Strickland, *The Last Dance*, 41–42.
2. P. D. Bardis, *History of Thanatology* (Washington, D.C.: University Press of America, 1981), 27; Habenstein and Lamers, *The History of American Funeral Directing*.
3. Habenstein and Lamers, *The History of American Funeral Directing*, 39
4. Ibid., 62–63
5. Kubler-Ross, *On Death and Dying*; Habenstein and Lamers, *The History of American Funeral Directing*, 62–63.
6. Bardis, *History of Thanatology*, 12–52.
7. DeSpelder and Strickland, *The Last Dance*, 49.
8. D. Chidester, *Patterns of Transcendence: Religion, Death, and Dying* (Belmont, Calif.: Wadsworth, 1990), 57.
9. E. A. W. Budge, *The Mummy* (New York: Causeway Books, 1972), 173.
10. Ibid., 177–78.
11. Bardis, *History of Thanatology*, 20.
12. Budge, *The Mummy*, 178–79.
13. Ibid., 179.
14. Ibid., 356; "The History of Cats," *Pet Care Report* (Knoxville: Whittle Communications, 1988), 4.
15. Montell, *Ghosts*; J. Stewart, "Superstitions," *Appalachian Heritage* 1, no. 3 (1973): 9–16.
16. Aiken, *Dying, Death*, 96.
17. M. Coffin, *Death in Early America* (Nashville: Thomas Nelson, 1976), 72.
18. Montell, *Ghosts*, 68.
19. M. Bettis et al., "The Care of the East Tennessee Dead," in *Glimpses of Southern Appalachian Folk Culture: Papers in Memory of Norbert F. Riedl*, ed. C. H. Faulkner and C. K. Buckles, Tennessee Anthropological Association Miscellaneous Paper no. 3, n.d., 108–9; J. C. Cash, *Among My Klediments* (Grand Rapids, Mich.: Zondervan, 1979), 24; A. Crosby, "Death in Cades Cove," in *Appalachia: When Yesterday Is Today*, ed. Students at the University of Tennessee (Knoxville, 1965), 1–3; G. T. Russell, *Call Me Hillbilly* (Alcoa, Tenn.: Russell, 1974), 68.
20. Bettis et al., "East Tennessee Dead," 108.
21. Montell, *Ghosts*, 68.
22. Crosby, "Death in Cades Cove," 1–3.
23. Day, *Bloody Ground*, 185; J. Vogel, *This Happened in the Hills of Kentucky* (Grand Rapids, Mich.: Zondervan, 1952), 127; F. Wolford, *Mountain Memories* (Parsons, W.Va.: McClain, 1975).
24. T. Evans and M. Travis, "John L. Richards, Stonecutter," in *Mountain Trace*, ed. K. G. Gilbert (Parsons, W.Va.: McClain, 1980), book 1, 295–310; T. Kromer, "Michael Kohler," in *Stories and Verse of West Virginia 2*, ed. J. Comstock (Richmond, Va.: Jim Comstock, 1974), 320–58; S. W. Stidham, *Trails into Cutshin County: A History of the Pioneers of Leslie County, Kentucky* (Corbin, Ky.: Sadie W. Stidham, 1978), 124.

25. Rigor mortis, the rigidity of the muscles, generally begins approximately five to seven hours after death and ends within twenty-four to thirty-six hours. It starts in the head, spreads to the arms and trunk, and finally reaches the legs and feet. Rigor leaves the body in the reverse direction, beginning in the feet and ending in the head. Heat accelerates rigor mortis and cold retards its dissolution. When it is gone, the body goes limp and decomposes rapidly. See, for example, Strub and Frederick, *The Principles and Practice of Embalming.*

26. Bettis et al., "East Tennessee Dead," 109; "Death and Burial in the Mountains," *Appalachian Heritage* 2, no. 1 (1974): 58; L. S. Murdoch, *Almetta of Gabriel's Run* (New York: Meridian Press, 1917), 60; interviews conducted in Perkinsville, N.C., 1970, and Linn, W.Va., 1981.

27. Bettis et al., "East Tennessee Dead," 109; "Death and Burial," 57. J. Ehle, *The Winter People* (New York: Harper and Row, 1982), 170–71; B. W. Peterson, "Quiet Dignity," *Appalachian Heritage* 3, no. 2 (1975): 5–8.

28. Bettis et al., "East Tennessee Dead," 109.

29. Ibid.

30. See, for example, ibid., 109; Montell, *Ghosts,* 69; Russell, *Call Me Hillbilly,* 33; H. Sandberg, *The Wheel of Earth* (New York: McDowell, Obolensky, 1958), 374; supported by numerous interviews.

31. Evans and Travis, "John L. Richards," 302–3.

32. J. F. West, *Appalachian Dawn* (Durham, N.C.: Moore, 1973), 37.

33. Bettis et al., "East Tennessee Dead," 109; Russell, *Call Me Hillbilly,* 33.

34. Ehle, *Winter People,* 172–82; Evans and Travis, "John L. Richards," 302–3; Marshall, *Christy;* Montell, *Ghosts,* 69; R. R. Ratliff, *Return to the Promised Land, Appalachia* (Frankfort, Ky.: Kentucky Images, 1977), 31; J. Sherburne, *Stand like Men* (Boston: Houghton Mifflin, 1973), 11; J. Still, *River of Earth* (New York: Viking Press, 1940), 236; supported by numerous interviews.

35. P. G. Brewster et al., eds., *The Frank C. Brown Collection of North Carolina Folklore,* vol. 3 (Durham, N.C.: Duke University Press, 1952), 258; "Death and Burial," 59; supported by several interviews.

36. Bettis et al., "East Tennessee Dead," 109

37. Coffin, *Death in Early America,* 101

38. A. Huffman, *My Mountain Memories* (Philadelphia: Dorrance, 1953), 104; "Death and Burial," 58; H. Arnow, *Hunter's Horn* (New York: MacMillan, 1949), 322–23.

39. R. Huntington and P. Metcalf, *Celebrations of Death: An Anthropology of Mortuary Ritual* (Cambridge: Cambridge University Press, 1979), 45.

40. Ibid.

41. L. Furman, *The Quare Woman* (Boston: Little, Brown, 1925), 282–83.

42. Bettis et al., "East Tennessee Dead," 169; Sherburne, *Stand like Men,* 11; Russell, *Call Me Hillbilly,* 33.

43. Stidham, *Trails into Cutshin County,* 124.

44. W. Faulkner, *As I Lay Dying* (New York: Random House, 1964).

45. "Death and Burial," 59.

46. Scalf, "The Death and Burial of 'Boney Bill' Scalf," 58; T. Kromer, "Michael Kohler," 343; C. N. Buck, *When "Bearcat" Went Dry* (New York: W. J. Watt, 1918), 222–23.

47. Mitford, *The American Way of Death*, 194.

48. Ibid., 196

49. Chidester, *Patterns of Transcendence*, 278; DeSpelder and Strickland, *The Last Dance*, 179; H. K. Douglas, *I Rode with Stonewall* (Simons Island, Ga.: Mockingbird Books, 1989), 222; R. Meredith, *Mr. Lincoln's Camera Man: Matthew B. Brady*, 2d rev. ed. (New York: Dover, 1974), 280, 286.

50. C. N. Buck, *A Pagan of the Hills* (New York: Grosset and Dunlap, 1919), 197.

51. R. E. Plowman, *Twice out of Sight* (Berea, Ky.: Kentucky Imprints, 1982), 42–43.

52. DeSpelder and Strickland, *The Last Dance*, 190.

53. Information concerning modern embalming procedures was derived from interviews with licensed embalmers in Central Appalachia and M. E. Grant, Sr., "Chronological Order of Events in Embalming," in *Champion Expanding Encyclopedia of Mortuary Practice* (Springfield, Ohio: Champion, 1986), 2298–301.

54. Mitford, *The American Way of Death*, 71; supported by interviews.

Chapter 3: Burial Receptacles and Grave Digging

1. Bardis, *History of Thanatology*, 26; L. Carlson, *Caring for Your Own Dead* (Hinesburg, Vt.: Upper Access, 1987), 24; Habenstein and Lamers, *The History of American Funeral Directing*, 31.

2. Bardis, *History of Thanatology*, 34; Carlson, *Caring for Your Own Dead*, 25; Habenstein and Lamers, *The History of American Funeral Directing*, 42.

3. Budge, *The Mummy*, 306.

4. A. J. Spencer, *Death in Ancient Egypt* (New York: Penguin Books, 1982), 165–70.

5. Spencer, *Death in Ancient Egypt*, 164–94.

6. Budge, *The Mummy*, 310.

7. Bardis, *History of Thanatology*, 37–53; Habenstein and Lamers, *The History of American Funeral Directing*, 53, 116.

8. Coffin, *Death in Early America*, 101; Mitford, *The American Way of Death*, 196–97.

9. Coffin, *Death in Early America*, 101; Mitford, *The American Way of Death*, 197.

10. Coffin, *Death in Early America*, 101; H. C. Raether and R. C. Slater, "The Funeral and the Funeral Director," in *Concerning Death: A Practical Guide for the Living*, ed. E. A. Grollman (Boston: Beacon Press, 1974), 187–209.

11. Coffin, *Death in Early America*, 104.

12. Ibid., 108–9.

13. Editors of Consumer Reports, *Funerals: Consumers' Last Rights* (Mount Vernon, N.Y.: Consumers Union of the United States, 1977), 75.

14. Ibid., 75–86.

15. Mitford, *The American Way of Death*.

16. M. Ragon, *The Space of Death* (Charlottesville: University Press of Virginia, 1983), 82.

17. "What Is a Burial Vault?" in *Facts Every Family Should Know* (Forest Park, Ill.: Wilbert, 1972), 29–37.

18. Some people, especially the poor, have been buried without a coffin or casket in twentieth-century central Appalachia.

19. Bettis et al., "East Tennessee Dead," 110.

20. H. M. Caudill, *The Senator from Slaughter Creek* (Boston: Little, Brown, 1973), 12; Habenstein and Lamers, *The History of American Funeral Directing*, 117; Wolford, *Mountain Memories*, 128; supported by numerous interviews.

21. C. Gardner, *Clever County* (New York: Fleming H. Revell, 1931), 61; H. Hatcher, *Tunnel Hill* (Indianapolis: Bobbs-Merrill, 1931), 199; H. Hornsby, *Lonesome Valley* (New York: William Sloane Associates, 1949), 29; supported by numerous interviews.

22. "Death and Burial," 59.

23. Bettis et al., "East Tennessee Dead," 111; E. O. Guerrant, *The Galax Gatherers* (Richmond, Va.: Onward Press, 1910), 173; G. Korson, *Coal Dust on the Fiddle* (Philadelphia: University of Pennsylvania Press, 1943), 266; M. C. Wharton, *Doctor Woman of the Cumberlands* (Pleasant Hill, Tenn.: Uplands, 1953), 119; supported by numerous interviews.

24. Hannum, "The Mountain People," 143.

25. F. R. Beiting, *Adventures of Daniel Boone* (Kentucky: Father Ralph W. Beiting, 1977); Bettis et al., "East Tennessee Dead," 110; H. T. Kane, *Miracle in the Mountains* (New York: Doubleday, 1956), 53; Montell, *Ghosts*, 74; supported by numerous interviews.

26. J. Parris, *These Storied Mountains* (Asheville, N.C.: Citizen-Times, 1972), 25.

27. Bettis et al., "East Tennessee Dead," 110.

28. L. W. Green, *And Scatter the Proud* (Winston-Salem, N.C.: John F. Blair, 1969), 427.

29. G. C. Banks, *Back to the Mountains* (Morehead, Ky.: Gabriel C. Banks, 1964), 16; C. N. Buck, *The Battle Cry* (New York: Grosset and Dunlap, 1914), 115; A. P. Hannum, "The Mountain People," in *The Great Smokies and the Blue Ridge*, ed. R. Peattie (New York: Vanguard Press, 1943), 142; R. Llewellyn, *How Green Was My Valley* (New York: Macmillan, 1943), 212; Ratliff, *Return to the Promised Land*, 31; Stidham, *Trails into Cutshin County*, 124.

30. Murdoch, *Almetta of Gabriel's Run*, 62.

31. "Death and Burial," 58.

32. P. W. Gainer, *Witches, Ghosts, and Signs: Folklore of the Southern Appalachians* (Grantsville, W.Va.: Seneca Books, 1975), 145; supported by interviews.

33. Bettis et al., "East Tennessee Dead," 111; Dunn, *Cades Cove*, 191; W. E. Phipps, "Traditional Appalachian Funerals," *Appalachian Heritage* 8, no. 4 (1980): 49; Ratliff, *Return to the Promised Land*, 31; Sanderson, *County Scott*, 61.

34. Bettis et al., "East Tennessee Dead," 111.

35. Interview with an elderly couple in Gilmer County, W.Va., 1980.

36. V. St. Cloud, *Pioneer Blood* (Raleigh, N.C.: Edwards and Broughton, 1948), 12–13.

37. Arnow, *Hunter's Horn*, 323.

38. G. E. Hatfield, *The Hatfields* (Stanville, Ky.: Big Sandy Valley Historical Society, 1974), 64.

39. Sanderson, *County Scott*, 61; Thomas, *Devil's Ditties*, 19.

40. "Death and Burial," 59; Gazaway, *The Longest Mile*, 124; Slone, *What My Heart Wants to Tell*, 57–58; Stidham, *Trails into Cutshin County*, 124.

41. "Death and Burial," 59; Evans and Travis, "John L. Richards," 305; supported by interviews.

42. Arnow, *Hunter's Horn*, 322; M. Frome, *Strangers in High Places* (Garden City, N.Y.: Doubleday, 1966), 237; Furman, *The Quare Woman*, 28; Gazaway, *The Longest Mile*, 124; H. F. Riggleman, *A West Virginia Mountaineer Remembers* (Parsons, W.Va.: McClain, 1980), 49; Vogel, *This Happened*, 118–19; supported by interviews.

43. H. Skidmore, *I Will Lift Up Mine Eyes* (New York: Book League of America, 1936), 88.

44. "Death and Burial," 59; S. G. Ross, *Come Go with Me* (Pineknot, Ky.: Kentucky Hills Industries, 1977), 109; Sherburne, *Stand like Men*, 12.

45. Bettis et al., "East Tennessee Dead," 112.

46. T. Allebaugh, *Disputanta: A Front Porch Chronicle* (Berea Ky.: Terry Allebaugh, 1980), 80; M. Campbell, *Cloud-Walking* (Bloomington: Indiana University Press, 1971), 172–73.

47. Bettis et al., "East Tennessee Dead," 112.

48. W. Moore, *Mountain Voices* (Chester, Conn.: Globe Pequot Press, 1988).

49. O. T. Dargan, *From My Highest Hill* (Philadelphia: J. B. Lippincott, 1925), 189.

Chapter 4: The Wake

1. M. R. Leming and G. E. Dickinson, *Understanding Dying, Death, and Bereavement* (New York: Holt, Rinehart, and Winston, 1985), 299.

2. Aiken, *Dying, Death*; Chidester, *Patterns of Transcendence*; R. W. Habenstein and W. M. Lamers, *Funeral Customs the World Over* (Milwaukee: Bulfin Printers, 1960).

3. Gainer, *Witches, Ghosts, and Signs*, 29.

4. Habenstein and Lamers, *The History of American Funeral Directing*, 66.

5. Ibid.

6. Ibid., 39.

7. Bardis, *History of Thanatology*.

8. Leming and Dickinson, *Understanding Dying*.

9. Habenstein and Lamers, *The History of American Funeral Directing*, 63.

10. Mitford, *The American Way of Death*, 191.

11. Habenstein and Lamers, *The History of American Funeral Directing*, 63.

12. Huntington and Metcalf, *Celebrations of Death*, 202.

13. Habenstein and Lamers, *The History of American Funeral Directing*, 61.

14. M. C. Kearl, *Endings: A Sociology of Death and Dying* (New York: Oxford University Press, 1989), 99.

15. Coffin, *Death in Early America*, 85.

16. Habenstein and Lamers, *The History of American Funeral Directing*, 105.

17. DeSpelder and Strickland, *The Last Dance*.

18. R. A. Kalish, *Death, Grief, and Caring Relationships*, 2d ed. (Monterey, Calif.: Brooks and Cole, 1985), 213.

19. Aiken, *Dying, Death*; DeSpelder and Strickland, *The Last Dance*, 222.

20. Giles, *Forty Acres and No Mules*, 170.

21. K. Morehouse, *Rain on the Just* (Carbondale: Southern Illinois University Press, 1936), 25.

22. Montell, *Ghosts*, 64.

23. Brewster et al., *The Frank C. Brown Collection*, 254.

24. W. D. Hand, ed. *The Frank C. Brown Collection of North Carolina Folklore*, vol. 7 (Durham, N.C.: Duke University Press, 1964), 84.

25. Bettis et al., "East Tennessee Dead," 100.

26. Montell, *Ghosts*, 64–71.

27. Allebaugh, *Disputanta*, 79–80.

28. Slone, *What My Heart Wants to Tell*, 58.

29. Guerrant, *The Galax Gatherers*.

30. Ratliff, *Return to the Promised Land*, 38.

31. Montell, *Ghosts*, 72.

32. J. Russell, *Snakes and the Devil* (New York: Vantage Press, 1959), 145.

33. F. B. Adams, *Appalachia Revisited: How People Lived Fifty Years Ago* (Ashland, Ky.: Economy, 1970), 125; F. B. Adams, *A Man from Jeremiah* (New York: Vantage Press, 1975), 96.

34. F. C. Watkins and C. H. Watkins, *Yesterday in the Hills* (Chicago: Quadrangle Books, 1963), 104.

35. H. Cooper, *North Carolina Mountain Folklore and Miscellany* (Murfreesboro, N.C.: Johnson, 1972), 43.

36. M. H. Ellyson, *Mud and Money* (New York: Vantage Press, 1973), 117.

37. Riggleman, *A West Virginia Mountaineer Remembers*, 50.

38. Russell, *Call Me Hillbilly*, 33.

39. Cooper, *North Carolina Mountain Folklore*, 43–44.

40. D. Loughrige, "A Perspective on Death in Appalachia," *Appalachian Heritage* 2, no. 1 (1983): 27.

41. Still, *River of Earth*, 177.

42. Day, *Bloody Ground*, 184.

43. This information was gathered from funeral directors in central Appalachia. An elderly funeral director in Fall Branch, Tenn., noted that the last body he had handled that was not embalmed was in 1968.

Chapter 5: The Funeral Service

1. E. Morgan, *Dealing Creatively with Death: A Manual of Death Education and Simple Burial*, 10th ed., rev. and exp. (Burnsville, N.C.: Celo Press, 1984), 67.

2. DeSpelder and Strickland, *The Last Dance,* 171.

3. Habenstein and Lamers, *The History of American Funeral Directing,* 41–42.

4. Ibid., 69.

5. Bardis, *History of Thanatology,* 47; T. Boase, *Death in the Middle Ages* (New York: McGraw-Hill, 1972), 100.

6. Bardis, *History of Thanatology,* 47.

7. Habenstein and Lamers, *The History of American Funeral Directing,* 149–50.

8. Bardis, *History of Thanatology,* 52.

9. Coffin, *Death in Early America,* 73.

10. Ibid., 78.

11. Ibid., 69; Habenstein and Lamers, *The History of American Funeral Directing,* 404.

12. A. C. Hall, *Grave Humor* (Charlotte, N.C.: McNally and Loftin, 1961), 4.

13. Habenstein and Lamers, *The History of American Funeral Directing,* 203, 435.

14. B. S. Puckle, *Funeral Customs: Their Origin and Development* (Detroit: Singing Tree Press, 1926), 271.

15. Aiken, *Dying, Death,* 222.

16. Leming and Dickinson, *Understanding Dying,* 303.

17. Habenstein and Lamers, *The History of American Funeral Directing,* 405.

18. Leming and Dickinson, *Understanding Dying,* 301; Mitford, *The American Way of Death,* 199.

19. Mitford, *The American Way of Death,* 199.

20. Morgan, *Dealing Creatively with Death,* 44–45.

21. Ibid., 45.

22. Scalf, "The Death and Burial of 'Boney Bill' Scalf," 59.

23. J. Ritchie, *Singing Family of the Cumberlands* (New York: Oak Publications, 1963), 214.

24. W. E. Cox, *Hensley Settlement: A Mountain Community* (Eastern National Park and Monument Association, 1990), 52.

25. Russell, *Call Me Hillbilly,* 33.

26. R. C. Davids, *The Man Who Moved a Mountain* (Philadelphia: Fortress Press, 1970), 21.

27. Buck, *When "Bearcat" Went Dry,* 233–34.

28. M. W. Toynbee, *A Day for Remembrance* (New York: Vantage Press, 1975), 47.

29. Russell, *Snakes and the Devil,* 145.

30. Watkins and Watkins, *Yesterday in the Hills,* 40.

31. J. S. Malone, *Sons of Vengeance: A Tale of the Cumberland Highlanders* (New York: Fleming A. Revell, 1903), 25.

32. Brewster et al., *The Frank C. Brown Collection.*

33. Davids, *The Man Who Moved a Mountain,* 21–22; L. Furman, *The Lonesome Road* (Boston: Little, Brown, 1927), 73; Marshall, *Christy,* 294; M. E. Sheppard, *Cloud by Day: The Story of Coal and Coke and People* (Chapel Hill: University of North Carolina Press, 1947), 67.

34. Campbell, *The Southern Highlander,* 181.

35. Raine, *Land of Saddlebags*, 202.

36. Furman, *The Lonesome Road*, 121; L. Furman, *The Glass Window: A Story of the Quare Woman* (Boston: Little, Brown, 1930), 146; Marshall, *Christy*, 294; Peterson, "Quiet Dignity," 88; Sanderson, *County Scott*, 61; B. Surface, *The Hollow* (New York: Coward-McCann, 1971), 148; supported by numerous interviews.

37. W. Dykeman, *Return the Innocent Earth* (New York: Holt, Rinehart, and Winston, 1973), 71.

38. Russell, *Call Me Hillbilly*, 33.

39. Furman, *The Lonesome Road*, 121.

40. L. Furman, *Mothering on Perilous* (New York: Macmillan, 1923), 152; Fettermen, *Stinking Creek*, 140; J. Fetterman, "The People of Cumberland Gap," *National Geographic*, Nov. 1971, 620; Dunn, *Cades Cove*, 191.

41. Campbell, *The Southern Highlander*, 183.

42. Riggleman, *A West Virginia Mountaineer Remembers*, 50.

43. H. Arnow, "The Washer Woman's Day," *Appalachian Heritage* 1, no. 4 (1973): 6; Fetterman, "The People of Cumberland Cap," 620; Montell, *Ghosts*, 82; Sherburne, *Stand like Men*, 2; supported by interviews.

44. Guerrant, *The Galax Gatherers*, 174; Dunn, *Cades Cove*, 191.

45. Phipps, "Traditional Appalachian Funerals," 48–53.

46. Adams, *A Man from Jeremiah*, 96.

47. Gazaway, *The Longest Mile*, 124.

48. Giles, *Forty Acres and No Mules*, 17.

49. Marshall, *Christy*, 294.

50. M. Pearsall, *Little Smoky Ridge* (Birmingham: University of Alabama Press, 1959), 122.

51. Campbell, *The Southern Highlander*, 183.

52. M. E. Sheppard, *Cabins in the Laurel* (Chapel Hill: University of North Carolina Press, 1935), 218.

53. Guerrant, *The Galax Gatherers*, 174.

54. Giles, *Forty Acres and No Mules*, 17.

55. Russell, *Call Me Hillbilly*, 33.

56. Giles, *Forty Acres and No Mules*, 17.

57. W. A. McCall, *I Thunk Me a Thaut* (New York: Teacher's College Press, 1975), 26.

Chapter 6: Burial Customs

1. Bardis, *History of Thanatology*, 21–22.

2. Habenstein and Lamers, *The History of American Funeral Directing*, 30–31.

3. Ibid., 53.

4. Ibid., 67–68.

5. E. Johnson, as quoted in Habenstein and Lamers, *The History of American Funeral Directing*, 41.

6. Coffin, *Death in Early America*, 104–5; I. Crichton, *The Art of Dying* (London: Peter Owen, 1976), 100.

7. Coffin, *Death in Early America*, 105.

8. Gardner, *Clever County*, 61.

9. Coffin, *Death in Early America*, 116.

10. Ibid., 117.

11. Aiken, *Dying, Death*, 91.

12. Ibid.; Ariés, *Western Attitudes toward Death*, 15; Bardis, *History of Thanatology*, 34.

13. Habenstein and Lamers, *The History of American Funeral Directing*, 54–55.

14. Ibid., 69–70.

15. "Death and Burial," 57.

16. Habenstein and Lamers, *The History of American Funeral Directing*, 423.

17. Chidester, *Patterns of Transcendence*, 281.

18. Guerrant, *The Galax Gatherers*, 169.

19. Banks, *Back to the Mountains*, 14.

20. Roberts and Roberts, *Where Time Stood Still*, 40.

21. Giles, *The Believers*, 125.

22. B. C. Clark, "The Death of Aunt Lottie," *Appalachian Heritage* 11, no. 1 (1983): 21.

23. R. A. Meyer, "Mountain Character: Carved from the Rock of Faith," *Appalachian Heritage* 4, no. 1 (1976): 7–8.

24. The Carter Family, "Bury Me under the Weeping Willow." Recorded on Aug. 1, 1927, in Bristol, Va., released on Victor 21074, Bluebird B-6053, Montgomery Ward M-7020, and reissued on RCA Victor LPM-2772.

25. Fetterman, *Stinking Creek*, 123.

26. P. J. Obermiller and R. Rappold, "Bury Me under a Sidewalk: The Appalachian Way of Death in the Cities," *Now and Then* 8, no. 2 (1990): 28–29.

27. M. Purcell and C. Purcell, *A Moonshine Preacher* (Toccoa, Ga.: Toccoa Printers, 1975), 196.

28. *New American Standard Bible*, Open Bible ed. (Nashville: Thomas Nelson, 1977).

29. C. Ward, *Silk Stockin' Row* (Parsons, W.Va.: McClain, 1975), 91.

30. Huffman, *My Mountain Memories*, 105.

31. Aiken, *Dying, Death*, 94–95.

32. Guerrant, *The Galax Gatherers*, 171.

33. Ritchie, *Singing Family*, 214.

34. W. Dykeman, *The Tall Woman* (New York: Holt, Rinehart, and Winston, 1962), 145.

35. Aiken, *Dying, Death*, 88; Bardis, *History of Thanatology*, 16.

36. N. A. Chagnon, *Yanomamo: The Fierce People*, 3d ed. (New York: Holt, Rinehart, and Winston, 1983), 105–6.

37. Chidester, *Patterns of Transcendence*, 78.

38. Ibid., 200.

39. Mitford, *The American Way of Death*, 129.

40. Ibid.

41. Chidester, *Patterns of Transcendence*, 287.

Chapter 7: Grave Markers and Other Forms of Memorialization

1. Puckle, *Funeral Customs*, 256.
2. E. R. Shushan, *Grave Matters* (New York: Ballantine Books, 1990), vii.
3. Bardis, *History of Thanatology*, 22.
4. Shushan, *Grave Matters*, vii.
5. Bardis, *History of Thanatology*, 26–27.
6. Shushan, *Grave Matters*, vii.
7. Habenstein and Lamers, *The History of American Funeral Directing*, 55.
8. Bardis, *History of Thanatology*, 47.
9. F. Y. Duval and I. B. Rigby, *Early American Gravestone Art in Photographs* (New York: Dover, 1978), 7–8; Hall, *Grave Humor*, 1–2.
10. E. Wasserman, *Gravestone Designs: Rubbings and Photographs from Early New York and New Jersey* (New York: Dover, 1972), 1.
11. Hall, *Grave Humor*, 1–2.
12. D. Edwards, "Haydenville, a Town of Clay," *Ceramics Monthly* 28 (1980): 47–51.
13. P. Schaltenbrand, "The Stoneware of Greensboro–New Geneva," *Ceramics Monthly* 28 (1980): 30–36.
14. Hall, *Grave Humor*, 1–2.
15. Editors of Consumer Reports, *Funerals*, 143–44.
16. I. A. Winter, "Choosing a Memorial," in *Concerning Death: A Practical Guide for the Living*, ed. E. A. Grollman (Boston: Beacon Press, 1974), 232.
17. Ibid., 228–29.
18. Wassermen, *Gravestone Designs*, 30.
19. Hall, *Grave Humor*, 2.
20. Most of the information about monument portraits was derived from my interview with Richard Stannard, president of J. A. Dedouch Co., and *Dedo Monument Portraits since 1893*, catalog no. 14 (Oak Park, Ill.: J. A. Dedouch, n.d.).
21. Campbell, *The Southern Highlander*, 148.
22. Furman, *Mothering on Perilous*, 113.
23. Furman, *The Lonesome Road*, 99.
24. Thomas, *Devil's Ditties*, 19.
25. Still, *River of Earth*, 183.
26. Habenstein and Lamers, *The History of American Funeral Directing*, 418–19; Puckle, *Funeral Customs*, 34.
27. Habenstein and Lamers, *The History of American Funeral Directing*, 30.
28. Ibid., 39.
29. Budge, *The Mummy*.
30. Kalish, *Death, Grief*, 11.
31. Mitford, *The American Way of Death*, 198–99.
32. Phipps, "Traditional Appalachian Funerals," 49.
33. E. Wigginton, ed., *A Foxfire Christmas* (New York: Doubleday, 1989), 19–20.

34. Bettis et al., "East Tennessee Death," 113.

35. Mitford, *The American Way of Death*, 198–99.

36. Editors of Consumer Reports, *Funerals*, 144–45.

37. Puckle, *Funeral Customs*, 269.

38. A. Gold, "Hair Has Its Strand of Jewelry History," *Chicago Tribune*, Oct. 16, 1977, sec. 11, p. 8.

39. I am indebted to the Kentucky Historical Society in Frankfort for the information and photograph concerning the graveyard quilt.

40. Coffin, *Death in Early America*, 206.

41. Ibid.; Puckle, *Funeral Customs*; Leming and Dickinson, *Understanding Dying*.

Chapter 8: Funeralizing and Memorial Traditions

1. Fink, "Religion in America," 36.

2. J. Fox, Jr., as quoted in Kephart, *Our Southern Highlanders*, 342.

3. Ibid.

4. Ibid.

5. Ibid.

6. A. W. Spaulding, *The Men of the Mountains* (Nashville: Southern Publishing Association, 1915), 49.

7. E. M. Gilmer, *A History of Elk Garden United Methodist Church, 1788–1988* (Rosedale, Va.: Elk Garden United Methodist Church Bicentennial Committee, 1988), 2.

8. J. G. Jones, *Haunted Valley and More Folk Tales* (Parsons, W.Va.: McClain, 1979), 149.

9. Fink, "Religion in America," 39.

10. V. M. Slone, *Common Folks* (Pippa Passes, Ky.: Appalachian Women Grants for Writers and the Appalachian Learning Laboratory, Alice Lloyd College, 1978), 33; Slone, *What My Heart Wants to Tell*, 58; Jones, *Haunted Valley*, 149.

11. Fink, "Religion in Appalachia," 39; R. L. Mason, *The Lure of the Great Smokies* (Boston: Houghton Mifflin, 1927), 190.

12. Kephart, *Our Southern Highlanders*, 343; Weller, *Yesterday's People*, 123.

13. Weller, *Yesterday's People*, 123.

14. Jones, *Haunted Valley*, 149.

15. J. Fox, Jr., *In Happy Valley* (New York: Charles Scribner's Sons, 1917), 56–57.

16. W. W. Sweet, *Religion on the American Frontier: The Baptists* (New York: Henry Holt, 1931), 36.

17. Bettis et al., "East Tennessee Dead," 111; Slone, *What My Heart Wants to Tell*, 58.

18. Malone, *Sons of Vengeance*, 26.

19. Kephart, *Our Southern Highlanders*, 335.

20. Phipps, "Traditional Appalachian Funerals," 50.

21. W. H. Haney, *The Mountain People of Kentucky* (Cincinnati: Roessler

Bros., 1906), 162; Kephart, *Our Southern Highlanders*, 335; Phipps, "Traditional Appalachian Funerals," 50; J. Thomas, *Big Sandy* (New York: Henry Holt, 1940), 55.

22. Raine, *Land of Saddlebags*, 8–9; Montell, *Ghosts*, 78; J. Thomas, *Blue Ridge Country* (New York: Duell, Sloan, and Pearce, 1942), 156; Stidham, *Trails into Cutshin County*, 125.

23. Raine, *Land of Saddlebags*, 202–3.

24. Thomas, *Devil's Ditties*, 20.

25. Haney, "The Mountain People," 162.

26. Campbell, *Cloud-Walking*, 165–66; Huston, *Observations of God's Timing*, 24; Norbeck, *The Lure of the Hills*, 193; Plowman, *Twice out of Sight*, 47; Sanderson, *County Scott*, 61; Thomas, *Devil's Ditties*, 20.

27. Guerrant, *The Galax Gatherers*, 169.

28. Campbell, *The Southern Highlanders*, 149.

29. Furman, *The Lonesome Road*, 15; J. W. Hall, "A Funeral Meeting in the Remote Parts of the Mountains," *Appalachian Heritage* 1, no. 4 (1973): 10; Campbell, *The Southern Highlander*, 149; Guerrant, *The Galax Gatherers*, 169; Malone, *Sons of Vengeance*, 26; Norbeck, *The Lure of the Hills*, 193.

30. Hall, "A Funeral Meeting," 18–19.

31. Huston, *Observations of God's Timing*, 34.

32. Marshall, *Christy*, 294.

33. Raine, *Land of Saddlebags*, 8–9.

34. Giles, *Forty Acres and No Mules*, 17.

35. Campbell, *The Southern Highlander*, 182.

36. J. M. Hatch, *The American Book of Days* (New York: H. W. Wilson, 1978), 59; M. Ickis, *The Book of Patriotic Holidays* (New York: Dodd, Mead, 1962), 501.

37. G. W. Douglas, *The American Book of Days* (New York: H. W. Wilson, 1948), 308; O. Friedrich, "A Day to Remember," *McCall's*, July 1986, 95–96; W. Walsh, *Curiosities of Popular Customs* (Philadelphia: J. B. Lippincott, 1925), 326.

38. Ickis, *The Book of Patriotic Holidays*, 503.

39. Ibid.

40. J. Bryant, "Flags, Flowers, and Thanks," *Reader's Digest*, May 1983, 75–76; Friedrich, "A Day to Remember," 95–96; W. E. Hamm, "Honoring the Noble Sacrifice: Once Again We Remember," *Vital Speeches of the Day* 55 (1988): 626–27; J. A. McCracken, "A Memorial Day in Maine," *Reader's Digest*, May 1984, 49–54; S. Swanson, "Slogans and Comrades," *Christian Century* 103 (1986): 510–11.

41. Ickis, *The Book of Patriotic Holidays*, 503.

42. Davids, *The Man Who Moved a Mountain*, 22.

43. Gazaway, *The Longest Mile*, 126.

44. Sheppard, *Cabins in the Laurel*, 214.

45. L. Lynn, *Coal Miner's Daughter* (Chicago: Henry Regnery, 1976), 24.

46. Clark, "The Death of Aunt Lottie," 17.

47. Sheppard, *Cabins in the Laurel*, 215.

48. Norbeck, *The Lure of the Hills*, 193.
49. Adams, *A Man from Jeremiah*, 96.
50. Plowman, *Twice out of Sight*, 47.
51. Thomas, *Devil's Ditties*, 20.
52. Slone, *Common Folks*, 34.

Chapter 9: Dying, Death, and Central Appalachian Music

1. C. Sharp and M. Karpeles, *Eighty English Folk Songs from the Southern Appalachians* (Cambridge, Mass.: MIT Press, 1968), 9.
2. Furman, *Mothering on Perilous*, 125.
3. Gainer, *Folk Songs from the West Virginia Hills*, xvi.
4. E. B. Miles, *The Spirit of the Mountains* (Knoxville: University of Tennessee Press, 1975), 34.
5. L. Jones, *Radio's "Kentucky Mountain Boy" Bradley Kincaid* (Berea, Ky.: Berea College Appalachian Center, 1980), 12.
6. J. F. Smith, "Introduction," in *Favorite Old-time Songs and Mountain Ballads*, book 2, by Bradley Kincaid (Chicago: WLS, 1929), 5.
7. T. Burton, *Some Ballad Folks* (Johnson City, Tenn.: Center for Appalachian Studies and Services, 1990), 1.
8. Sharp and Karpeles, *Eighty English Folk Songs*, 9.
9. Ibid.
10. P. Seeger, *How to Play the Five-String Banjo*, 3d ed. rev. (Beacon, N.Y.: Pete Seeger, 1962), 5.
11. Campbell, *The Southern Highlander*, 184.
12. P. Gainer, *Witches, Ghosts, and Signs*, 25.
13. Ibid.
14. Smith, "Introduction," 5.
15. "Home." Used by permission from Texas Wedge Music (ASCAP) © 1990. Written by Andy Spooner and Fred Lehner and performed by Joe Diffie on Epic Records. All rights reserved.
16. Quoted from the sheet music for Chas. K. Harris, "'Mid the Green Fields of Virginia (in the Vale of Shenandoah)" (London, England: Chas. K. Harris, 1898), 3–4. See also the Carter Family, "'Mid the Green Fields of Virginia." Recorded on Feb. 23, 1932, in Atlanta, issued on Victor 23686, Bluebird B-5243, and Montgomery Ward M-4737, and reissued on RCA Victor LPM-2772.
17. Rutherford and Foster, "Cabin with the Roses at the Door." Recorded on Nov. 13, 1930, in Atlanta, issued on Brunswick 490, and reissued on Rounder 1004.
18. See G. Carawan and C. Carawan, *Voices from the Mountains* (New York: Alfred A. Knopf, 1975), 74, 60.
19. Sarah Ogan Gunning, "Dreadful Memories." © 1965 Folk-Legacy Records, Inc. Used by permission.
20. Quoted from sheet music for Herbert S. Lambert, "I Wonder How the Old Folks Are at Home" (Williamsport, Pa.: Vandersloot Music, 1909), 4–5.

21. H. Shellans, *Folk Songs of the Blue Ridge Mountains* (New York: Oak Publications, 1968), 30–31.

22. Gene Autry and Jimmy Long, "Silver Haired Daddy of Mine." Recorded Oct. 29, 1931, in New York, issued on Conqueror 7908 and Vocalion 5489, and reissued on Smithsonian RM 025-E.

23. Jimmie Rodgers, "Daddy and Home." Recorded June 12, 1928, in Camden, N.J., released on a multitude of different labels, and reissued on several albums.

24. Blue Sky Boys, "East Bound Train." Recorded Feb. 5, 1940, in Atlanta, released on Bluebird B-8552, and reissued on Smithsonian RM 025-C.

25. Blind Alfred Reed, "The Prayer of the Drunkard's Little Girl." Recorded Dec. 19, 1927, in Camden, N.J., released on Victor 21191, and reissued on Rounder 1001.

26. Jimmie Davis, "Nobody's Darlin' but Mine." Recorded Sept. 21, 1934, in Chicago, released on Decca 5090, and reissued on Smithsonian RM 025-E.

27. Ernest V. Stoneman, "The Dying Girl's Farewell." Recorded July 25, 1927, in Bristol, Tenn., with vocals by Ernest V. Stoneman, E. K.(Kahle) Brewer, and M. (Walter) Brewer, released on Victor 21129, and reissued on Rounder 1008.

28. The Carter Family, "Motherless Children." Recorded Nov. 22, 1929, in Atlanta, released on Victor 23641, Bluebird B-5924, and Montgomery Ward M5010, and reissued on RCA Victor LPM 2772.

29. Bradley Kincaid, "Two Little Orphans." Recorded Sept. 14, 1932, in New York and issued on Bluebird B-4906. See also Jones, *Radio's "Kentucky Mountain Boy" Bradley Kincaid*, 108, and B. Kincaid, *Favorite Old-time Songs and Mountain Ballads*, book 3 (Chicago: WLS, 1930), 32.

30. Blue Sky Boys, "Row Us over the Tide." Recorded June 16, 1936, in Charlotte, N.C., and released on Bluebird B-6567 and Montgomery Ward M-7018.

31. G. B. Grayson and Henry Whitter, "He Is Coming to Us Dead." Recorded Oct. 18, 1927, in Atlanta, released on Victor 21139, and reissued on County 513.

32. Vernon Dalhart, "The Dying Girl's Message." Released on Columbia 15051-D.

33. J. E. Mainer's Mountaineers, "Maple on the Hill." Recorded Aug. 6, 1935, in Atlanta, released on Bluebird B-6065 and Montgomery Ward M-4969-A, and reissued on Smithsonian RM 025-D.

34. The Callahan Brothers, "The Dying Girl's Farewell." Recorded Dec. 20, 1936, in New York, released on Vocalion 04483, Okeh 04483, and Conqueror 9144, and reissued on Old Homestead OHS 90031

35. Ibid.

36. The Blue Sky Boys, "Little Bessie." © Berwick Music Corp. Used by permission.

37. Vernon Dalhart, "The Prisoner's Song." Released on Edison 51459 and reissued on Mark56 793.

38. Vernon Dalhart, "Behind These Grey Walls." Recorded Dec. 12, 1935, released on Edison 51669, and reissued on Mark56 793.

39. Grayson and Whitter, "Dark Road Is a Hard Road to Travel." Recorded July 31, 1928, in New York City, released on Victor V-40063, and reissued on County 513.

40. Karl and Harty, "I'm Here to Get My Baby out of Jail." Recorded Mar. 22, 1934, released on Banner 33118, Melotone M13085, Oriole 8360, Perfect 13023, and Romeo 5360, and reissued on Smithsonian RM 025-D.

41. Bradley Kincaid, "Bury Me out on the Prairie." See Jones, *Radio's "Kentucky Mountain Boy" Bradley Kincaid*, 116.

42. Burnett and Rutherford, "Willie Moore." Recorded in 1927 and issued on Columbia 15314D.

43. "Parents, Warning," in Shellans, *Folk Songs of the Blue Ridge Mountains*, 34.

44. The Coon Creek Girls, "Pretty Polly." Recorded on May 30, 1938, in Chicago, issued on Vocalion 04659, and reissued on Smithsonian RM 025-C and Old Homestead OHCS-142.

45. The Carter Family, "Can the Circle Be Unbroken (Bye and Bye)?" Recorded in May 1935, issued on Banner 33465, Melotone M-13432, Oriole 8484, Perfect 13155, and Romeo 5484, and reissued on Smithsonian RM 025-D.

46. Bradley Kincaid, "In the Streets of Laredo." Recorded on Jan. 28, 1929, in Richmond, Ind., and released on Gennett 6790 and Supertone 9404. See also Kincaid, *Favorite Old-time Songs and Mountain Ballads*, 28.

47. "Broken Engagement," in Shellans, *Folk Songs of the Blue Ridge Mountains*, 29.

48. Roy Harvey and the North Carolina Ramblers, "George Collins." Recorded on Feb. 16, 1928, in Ashland, Ky., and issued on Brunswick 250.

49. The Dixon Brothers, "Answer to Maple on the Hill, Part 1." Released on Montgomery Ward M-5025-A and Bluebird B-6462.

50. Dock Boggs, "Lost Love Blues." Recorded in 1929 in Chicago, released on Lonesome Ace 21406, and reissued on Folkways RBF 654.

51. The Callahan Brothers, "The Dying Girl's Farewell."

52. Blind Alfred Reed, "There'll Be No Distinction There." Recorded Dec. 3, 1929, in New York City, released on Victor 23550, and reissued on Rounder 1001.

53. Roy Acuff and his Crazy Tennesseans, "Great Speckled Bird." Recorded Oct. 20, 1936, in Chicago, released on Vocalion 04252, and reissued on Smithsonian RM 025-D.

54. "I'll Have a New Life," in Shellans, *Folk Songs of the Blue Ridge Mountains*, 91-92.

55. The Monroe Brothers, "We Read of a Place That's Called Heaven." Released on Montgomery Ward M-7087-B and Bluebird B-6676.

56. The Frank Luther Trio, "When I Take My Vacation in Heaven." Released on Conqueror 8170-A.

57. From the video of Vern Gosdin, "The Garden." Released in 1991 for Columbia on *Out of My Heart*.

58. The Blue Sky Boys, "Katie Dear." Recorded Jan. 25, 1938, in Charlotte, N.C., released on Bluebird B-7661 and Montgomery Ward M-7468, and reissued on Rounder 1006. © Berwick Music Corp. Used by permission.

59. Buell Kazee, "The Butcher's Boy." Recorded in 1928 and issued on Brunswick 213.

60. Kincaid, *Favorite Old-time Songs and Mountain Ballads,* book 3, 23. See also Jones, *Radio's "Kentucky Mountain Boy" Bradley Kincaid,* 95.

61. Bradley Kincaid, "The Fatal Wedding." Recorded in Dec. 1930 in Chicago, released on Melotone M12315, Vocalion 02684, and Conqueror, and reissued on Old Homestead OHCS 107.

62. Sharp and Karpeles, *Eighty English Folk Songs,* 42–43.

63. Ibid.

64. B. A. Botkin, *A Treasury of Southern Folklore* (New York: American Legacy Press, 1949), 737–38.

65. "Leaving Home," in K. Rorrer, *Rambling Blues: The Life and Songs of Charlie Poole* (London: Old Time Music, 1982), 72.

66. Gainer, *Folk Songs from the West Virginia Hills,* 13–14.

67. Ibid.

68. Sharp and Karpeles, *Eighty English Folk Songs,* 28–29, and Gainer, *Folk Songs from the West Virginia Hills,* 18–19.

69. R. L. Sturgill, *Crimes, Criminals, and Characters of the Cumberlands and Southwest Virginia* (Roy L. Sturgill, 1970), 61–66.

70. Botkin, *A Treasury of Southern Folklore,* 392–97.

71. Sheppard, *Cabins in the Laurel,* 35–36.

72. Ibid., 37.

73. Gainer, *Folk Songs from the West Virginia Hills,* 63.

74. Rosa Lee Carson, "Little Mary Phagan," recorded on June 24, 1925, in New York City for the General Phonograph Corp. and released on Okeh 40446, in Gene Wiggins, *Fiddlin' Georgia Crazy: Fiddlin' John Carson, His Real World, and the World of His Songs* (Urbana: University of Illinois Press, 1987), 35–36. Fiddlin' John Carson, Rosa Lee's father, also recorded a version of the Mary Phagan story for the General Phonograph Corp. in Dec. 1925 or Jan. 1926. "The Grave of Little Mary Phagan" was released on Okeh 45028.

75. W. K. McNeil, *Southern Folk Ballads, Volume 2* (Little Rock: August House, 1988), 71–75.

76. Charlie Poole and the North Carolina Ramblers, "White House Blues." Recorded Sept. 20, 1926, in New York, released on Columbia 15099-D, and reissued on Folkways FA 2951.

77. Kelly Harrell, "Charles Guiteau." Recorded in Mar. 1927, released on Victor 20797, and reissued on County 408 and Folkways FA 2951.

78. L. Jones, *Minstrel of the Appalachians: The Story of Bascom Lamar Lunsford* (Boone, N.C.: Appalachian Consortium Press, 1984), 178.

79. For more information see M. B. Jones and T. J. Smith, *White Christmas, Bloody Christmas* (Trinity, N.C.: Upwords Publications, 1990), 101–5.

80. The Monroe Brothers, "The Forgotten Soldier Boy." Recorded Oct. 12, 1936, in Charlotte, N.C., issued on Bluebird B-6829, and reissued on New World NW 287 and Rounder 1026.

81. For more information about the portrayal of the railroad (including songs about death) in American folk music, see Norm Cohen's *Long Steel*

Rail: The Railroad in American Folksong (Urbana: University of Illinois Press, 1981).

82. Bradley Kincaid, "True and Trembling Brakeman." Recorded in mid-December 1930 in Chicago, released on Melotone M12184, Conqueror 8091, Vocalion 02683, Polk 9064, English Panachord 25, and Australian Panachord P12184, and reissued on Old Homestead OHCS 155. See also Jones, *Radio's "Kentucky Mountain Boy" Bradley Kincaid*, 107.

83. Florence Reece, "Which Side Are You On?" in A. Lomax, W. Guthrie, and P. Seeger, *Hard Hitting Songs for Hard-hit People* (New York: Oak Publishers, 1967), 176.

84. Gene Autry's "The Death of Mother Jones" was recorded in 1931 and released on several ARC labels: Banner, Conqueror, Jewel, Oriole, Perfect, Regal, and Romeo. The quotation here is from Conqueror 7702 as it is printed in Archie Green's *Only a Miner: Studies in Recorded Coal-Mining Songs* (Urbana: University of Illinois Press, 1972), 252.

85. Dick Bell (Green Bailey), "Shut Up in the Coal Creek Mine." Recorded Aug. 29, 1929, in Richmond, Ind., released on Challenge 425, and reissued on Rounder 1026.

Chapter 10: Mining Disasters and Death

1. B. A. Franklin, "The Scandal of Death and Injury in the Mines," in *Appalachia in the Sixties*, 92.

2. Lee, *Bloodletting in Appalachia*, 6.

3. Erikson, *Everything in Its Path*, 96.

4. Lee, *Bloodletting in Appalachia*, 6.

5. L. A. Dillon, *They Died in the Darkness* (Parsons, W.Va.: McClain, 1976), 84–90.

6. Ibid., vii–viii.

7. Erikson, *Everything in Its Path*, 97.

8. Ibid.

9. T. N. Bethell, "Conspiracy in Coal," in *Appalachia in the Sixties*, 78.

10. Franklin, "The Scandal of Death and Injury," 94.

11. Ibid., 92.

12. Shackelford and Weinberg, *Our Appalachia*, 11.

13. N. P. Chironis, ed., *Coal Age Operating Handbook of Underground Mining* (New York: McGraw-Hill, 1977), 266.

14. Dillon, *They Died in the Darkness*, 252.

15. Franklin, "The Scandal of Death and Injury," 96.

16. Shackelford and Weinberg, *Our Appalachia*, 205.

17. Franklin, "The Scandal of Death and Injury," 96.

18. Dillon, *They Died in the Darkness*, 122.

19. Ibid.

20. Ibid., 19–20.

21. Ibid., 44.

22. Ibid., 187.

23. Ibid., 179.

24. Franklin, "The Scandal of Death and Injury," 98.

25. See Erikson, *Everything in Its Path*, for a more complete description of this event.

26. Dillon, *They Died in the Darkness*, 74.

27. Ibid., 42.

28. Caudill, *Night Comes to the Cumberlands*, 120.

29. Ibid.

30. Dillon, *They Died in the Darkness*, 130.

31. Ibid., 130.

32. Ibid., 126.

33. Ibid., 99.

34. Ibid., 163.

35. Ibid., 207.

36. Korson, *Coal Dust on the Fiddle*, 266–67.

37. H. B. Lee, *My Appalachia* (Parsons, W.Va.: McClain, 1971), 102.

38. Korson, *Coal Dust on the Fiddle*, 267.

39. Sheppard, *Cloud by Day*, 67.

40. R. A. Lucas, *Men in Crisis: A Study of a Mine Disaster* (New York: Basic Books, 1969).

41. Dillon, *They Died in the Darkness*, 116–17.

42. Cf. Chironis, *Coal Age Operating Handbook of Underground Mining*, and W. Graebner, *Coal-mining Safety in the Progressive Period: The Political Economy of Reform* (Lexington: University Press of Kentucky, 1976).

Bibliography

Adams, F. B. 1970. *Appalachia Revisited: How People Lived Fifty Years Ago.* Ashland, Ky.: Economy.

————. 1975. *A Man from Jeremiah.* New York: Vantage Press.

Aiken, L. R. 1985. *Dying, Death, and Bereavement.* Boston: Allyn and Bacon.

Allebaugh, T. 1980. *Disputanta: A Front Porch Chronicle.* Berea Ky.: Terry Allebaugh.

Arcury, T. A., and J. D. Porter. 1985. "Household Composition in Appalachian Kentucky in 1900." *Journal of Family History* 10 (2): 183–95.

Ariés, P. 1974. *Western Attitudes toward Death.* Translated by Patricia M. Ranum. Baltimore: Johns Hopkins University Press.

Arnow, H. 1949. *Hunter's Horn.* New York: MacMillan.

————. 1973. "The Washer Woman's Day." *Appalachian Heritage* 1 (4): 6.

Banks, G. C. 1964. *Back to the Mountains.* Morehead, Ky.: Gabriel C. Banks.

Bardis, P. D. 1981. *History of Thanatology.* Washington, D.C.: University Press of America.

Beiting, F. R. 1977. *Adventures of Daniel Boone.* Kentucky: Father Ralph W. Beiting.

Berry, W. 1967. *A Place on Earth.* New York: Harcourt, Brace, and World.

————. 1974. *A Memory of Old Jack.* New York: Harcourt, Brace, Jovanovich.

Bethell, T. N. 1972. "Conspiracy in Coal." In *Appalachia in the Sixties: Decade of Reawakening,* ed. D. S. Walls and J. B. Stephenson. Lexington: University Press of Kentucky.

Bettis, M., M. Blackwell, R. Hoffman, P. Sonka, and L. Swingle. n.d. "The Care of the East Tennessee Dead. In *Glimpses of Southern Appalachian Folk Culture: Papers in Memory of Norbert F. Riedl,* ed. C. H. Faulkner and C. K. Buckles, 108–21. Tennessee Anthropological Association Miscellaneous Paper no. 3.

Blisten, D. R. 1974. "Three Major Types of Family Organization: Comparisons and Contrasts." In *Sociological Essays and Research,* ed. C. H. Anderson, 332–41. Homewood, Ill.: Dorsey Press.

Blood, R. O., and D. M. Wolfe. 1960. *Husbands and Wives: The Dynamics of Married Living.* New York: Free Press.

Boase, T. 1972. *Death in the Middle Ages.* New York: McGraw-Hill.

Boden, F. C. 1932. *Miner.* New York: E. P. Dutton.

Botkin, B. A. 1949. *A Treasury of Southern Folklore.* New York: American Legacy Press.

Breathitt, E. T. 1968. "Urban and Rural America." *Appalachia: A Journal of the Appalachian Regional Commission* 1 (June–July): 88–89.

Brewster, P. G., A. Taylor, B. J. Whiting, G. P. Wilson, and S. Thompson, eds. 1952. *The Frank C. Brown Collection of North Carolina Folklore.* Vol. 3. Durham, N.C.: Duke University Press.

Brown, J. S., and H. K. Schwarzweller. 1974. "The Appalachian Family." In *Appalachia: Its People, Heritage, and Problems,* ed. F. S. Riddel, 63–75. Dubuque: Kendall/Hunt.

Bryant, J. 1983. "Flags, Flowers and Thanks." *Reader's Digest,* May, 75–76.

Buck, C. N. 1914. *The Battle Cry.* New York: Grosset and Dunlap.

———. 1915. *The Code of the Mountains.* New York: W. J. Watt.

———. 1918. *When "Bearcat" Went Dry.* New York: W. J. Watt.

———. 1919. *A Pagan of the Hills.* New York: Grosset and Dunlap.

Budge, E. A. W. 1972. *The Mummy.* New York: Causeway Books.

Burke, F. 1932. *Call Home the Heart.* New York: Longmans, Green.

———. 1935. *A Stone Came Rolling.* New York: Longmans, Green.

Burman, B. L. 1951. *Children of Noah: Glimpses of Unknown America.* New York: Julian Messner.

Burnett, F. H. 1899. *In Connection with the De Willoughby Claim.* New York: Charles Scribner's Sons.

Burton, T. 1990. *Some Ballad Folks.* Johnson City, Tenn.: Center for Appalachian Studies and Services.

Byers, T. 1932. *Martha Berry: The Sunday Lady of Possum Trot.* New York: G. P. Putnam's Sons.

Campbell, J. C. 1921. *The Southern Highlander and His Homeland.* New York: Russell Sage Foundation.

Campbell, M. 1971. *Cloud-Walking.* Bloomington: Indiana University Press.

Campbell, W. D. 1977. *Brother to a Dragonfly.* New York: Seabury Press.

Carawan, G., and C. Carawan. 1975. *Voices from the Mountains.* New York: Alfred A. Knopf.

Carlson, L. 1987. *Caring for Your Own Dead.* Hinesburg, Vt.: Upper Access.

Carter, M. V., and G. L. Osborne. 1987. "Appalachia in the Information Age: A New Chance for Change?" *The Rural Sociologist* 7 (1): 38–43.

Cash, J. C. 1979. *Among My Klediments.* Grand Rapids, Mich.: Zondervan.

Caudill, H. M. 1963. *Night Comes to the Cumberlands.* Boston: Little, Brown.

———. 1972. "Jaded Old Land of Bright New Promise." In *Appalachia in the Sixties: Decade of Reawakening,* ed. D. S. Walls and J. B. Stephenson, 240–46. Lexington: University of Kentucky Press.

———. 1973. *The Senator from Slaughter Creek.* Boston: Little, Brown.

Chagnon, N. A. 1983. *Yanomamo: The Fierce People.* 3d ed. New York: Holt, Rinehart, and Winston.

Chidester, D. 1990. *Patterns of Transcendence: Religion, Death, and Dying.* Belmont, Calif.: Wadsworth.

Chironis, N. P., ed. 1977. *Coal Age Operating Handbook of Underground Mining.* New York: McGraw-Hill.

Clark, B. C. 1983. "The Death of Aunt Lottie." *Appalachian Heritage* 11 (1): 17–22.

Cleaver, V., and B. Cleaver. 1969. *Where the Lilies Bloom.* Philadelphia: J. B. Lippincott.

Coffin, M. 1976. *Death in Early America.* Nashville: Thomas Nelson.

Cohen, N. 1981. *Long Steel Rail: The Railroad in American Folksong.* Urbana: University of Illinois Press.

Coleman, J., and D. Cressey. 1984. *Social Problems.* New York: Harper and Row.

Collins, R., and M. Makowsky. 1978. *The Discovery of Society.* 2d ed. New York: Random House.

Cooper, H. 1972. *North Carolina Mountain Folklore and Miscellany.* Murfreesboro, N.C.: Johnson.

Cox, W. E. 1990. *Hensley Settlement: A Mountain Community.* Eastern National Park and Monument Association.

Crichton, I. 1976. *The Art of Dying.* London: Peter Owen.

Crissman, J. K. 1987. "The Impact of the Urban Milieu on the Appalachian Family Type." In *Too Few Tomorrows: Urban Appalachians in the 1980's,* ed. P. J. Obermiller and W. W. Philliber, 81–88. Boone, N.C.: Appalachian Consortium Press.

———. 1989. "Family Type and Familism in Contemporary Appalachia." *Southern Rural Sociology* 6:29–44.

Crissman, J. K., and A. P. Buteau. 1989. "Actual Family Size and Desired Family Size: A Comparison of Central Appalachian and Non–Central Appalachian Residents in an Urban Environment." In *Building Family Strengths: A Time of Change,* ed. J. G. King and L. Sydorenko, 93–103. Jonesboro: Arkansas State University.

Crissman, J. K., and T. G. Jelen. 1987. "Familistic Tendencies of Central Appalachian Migrants in an Urban Environment." Paper presented at the annual meeting of the Illinois Sociological Association, Chicago, Oct.

Crosby, A. 1965. "Death in Cades Cove." In *Appalachia: When Yesterday Is Today,* ed. Students at the University of Tennessee, 1–3. Knoxville.

Cyporyn, D. 1972. *The Bluegrass Songbook.* New York: Macmillan.

Dargan, O. T. 1925. *From My Highest Hill.* Philadelphia: J. B. Lippincott.

Davids, R. C. 1970. *The Man Who Moved a Mountain.* Philadelphia: Fortress Press.

Day, J. F. 1941. *Bloody Ground.* Garden City, N.Y.: Doubleday, Doran.

Day, R. M. 1975. "Pride and Poverty: An Impressionistic View of the Family in the Cumberlands of Appalachia." In *Appalachia: Family Traditions in Transition,* ed. E. M. Essin III, 71–80. Johnson City: East Tennessee State University Advisory Council.

"Death and Burial in the Mountains." 1974. *Appalachian Heritage* 2 (1): 57–61.

Dedo Monument Portraits since 1893. n.d. Catalog no. 14. Oak Park, Ill.: J. A. Dedouch.

DeSpelder, L. A., and A. L. Strickland. 1987. *The Last Dance: Encountering Death and Dying.* 2d ed. Palo Alto, Calif.: Mayfield.

Dillon, L. A. 1976. *They Died in the Darkness.* Parsons, W.Va.: McClain.

Douglas, G. W. 1948. *The American Book of Days.* New York: H. W. Wilson.

Douglas, H. K. 1989. *I Rode with Stonewall*. Simons Island, Ga.: Mocking-bird Books.

Dunn, D. 1988. *Cades Cove: The Life and Death of a Southern Appalachian Community*. Knoxville: University of Tennessee Press.

Durkheim, E. 1947. *The Division of Labor in Society*. Translated by George Simpson. New York: Free Press.

Duval, F. Y., and I. B. Rigby. 1978. *Early American Gravestone Art in Photographs*. New York: Dover.

Dykeman, W. 1962. *The Tall Woman*. New York: Holt, Rinehart, and Winston.

———. 1966. *The Far Family*. New York: Holt, Rinehart, and Winston.

———. 1973. *Return the Innocent Earth*. New York: Holt, Rinehart, and Winston.

Editors of Consumer Reports. 1977. *Funerals: Consumers' Last Rights*. Mount Vernon, N.Y.: Consumers Union of the United States.

Edwards, D. 1980. "Haydenville, a Town of Clay." *Ceramics Monthly* 28:47–51.

Ehle, J. 1982. *The Winter People*. New York: Harper and Row.

Ellyson, M. H. 1968. *It Might Have Been*. New York: Vantage Press.

———. 1973. *Mud and Money*. New York: Vantage Press.

Ergood, B. 1976. "Toward a Definition of Appalachia." In *Appalachia: Social Context Past and Present*, ed. B. Ergood and B. E. Kuhre, 31–41. Dubuque: Kendall/Hunt.

Erikson, K. T. 1976. *Everything in Its Path*. New York: Simon and Schuster.

Evans, T., and M. Travis. 1980. "John L. Richards, Stonecutter." In *Mountain Trace*, ed. K. G. Gilbert, book 1, 295–310. Parsons, W.Va.: McClain.

Faulkner, W. 1964. *As I Lay Dying*. New York: Random House.

Fetterman, J. 1967. *Stinking Creek*. New York: E. P. Dutton.

———. 1971. "The People of Cumberland Gap." *National Geographic*, Nov., 617–20.

Fink, P. M. 1975. "Religion in America." In *Appalachia: Family Traditions in Transition*, ed. E. M. Essin III, 33–42. Johnson City: East Tennessee State University Advisory Council.

Fox, J., Jr. 1901. *Blue-Grass and Rhododendron*. New York: Charles Scribner's Sons.

———. 1913. *The Heart of the Hills*. New York: Charles Scribner's Sons.

———. 1917. *In Happy Valley*. New York: Charles Scribner's Sons.

Franklin, B. A. 1972. "The Scandal of Death and Injury in the Mines." In *Appalachia in the Sixties: Decade of Reawakening*, ed. D. S. Walls and J. B. Stephenson. Lexington: University Press of Kentucky.

Friedrich, O. 1986. "A Day to Remember." *McCall's*, July, 95–96.

Frome, M. 1966. *Strangers in High Places*. Garden City, N.Y.: Doubleday.

Frost, W. G. 1899. "Our Contemporary Ancestors in the Southern Mountains." *Atlantic Monthly*, Mar., 311–19.

Furman, L. 1914. *Sight to the Blind*. New York: MacMillan.

———. 1923. *Mothering on Perilous*. New York: MacMillan.

———. 1925. *The Quare Woman*. Boston: Little, Brown.

———. 1927. *The Lonesome Road.* Boston: Little, Brown.

———. 1930. *The Glass Window: A Story of the Quare Woman.* Boston: Little, Brown.

Furstenberg, F. F., Jr. 1972. "Industrialization and the American Family." In *Readings on the Family System,* ed. I. L. Reiss, 397–413. New York: Holt, Rinehart, and Winston.

Gainer, P. W. 1975a. *Folk Songs from the West Virginia Hills.* Grantsville, W.Va.: Seneca Books.

———. 1975b. *Witches, Ghosts, and Signs: Folklore of the Southern Appalachians.* Grantsville, W.Va.: Seneca Books.

Gardner, C. 1931. *Clever County.* New York: Fleming H. Revell.

Gaventa, J. 1980. *Power and Powerlessness: Quiescence and Rebellion in an Appalachian Valley.* Urbana: University of Illinois Press.

Gazaway, R. 1974. *The Longest Mile.* Baltimore: Penguin Books.

Giles, J. H. 1956. *Hannah Fowler.* Boston: Houghton Mifflin.

———. 1957. *The Believers.* Boston: Houghton Mifflin.

———. 1967. *Forty Acres and No Mules.* 2d ed. Boston: Houghton Mifflin.

Gillon, E. V., Jr. 1972. *Victorian Cemetery Art.* New York: Dover.

Gilmer, E. M. 1988. *A History of Elk Garden United Methodist Church, 1788–1988.* Rosedale, Va.: Elk Garden United Methodist Church Bicentennial Committee.

Glasgow, E. 1935. *Vein of Iron.* New York: Harcourt, Brace.

Gold, A. 1977. "Hair Has Its Strand of Jewelry History." *Chicago Tribune,* Oct. 16, sec. 11, p. 8.

Graebner, W. 1976. *Coal-Mining Safety in the Progressive Period: The Political Economy of Reform.* Lexington: University Press of Kentucky.

Graff, O. B. 1962. "The Needs of Education." In *The Southern Appalachian Region: A Survey,* ed. T. R. Ford, 188–200. Lexington: University of Kentucky Press.

Grant, M. E., Sr. 1986. "Chronological Order of Events in Embalming." *Champion Expanding Encyclopedia of Mortuary Practice.* Springfield, Ohio: Champion.

Green, A. 1972. *Only a Miner: Studies in Recorded Coal-Mining Songs.* Urbana: University of Illinois Press.

Green, L. W. 1969. *And Scatter the Proud.* Winston-Salem, N.C.: John F. Blair.

Guerrant, E. O. 1910. *The Galax Gatherers.* Richmond, Va.: Onward Press.

Habenstein, R. W., and W. M. Lamers. 1960. *Funeral Customs the World Over.* Milwaukee: Bulfin Printers.

———. 1962. *The History of American Funeral Directing.* Milwaukee: Bulfin Printers.

Hacker, A., ed. 1983. *U/S: A Statistical Portrait of the American People.* New York: Viking Press.

Hall, A. C. 1961. *Grave Humor.* Charlotte, N.C.: McNally and Loftin.

Hall, J. W. 1973. "A Funeral Meeting in the Remote Parts of the Mountains." *Appalachian Heritage* 1 (4): 17–21.

Hamm, W. E. 1988. "Honoring the Noble Sacrifice: Once Again We Remember." *Vital Speeches of the Day* 55:626–27.

Hand, W. D., ed. 1964. *The Frank C. Brown Collection of North Carolina Folklore*. Vol. 7. Durham, N.C.: Duke University Press.

Haney, W. H. 1906. *The Mountain People of Kentucky*. Cincinnati: Roessler Bros.

Hannum, A. P. 1943. "The Mountain People." In *The Great Smokies and the Blue Ridge*, ed. Roderick Peattie, 73–151. New York: Vanguard Press.

———. 1969. *Look Back with Love: A Recollection of the Blue Ridge*. New York: Vanguard Press.

Harris, C. K. (words and music). 1898. "'Mid the Green Fields of Virginia (in the Vale of Shenandoah)." Milwaukee: Charles K. Harris.

Hatch, J. M. 1978. *The American Book of Days*. New York: H. W. Wilson.

Hatcher, H. 1931. *Tunnel Hill*. Indianapolis: Bobbs-Merrill.

Hatfield, G. E. 1974. *The Hatfields*. Stanville, Ky.: Big Sandy Valley Historical Society.

Heller, P. L. 1970. "Familism Scale: A Measure of Family Solidarity." *Journal of Marriage and the Family* 32 (Feb.): 73–80.

———. 1976. "Familism Scale: Revalidation and Revision." *Journal of Marriage and the Family* 38 (Aug.): 423–29.

Heller, P. L., and G. M. Quesada. 1977. "Rural Familism: An Interregional Analysis." *Rural Sociology* 42 (Summer): 220–40.

Heller, P. L., G. M. Quesada, D. L. Harvey, and L. G. Warner. 1981. "Familism in Rural and Urban America: Critique and Reconceptualization of a Construct." *Rural Sociology* 46 (Fall): 446–64.

Hicks, G. L. 1976a. *Appalachian Valley*. New York: Holt, Rinehart, and Winston.

———. 1976b. "Kinship and Sex Roles." In *Appalachia: Social Context Past and Present*, ed. B. Ergood and B. E. Kuhre, 210–19. Dubuque: Kendall/Hunt.

Hirt, D. F. 1975. "Semi-retained Rural Society on the Appalachian Family-Life during the Post–World War II Period." In *Appalachia: Family Traditions in Transition*, ed. E. M. Essin III, 51–61. Johnson City: East Tennessee State University Research Advisory Council.

"The History of Cats." 1988. *Pet Care Report*. Knoxville: Whittle Communications.

Hornsby, H. 1949. *Lonesome Valley*. New York: William Sloane Associates.

Huffman, A. 1953. *My Mountain Memories*. Philadelphia: Dorrance.

Huntington, R., and P. Metcalf. 1979. *Celebrations of Death: An Anthropology of Mortuary Ritual*. Cambridge: Cambridge University Press.

Huston, R. 1962. *Observations of God's Timing in the Kentucky Mountains*. Salisbury, N.C.: Rowan Printing.

Ickis, M. 1962. *The Book of Patriotic Holidays*. New York: Dodd, Mead.

Jewell, P. L. 1975. "Early Family Settlers and Settlements of Southern Appalachia." In *Appalachia: Family Traditions in Transition*, ed. E. M. Essin III, 25–29. Johnson City: East Tennessee State University Advisory Council.

Johnson, E. 1944. *A History of the Art and Science of Embalming*. New York: Casket and Sunnyside.

Jones, J. G. 1979. *Haunted Valley and More Folk Tales*. Parsons, W.Va.: McClain.

Jones, L. 1975. "Appalachian Values." In *Voices from the Hills: Selected Read-*

ings in Southern Appalachia, ed. R. J. Higgs and A. N. Manning, 507–17. New York: Frederick Unger.

———. 1980. *Radio's "Kentucky Mountain Boy" Bradley Kincaid.* Berea, Ky.: Berea College Appalachian Center.

———. 1984. *Minstrel of the Appalachians: The Story of Bascom Lamar Lunsford.* Boone, N.C.: Appalachian Consortium Press.

Jones, M. B., and T. J. Smith. 1990. *White Christmas, Bloody Christmas.* Trinity, N.C.: Upwords Publications.

Jones, V. C. 1976. *The Hatfields and the McCoys.* Atlanta: Mockingbird Books.

Kahn, K. 1973. *Hillbilly Women.* Garden City, N.Y.: Doubleday.

Kalish, R. A. 1985. *Death, Grief, and Caring Relationships.* 2d ed. Monterey, Calif.: Brooks/Cole.

Kamerman, J. B. 1988. *Death in the Midst of Life.* Englewood Cliffs, N.J.: Prentice Hall.

Kane, H. T. 1956. *Miracle in the Mountains.* New York: Doubleday.

Kastenbaum, R. J. 1991. *Death, Society, and Human Experience.* New York: Macmillan.

Kaplan, B. H. 1971. *Blue Ridge: An Appalachian Community in Transition.* Morgantown: Office of Research and Development, West Virginia University.

Kearl, M. C. 1989. *Endings: A Sociology of Death and Dying.* New York: Oxford University Press.

Kelley, R. K. 1969. *Courtship, Marriage, and the Family.* New York: Harcourt, Brace, and World.

Keniston, K. 1985. "The Myth of Family Independence. In *Marriage and Family in a Changing Society,* ed. J. M. Henslin, 27–33. 2d ed. New York: Free Press.

Kephart, H. 1980. *Our Southern Highlanders.* Knoxville: University of Tennessee Press.

Kincaid, B. 1929. *Favorite Old-time Songs and Mountain Ballads.* Book 2. Chicago: WLS.

———. 1930. *Favorite Old-time Songs and Mountain Ballads.* Book 3. Chicago: WLS.

Korson, G. 1943. *Coal Dust on the Fiddle.* Philadelphia: University of Pennsylvania Press.

Kromer, T. 1974. "Michael Kohler." In *Stories and Verse of West Virginia 2,* ed. J. Comstock, 320–58. Richmond, W.Va.: Jim Comstock.

Kronenfeld, J. J., and M. L. Whicker. 1986. "Feminist Movements and Changes in Sex Roles: The Influence of Technology." *Sociological Focus* 19 (1): 47–58.

Kubler-Ross, E. 1969. *On Death and Dying.* New York: MacMillan.

Lambert, H. S. (words), and F. W. Vandersloot (music). 1909. "I Wonder How the Old Folk Are at Home." Williamsport, Pa.: Vandersloot Music.

Lee, H. B. 1968. *The Burning Springs and Other Tales of the Little Kanawha.* Parsons, W.Va.: McClain.

———. 1969. *Bloodletting in Appalachia.* Parsons, W.Va.: McClain.

———. 1971. *My Appalachia.* Parsons, W.Va.: McClain.

Lee, K. W. 1972. "Fair Elections in West Virginia. In *Appalachia in the Sixties: Decade of Reawakening*, ed. D. S. Walls and J. B. Stephenson, 164–76. Lexington: University of Kentucky Press.

Lee, M. 1980. *The People Therein*. New York: Houghton Mifflin.

Leming, M. R., and G. E. Dickinson. 1985. *Understanding Dying, Death, and Bereavement*. New York: Holt, Rinehart, and Winston.

Levitan, S. A., and R. S. Belous. 1985. "Trends in Fertility." In *Marriage and the Family in a Changing Society*, ed. J. M. Henslin, 77–84. 2d ed. New York: Free Press.

Litsey, E. C. 1940. *Stones and Bread*. Caldwell, Idaho: Caxton Printers.

Llewellyn, R. 1943. *How Green Was My Valley*. New York: MacMillan.

Lomax, A., W. Guthrie, and P. Seeger. 1967. *Hard Hitting Songs for Hard-hit People*. New York: Oak Publications.

Lose, G. W. n.d. *The Mountaineer's Song*. Columbus, Ohio: Book Concern.

Loughrige, D. 1983. "A Perspective on Death in Appalachia." *Appalachian Heritage* 2 (1): 25–28.

Lucas, R. A. 1969. *Men in Crisis: A Study of a Mine Disaster*. New York: Basic Books.

Lynn, L. 1976. *Coal Miner's Daughter*. Chicago: Henry Regnery.

McCall, W. A. 1975. *I Thunk Me a Thaut*. New York: Teacher's College Press.

McCracken, J. A. 1984. "A Memorial Day in Maine." *Reader's Digest*, May, 49–54.

McFarland, L., and R. Gardner. 1931. *Mac and Bob's Book of Songs (Old and New)*. Chicago: Agricultural Broadcasting.

McKee, M., and I. Robertson. 1975. *Social Problems*. New York: Random House.

McNeil, W. K. 1987. *Southern Folk Ballads, Volume 1*. Little Rock: August House Publisher.

———. 1988. *Southern Folk Ballads, Volume 2*. Little Rock: August House Publisher.

Malone, J. S. 1903. *Sons of Vengeance: A Tale of the Cumberland Highlanders*. New York: Fleming A. Revell.

Marshall, C. 1967. *Christy*. New York: McGraw-Hill.

Martin, I. P. 1954. *A Minister in the Tennessee Valley*. Nashville: Parthenon Press.

Mason, R. L. 1927. *The Lure of the Great Smokies*. Boston: Houghton Mifflin.

Melville, K. 1983. *Marriage and the Family Today*. New York: Random House.

Meredith, R. 1974. *Mr. Lincoln's Camera Man: Matthew B. Brady*. 2d rev. ed. New York: Dover.

Meyer, R. A. 1976. "Mountain Character: Carved from the Rock of Faith." *Appalachian Heritage* 4 (1): 4–9.

Miles, E. B. 1975. *The Spirit of the Mountains*. Knoxville: University of Tennessee Press.

Miller, C. 1933. *Lamb in His Bosom*. New York: Harper and Brothers.

Mitford, J. 1963. *The American Way of Death*. New York: Simon and Schuster.

Montell, W. L. 1975. *Ghosts along the Cumberland: Deathlore in the Kentucky Foothills*. Knoxville: University of Tennessee Press.

Moore, Warren. 1988. *Mountain Voices.* Chester, Conn.: Globe Pequot Press.

Morehouse, K. 1936. *Rain on the Just.* Carbondale: Southern Illinois University Press.

Morgan, E. 1984. *Dealing Creatively with Death: A Manual of Death Education and Simple Burial.* 10th ed., rev. and exp. Burnsville, N.C.: Celo Press.

Murdoch, L. S. 1917. *Almetta of Gabriel's Run.* New York: Meridian Press.

New American Standard Bible. 1977. Open Bible ed. Nashville: Thomas Nelson.

Nimkoff, M. F. 1974. *Marriage and the Family.* Boston: Houghton Mifflin.

Norbeck, M. E. 1931. *The Lure of the Hills: A Tale of Life in the Mountains of Kentucky.* Oakdale, Ky.: Revivalist Press.

Obermiller, P. J., and R. Rappold. 1990. "Bury Me under a Sidewalk: The Appalachian Way of Death in the Cities." *Now and Then* 8 (2): 28–29.

Ogburn, W., and M. F. Nimkoff. 1955. *Technology and the Changing Family.* Boston: Houghton Mifflin.

Parris, J. 1972. *These Storied Mountains.* Asheville, N.C.: Citizen-Times.

Parsons, T. 1951. *The Social System.* Glencoe, Ill.: Free Press.

———. 1955a. "The American Family: Its Relations to Personality and to Social Structure." In *Family, Socialization, and Interaction Process,* ed. T. Parsons and R. F. Bales, 3–34. Glencoe, Ill.: Free Press.

———. 1955b. "Conclusion: Levels of Culture Generality and the Process of Differentiation." In *Family, Socialization, and Interaction Process,* ed. T. Parsons and R. F. Bales, 353–96. Glencoe, Ill.: Free Press.

———. 1961. "Some Considerations on the Theory of Social Change." *Rural Sociology* 26 (Sept.): 219–39.

Pearsall, M. 1959. *Little Smoky Ridge.* Birmingham: University of Alabama Press.

Peterson, B. W. 1975. "Quiet Dignity." *Appalachian Heritage* 3 (2): 5–8.

Phipps, W. E. 1980. "Traditional Appalachian Funerals." *Appalachian Heritage* 8 (4): 48–53.

Plowman, R. E. 1982. *Twice out of Sight.* Berea, Ky.: Kentucky Imprints.

Pratt, D. C. 1954. *Bluegrass Adventures.* Bristol, Tenn.: King Printing.

Puckle, B. S. 1926. *Funeral Customs: Their Origin and Development.* Detroit: Singing Tree Press.

Purcell, M., and C. Purcell. 1975. *A Moonshine Preacher.* Toccoa, Ga.: Toccoa Printers.

Raether, H. C., and R. C. Slater. 1974. "The Funeral and the Funeral Director." In *Concerning Death: A Practical Guide for the Living,* ed. E. A. Grollman, 187–209. Boston: Beacon Press.

Ragon, M. 1983. *The Space of Death.* Charlottesville: University Press of Virginia.

Raine, J. W. 1924. *The Land of Saddlebags: A Study of the Mountain People of Appalachia.* New York: Council of Women for Home Mission and Missionary Education Movement of the United States and Canada.

Ratliff, R. R. 1977. *Return to the Promised Land, Appalachia.* Frankfort, Ky.: Kentucky Images.

Reeder, C., and J. Reeder. 1978. *Shenandoah Heritage: The Story of the People before the Park.* Washington, D.C.: Potomac Appalachian Trail Club.

Reilly, R. T. 1979. *Rebels in the Shadows*. Pittsburgh: University of Pittsburgh Press.

Riggleman, H. F. 1980. *A West Virginia Mountaineer Remembers*. Parsons, W.Va.: McClain.

Ritchie, J. 1963. *Singing Family of the Cumberlands*. New York: Oak Publications.

Roberts, B., and N. Roberts. 1970. *Where Time Stood Still*. New York: Crowell-Collier Press.

Rodgers, J. 1934. *Jimmie Rodgers' Album of Songs*. No. 2, 3d ed. New York: Southern Music.

Rorrer, K. 1982. *Rambling Blues: The Life and Songs of Charlie Poole*. London: Old Time Music.

Ross, S. G. 1977. *Come Go with Me*. Pineknot, Ky.: Kentucky Hills Industries.

Rowland, J. M. 1927. *Blue Ridge Breezes*. Nashville: Publishing House M. E. Church, South.

Russell, G. T. 1974. *Call Me Hillbilly*. Alcoa, Tenn.: Russell.

Russell, J. 1959. *Snakes and the Devil*. New York: Vantage Press.

Ryan, M. E. 1891. *A Pagan of the Alleghenies*. Chicago: Rand, McNally.

St. Cloud, V. 1948. *Pioneer Blood*. Raleigh, N.C.: Edwards and Broughton.

Sandberg, H. 1958. *The Wheel of Earth*. New York: McDowell, Obolensky.

Sanderson, E. S. 1958. *County Scott and Its Mountain Folk*. Huntsville, Tenn.: Esther Sharp Sanderson.

Scalf, H. P. 1974. "The Death and Burial of 'Boney Bill' Scalf." *Appalachian Heritage* 2 (2): 57–60.

———. 1975. "The Bewitched Cow." *Appalachian Heritage* 3 (2): 14.

Schaltenbrand, P. 1980. "The Stoneware of Greensboro–New Geneva." *Ceramics Monthly* 28:30–36.

Schrag, P. 1972. "The School and Politics." In *Appalachia in the Sixties: Decade of Reawakening*, ed. D. S. Walls and J. B. Stephenson, 219–23. Lexington: University of Kentucky Press.

Seeger, P. 1962. *How to Play the Five-String Banjo*. 3d ed. rev. Beacon, N.Y.: Pete Seeger.

Shackelford, L., and B. Weinberg. 1977. *Our Appalachia*. New York: Hill and Wang.

Sharp, C., and M. Karpeles. 1968. *Eighty English Folk Songs from the Southern Appalachians*. Cambridge, Mass.: MIT Press.

Shellans, H. 1968. *Folk Songs of the Blue Ridge Mountains*. New York: Oak Publications.

Sheppard, M. E. 1935. *Cabins in the Laurel*. Chapel Hill, N.C.: University of North Carolina Press.

———. 1947. *Cloud by Day: The Story of Coal and Coke and People*. Chapel Hill: University of North Carolina Press.

Sherburne, J. 1973. *Stand like Men*. Boston: Houghton Mifflin.

Shushan, E. R. 1990. *Grave Matters*. New York: Ballantine Books.

Skidmore, H. 1936. *I Will Lift Up Mine Eyes*. New York: Book League of America.

Skolnick, A. 1978. *The Intimate Environment: Exploring Marriage and the Family*. 2d ed. Boston: Little, Brown.

Slone, V. M. 1978. *Common Folks.* Pippa Passes, Ky.: Appalachian Women Grants for Writers and the Appalachian Learning Laboratory, Alice Lloyd College.

———. 1979. *What My Heart Wants to Tell.* Washington, D.C.: New Republic Books.

Smith, J. F. 1930. "Introduction." In *Favorite Old-time Songs and Mountain Ballads* by Bradley Kincaid, book 2. Chicago: WLS.

Smith, L. 1980. *Black Mountain Breakdown.* New York: G. P. Putnam's Sons.

Spaulding, A. W. 1915. *The Men of the Mountains.* Nashville: Southern Publishing Association.

Spencer, A. J. 1982. *Death in Ancient Egypt.* New York: Penguin Books.

Stephenson, J. B. 1968. *Shiloh: A Mountain Community.* Lexington: University of Kentucky Press.

Stewart, J. 1973a. "Superstitions." *Appalachian Heritage* 1 (3): 9–16.

———. 1973b. "Superstitions 2." *Appalachian Heritage* 1 (4): 23–41.

Stidham, S. W. 1978. *Trails into Cutshin County: A History of the Pioneers of Leslie County, Kentucky.* Corbin, Ky.: Sadie W. Stidham.

Still, J. 1940. *River of Earth.* New York: Viking Press.

Stoddard, S. 1978. *The Hospice Movement.* New York: Vintage Books.

Straus, R. 1968. "Health Barriers." *Appalachia: A Journal of the Appalachian Regional Commission* 1 (Apr.): 21.

Strub, C. G., and L. G. "Darke" Frederick. 1967. *The Principles and Practice of Embalming.* 4th ed. Dallas: L. G. Frederick.

Stuart, J. 1950. *Clearing in the Sky.* New York: McGraw-Hill.

———. 1971. *Come Back to the Farm.* New York: McGraw-Hill.

———. 1975. *Taps for Private Tussie.* Atlanta: Mockingbird Books.

Sturgill, R. L. 1970. *Crimes, Criminals, and Characters of the Cumberlands and Southwest Virginia.* Roy L. Sturgill.

Sudnow, D. 1967. *Passing On: The Social Organization of Dying.* Englewood Cliffs, N.J.: Prentice Hall.

Surface, B. 1971. *The Hollow.* New York: Coward-McCann.

Swanson, S. 1986. "Slogans and Comrades." *Christian Century* 103:510–11.

Sweet, W. W. 1931. *Religion on the American Frontier: The Baptists.* New York: Henry Holt.

Theodorson, G. A., and A. G. Theodorson. 1969. *Modern Dictionary of Sociology.* New York: Thomas Crowell.

Thomas, J. 1931. *Devil's Ditties.* Chicago: W. Wilbur Hatfield.

———. 1940. *Big Sandy.* New York: Henry Holt.

———. 1942. *Blue Ridge Country.* New York: Duell, Sloan, and Pearce.

Toynbee, M. W. 1975. *A Day for Remembrance.* New York: Vantage Press.

Troxel, T. H. 1958. *Legion of the Lost Mine: Stories of the Cumberland.* Comet Press Books.

Turner, J. H. 1985. *Sociology: The Science of Human Organization.* Chicago: Nelson-Hall.

Vincent, G. E. 1898. "The Retarded Frontier." *American Journal of Sociology* 4 (1): 1–20.

Vogel, J. 1952. *This Happened in the Hills of Kentucky.* Grand Rapids, Mich.: Zondervan.

Walker, R. S. 1941. *Lookout: The Story of a Mountain.* Kingsport, Tenn.: Southern.

Walsh, W. 1925. *Curiosities of Popular Customs.* Philadelphia: J. B. Lippencott.

Ward, C. 1975. *Silk Stockin' Row.* Parsons, W.Va.: McClain.

Wasserman, E. 1972. *Gravestone Designs: Rubbings and Photographs from Early New York and New Jersey.* New York: Dover.

Watkins, F. C., and C. H. Watkins. 1963. *Yesterday in the Hills.* Chicago: Quadrangle Books.

Weller, J. E. 1966. *Yesterday's People.* Lexington: University of Kentucky Press.

West, J. F. 1973. *Appalachian Dawn.* Durham, N.C.: Moore.

Wharton, M. C. 1953. *Doctor Woman of the Cumberlands.* Pleasant Hill, Tenn.: Uplands.

"What Is a Burial Vault?" 1972. In *Facts Every Family Should Know.* Forest Park, Ill.: Wilbert.

White, E. E. 1937. *Highland Heritage.* New York: Friendship Press.

"Why Study Appalachia?" 1976. In *Appalachia: Social Context Past and Present,* ed. B. Ergood and B. E. Kuhre, 3–8. Dubuque: Kendall/Hunt.

Widner, R. R. 1974. "The Four Appalachias." In *Appalachia: Its People, Heritage, and Problems,* ed. F. S. Riddel, 1–8. Dubuque: Kendall/Hunt.

Wiggins, G. 1987. *Fiddlin' Georgia Crazy: Fiddlin' John Carson, His Real World, and the World of His Songs.* Urbana: University of Illinois Press.

Wigginton, E., ed. 1989. *A Foxfire Christmas.* New York: Doubleday.

Wilcox, S. G., and M. Sutton. 1985. *Understanding Death and Dying: An Interdisciplinary Approach.* 3d ed. Palo Alto, Calif.: Mayfield.

Wilson, A. E. 1902. *A Speckled Bird.* New York: G. W. Dillingham.

Winter, I. A. 1974. "Choosing a Memorial." In *Concerning Death: A Practical Guide for the Living,* ed. E. A. Grollman, 225–37. Boston: Beacon Press.

Wirth, L. 1938. "Urbanism as a Way of Life." *American Journal of Sociology* 44 (July): 1–24.

Wolford, F. 1975. *Mountain Memories.* Parsons, W.Va.: McClain.

Zakuta, L. 1985. "Equality in North American Marriage." In *Marriage and the Family in a Changing Society,* ed. J. M. Henslin, 67–76. 2d ed. New York: Free Press.

Zelditch, M., Jr. 1955. "Role Differentiation in the Nuclear Family: A Comparative Study." In *Family, Socialization, and Interaction Process,* ed. T. Parsons and R. F. Bales, 307–52. Glencoe, Ill.: Free Press.

Zimmerman, C. C. 1948. *Family and Civilization.* New York: Harper and Brothers.

Index

James K. Crissman received his Ph.D. in sociology from the University of Akron in 1980. Since then he has published a number of articles on Appalachian life and the family. He is presently an associate professor in the Sociology and Psychology Department at Illinois Benedictine College. This is his first book.

Wild, Sweet Notes
    Avail. 5/2000